THE RENAISSANCE TEXT

MANCHESTER
UNIVERSITY PRESS

The Renaissance text

Theory, editing, textuality

EDITED BY
ANDREW MURPHY

Manchester University Press
Manchester and New York

distributed exclusively in the USA by St. Martin's Press

Published by Manchester University Press
Oxford Road, Manchester M13 9NR, UK
and Room 400, 175 Fifth Avenue, New York, NY 10010, USA
http://www.man.ac.uk/mup

Distributed exclusively in the USA by
St. Martin's Press, Inc., 175 Fifth Avenue, New York,
NY 10010, USA

Distributed exclusively in Canada by
UBC Press, University of British Columbia, 2029 West Mall,
Vancouver, BC, Canada V6T 1Z2

British Library Cataloguing-in-Publication Data
A catalogue record for this book is available from the British Library

Library of Congress Cataloging-in-Publication Data applied for

ISBN   0 7190 5398 6   *hardback*
        0 7190 5917 8   *paperback*

First published 2000

07 06 05 04 03 02 01 00   10 9 8 7 6 5 4 3 2 1

Typeset by
D R Bungay Associates, Burghfield, Berks

Printed in Great Britain
by Bookcraft (Bath) Ltd, Midsomer Norton

Contents

Figures

The author and publisher express their gratitude to Stanford
University Library for providing some of the above images.

Politics of Mirth: Jonson, Herrick, Milton, Marvell (University of Chicago Press, 1986), *Puzzling Shakespeare: Local Reading and its Discontents* (University of California Press, 1988) and *Unediting the Renaissance: Shakespeare, Marlowe, Milton* (Routledge, 1996). She is co-editor (with Janel Mueller and Mary Beth Rose) of *The Speeches, Letters, Verses, and Prayers of Queen Elizabeth I*, forthcoming from the University of Chicago Press.

Andrew Murphy is Lecturer in English at the University of St Andrews. He is the author of *But the Irish Sea Betwixt Us: Ireland, Colonialism and Renaissance Literature* (University Press of Kentucky, 1999). He is currently working on a book entitled *Shakespeare in Print: A History and Chronology of Shakespeare Publishing, 1590–2000*, to be published by Cambridge University Press.

Stephen Orgel is the Jackson Eli Reynolds Professor of Humanities at Stanford University. His books include *The Illusion of Power* (University of California Press, 1975), *The Jonsonian Masque* (Columbia University Press, 1981) and *Impersonations: The Performance of Gender in Shakespeare's England* (Cambridge University Press, 1996). He has edited *The Tempest* and *The Winter's Tale* for the Oxford Shakespeare, *Ben Jonson's Court Masques* for the Yale Ben Jonson, Christopher Marlowe's *Complete Poems and Translations* for Penguin English Poets and (with Jonathan Goldberg) *John Milton* for the Oxford Authors. He is the general editor of Cambridge Studies in Renaissance Literature and Culture.

John Pitcher is a Fellow of St John's College, Oxford. He has published extensively on Samuel Daniel in preparation for the four-volume Oxford English Text edition of Daniel. He is the editor of the Penguin edition of Francis Bacon's *Essays* and of the Arden *The Winter's Tale* (2000) and the New Penguin *Cymbeline* (2000). He is the editor of the annual *Medieval and Renaissance Drama in England*.

Stanley E. Porter is Professor of Theology and Head of the Department of Theology and Religious Studies at University of Surrey, Roehampton. His books include *Verbal Aspect in the Greek of the New Testament, with Reference to Tense and Mood* (Lang, 1989), *Idioms of the Greek New Testament* (Sheffield Academic Press, 2nd edn, 1994), *Studies in the Greek New Testament* (Lang, 1996) and (with Jeffrey A. D. Weima) *An Annotated Bibliography of 1 and 2 Thessalonians* (Brill, 1998). He is the editor of *Handbook of Classical Rhetoric in the Hellenistic Period 330 B.C.–A.D. 400* (Brill, 1997) and of *Handbook to Exegesis of the New Testament* (Brill, 1997). He is currently writing a major commentary on the book of Acts in the New Testament, and editing a number of biblical papyri for publication.

Emma Smith is Fellow in English at Hertford College Oxford. She is the editor of the Penguin edition of *The Spanish Tragedie* (1998) and is currently completing the *Henry V* volume in the Cambridge University Press 'Shakespeare in Production' series.

Peter Stallybrass is Professor of English and of Comparative Literature and Literary Theory at the University of Pennsylvania. With Allon White, he wrote *The Politics and Poetics of Transgression* (Methuen/Cornell University Press, 2nd edn, 1990), and he has co-edited with David Kastan *Staging the Renaissance: Studies in Elizabethan and Jacobean Drama* (Routledge, 1991), with Margreta de Grazia and Maureen Quilligan *Subject and Object in Renaissance Culture* (Cambridge University Press, 1996) and with Jeffrey Masten and Nancy Vickers *Language Machines: Technologies of Literary and Cultural Production* (Routledge, 1997). He is co-author (with Ann Rosalind Jones) of *Worn Worlds: Clothes and the Constitution of the Subject in the Renaissance* (forthcoming from Cambridge University Press) and a selection of his essays on Marx has been published in Brazil, under the title *Marx's Coat*.

Michael Steppat is Professor of English Literature at the University of Bayreuth. He is the editor (with Marvin Spevack) of the New variorum edition of Shakespeare's *Antony and Cleopatra* (MLA, 1990) and has also edited texts in the 'Renaissance Latin Drama in England' series. He is currently editing the New variorum *Merry Wives of Windsor* volume and (with Louise Schleiner) is working on a book entitled *Discourse of Voicing in the Early Modern Theatre*. He is founding co-editor of the journal *Connotations*.

Gary Taylor is Director of the Hudson Strode Program in Renaissance Studies at the University of Alabama. He is general editor of the works of Shakespeare (Oxford University Press, 1986) and of Thomas Middleton (Oxford University Press, forthcoming) and has co-edited (with Michael Warren) *The Division of the Kingdoms: Shakespeare's Two Versions of 'King Lear'* (Oxford University Press, 1983). He is the author of *Reinventing Shakespeare* (Chatto & Windus, 1990) and *Cultural Selection* (Basic Books, 1996) and is co-author of *William Shakespeare: A Textual Companion* (Oxford University Press, 1987) and (with John Jowett) of *Shakespeare Reshaped, 1606–1623* (Oxford University Press, 1993). He is currently co-editing, with Celia R. Daileader, John Fletcher's *The Tamer Tamed* (forthcoming from Manchester University Press).

Ramona Wray is Lecturer in English at the Queen's University of Belfast. She is the co-editor (with Mark Thornton Burnett) of *Shakespeare and Ireland: History, Politics, Culture* (Macmillan, 1997) and *Shakespeare, Film, Fin de Siècle* (Macmillan, 2000). She is the author of *Women Writers of the Seventeenth Century* (Northcote House, 2000) and is currently working on *Women, Writing, Revolution: An Anthology of Writing by Women during the English Civil War*, to be published by Blackwell.

New Bibliography offers 'a fresh start, the *right* start', and it advances along a road which only ever leads in a single direction. Critiques of New Bibliography have, as much as anything else, alerted us to the impossibility of a singular editorial approach that can be applied in the same way to all texts at all times. We have begun increasingly to appreciate that texts and their histories are multiplicitous and require diverse and adaptive interpretive frameworks and editorial strategies.

The New Bibliography was driven by scholars whose specialisms lay in Renaissance literature generally and, more specifically, in the texts of Shakespeare. It comes as no surprise, then, to find that challenges to the New Bibliographic orthodoxy should come from Renaissance scholars and, particularly, from Shakespeare specialists. It is, perhaps, the liminal positioning of the Renaissance text that enables it to function so productively as a focal point for textual issues. The Renaissance is, after all, the period in which an organised commercial theatre is first established in England; in which the idea of a profession of letters first begins to emerge; and in which printing begins to establish itself as a primary form of textual dissemination (though by no means a wholly dominant form, as Arthur F. Marotti's work on Renaissance poetry indicates[2]). The Renaissance text is sited at the intersection of the 'amateur' (or – in some instances of the theatre – the 'civic') and the professional; of the oral and the printed; of the manuscript and the book; of the coterie and the public; and at the point of initiation of concepts of authorship tied to the isolable individual. The complex interaction of these factors is written across the surface of the texts produced within this period in manifold ways. A close engagement with the Renaissance text and its heterogeneous histories can thus provide the basis for a fuller appreciation of the complexity of all texts and their historical positionings.

The present collection addresses itself precisely to this field of textual complexity, taking the Renaissance as its primary focal point and foregrounding, but by no means limiting itself to, the instance of Shakespeare. But the book also ranges beyond this chronological focus, as some contributors engage with the extended history of certain Renaissance texts, while Graham Caie, in his chapter, explores the issue of how current developments in medieval studies might offer a fruitful model for approaches to texts from the Renaissance period. The aim of the collection is to be eclectic and diverse: this book does not seek to be a manifesto for what has sometimes been called the 'New Textualism'. There are dissonant and dissident voices recorded here – Graham Caie and Gary Taylor staking out diametrically opposed positions on electronic textuality, Michael Steppat offering a probing critique of the positions advanced elsewhere in their work by several of his co-contributors to this book. What does serve to unify this collection, however, is a shared commitment on the part of its contributors to the view that the nature of texts and the parameters of textuality cannot be taken for granted, and that texts, textual histories and regimes of textuality demand from us a complex, mobile and multifaceted set of responses. Hence all of the contributors here are committed to exploring the interpenetration of theoretical and editorial concerns, bringing a theoretical inflection of one sort or another to their textual and bibliographical analyses. All of the contributors to this book firmly believe in the centrality of textual studies to the exploration of literature and culture and all are committed to a revitalised bibliography which brings the insights of current theory to bear on textual and editorial thinking. We would thus all likely agree with Ralph G. Williams's assertion that '[t]he theory and practice of textual scholarship are in fact at the fulcrum of fundamental shifts in how we understand and transmit the monuments of our culture' and that 'textual studies are at present one of the most self-conscious and experimental branches of the humanities'.[3]

The Renaissance Text opens, then, with John Pitcher's exploration of the complex history of Samuel Daniel's publishing career. Pitcher's concern lies in the issue of how to accommodate Daniel's many castings and recastings of his texts within a standard edition of the author's works – the OET edition, of which he is editor. Pitcher finds his solution in one of Daniel's own textual metaphors: he imagines the text as an edifice, within the contours of which previous textual building blocks can be discerned – thus the edition is consciously constructed to be 'a house of remade but fixed parts, notes and elucidations, with, most important of all, a textual apparatus of discarded pieces beneath the established fabric of texts' (27). Pitcher thus forswears the New Bibliographic aim of establishing a definitive edition which would reclaim the author's final intentions from behind the veil of print but, in the process, he hopes to produce an edition which is in fact more closely aligned with the textual strategies that characterise his author.

One solution to the problems of textual complexity that Pitcher considers but ultimately rejects is the electronic edition, which enables the editor to present a vast array of materials to the reader. In his chapter, Graham Caie celebrates the electronic text and offers the general embracing of new editorial technologies among medievalists as an fixated at the stage of textual loss and the desire for recovery. The value of evolving a form of postmodern editing, in Maguire's view, is that it might release us from such constraining paradigms.

The chapters by Graham Holderness, Stanley E. Porter and Carol Banks, Emma Smith, and myself focus on the history and historicity of texts and of textuality itself. Holderness and his colleagues trace the history of – and filiations between – two foundational Renaissance volumes: the King James Bible and the Shakespeare First Folio. In particular, they examine the way in which a set of diverse and often dissonant texts were reduced to singularity and unilinearity in these two projects, producing monumentalised textual entities from which 'the Pentecostal babbling of many tongues' (171) was rigorously excluded. In closing, they note the unpicking of this uniformity in recent biblical and Shakespearean studies. Emma Smith takes an equally monumentalised individual Shakespearean text – *Hamlet* – and charts the history of its strange textual *doppelgänger*: the supposed *Hamlet* 'ur-text'. Smith notes the curious way in which the ur-text, evolved in some respects as a mechanism for displacing problematic moments out of the 'true' Shakespeare text, comes instead to haunt that text, operating, it might be said, in the manner of the Derridean supplement. My own chapter extends the Shakespearean strand of the book, as I attempt to map out (using the Shakespeare text as a kind of central emblematic instance) a history of textuality itself, tracing a shifting set of textual regimes from the Renaissance through to the present.

Leah Marcus's 'Afterword' serves, in one sense, to bring the collection full circle in that, like John Pitcher, her primary focus is on the editorial logistics of bringing a complex body of work – the writings of Elizabeth I – to print in a new edition. As an active interrogator of prior textual and editorial orders (in *Unediting the Renaissance*, *Puzzling Shakespeare* and elsewhere) Marcus brings a new sensibility to the business of editing Elizabeth's work and she explicitly forges a link between theory and practice – a connection which she views as crucial to the future of literary studies, as she exhorts more theorists to become practitioners.

Much of the work presented in this volume is indebted to the pioneering studies of Randall McLeod/Random Cloud. McLeod's project throughout his career has been to try to encourage us to *look* at texts as well as reading them – prompting us to avoid what he has wittily termed 'The Missionary Position of Reading'. As McLeod has stressed, '[a]t all levels, the text is mediated, and always the mediation is inseparable from the text'.[5] The New Bibliographers certainly looked at texts – indeed, they looked at the physical book far more closely than any previous generation of scholars had ever done. But, as many critics have remarked, this interest in the physical book was rendered totally subservient to the pursuit of a single, unified ideal object which was imagined as lying behind the material book and its 'veil of print'. The aim of the contributors to this volume is to maintain a broad point of focus on the complex object of the Renaissance text: to attempt to read its codes in their own terms; to follow its contemporary and extended history; to attempt to recover its context and its gendered force; to understand its editorial history (and the cultural function of editing more generally); to recover the traces of its previous generations of readers; and to map out diverse strategies for how we might usefully reproduce the text in our own time. Our interest in the text lies, we might say, as much in the fabric and changing fashions of the veil of print – and of the textile of inscription more generally – as in what we might imagine lies behind it.

Notes

1 John Dover Wilson, 'The new way with Shakespeare's texts: an introduction for lay readers', *Shakespeare Survey*, 11 (1958), p. 78.

2 Marotti notes that 'Of those who wrote lyric poetry in the period between Donne and Marvell, the majority preferred to restrict their work to manuscript circulation, many first functioned within a system of manuscript transmission and then organized their work for publication, and very few took a direct route from private composition to typographical presentation of their work to a large public', 'Manuscript, print, and the social history of the lyric', in Thomas N. Corns (ed.), *The Cambridge Companion to English Lyric Poetry, Donne to Marvell* (Cambridge, Cambridge University Press, 1993), p. 56. See also Marotti's *Manuscript, Print and the English Renaissance Lyric* (Ithaca, NY, Cornell University Press, 1995).

3 Ralph G. Williams, 'I shall be spoken', in George Bornstein and Ralph G. Williams (eds), *Palimpsest: Editorial Theory in the Humanities* (Ann Arbor, University of Michigan Press, 1993), p. 45.

4 A related key issue which is not taken up in this collection is the intersection between textual studies and Queer Theory. On this topic, see the work of Jeffrey Masten – especially 'Textual deviance: Ganymede's hand in *As You Like It*', in Marjorie Garber, Paul B. Franklin and Rebecca L. Walkowitz (eds), *Field Work: Sites in Literary and Cultural Studies* (London, Routledge, 1996), pp. 153–63.

5 Random Cloud, 'from tranceformations in the text of *Orlando Furioso*', *Library Chronicle of the University of Texas at Austin*, 20:1/2 (1990), pp. 61, 80.

Essays, works and small poems: divulging, publishing and augmenting the Elizabethan poet, Samuel Daniel

John Pitcher

Samuel Daniel's poems, plays and prose writings come to us in all sizes and shapes, and they range across almost the full spectrum of literary genres known to the Renaissance. Daniel wrote love sonnets, pastoral tragicomedies, verse epistles, neoclassical tragedies, an epic poem in over a thousand stanzas of *ottava rima*, a prose history of medieval English kings, verse complaints, court masques, songs for the lute, translations from Italian and French poets, a prose pamphlet on rhyme and the enduring character of the English constitution, elegies and memorials for his patrons, lyrical dialogues, panegyrics and dedications for two monarchs and for the aristocracy, and even one extraordinary innovation, a hybrid of colloquy and treatise, in the poem *Musophilus*. He wrote in blank verse, *terza rima*, cross rhymes, couplets and rime royale, as well as in a prose which makes much of the prose writing of the next generation, including that of Milton, seem by comparison unwieldy and on occasions even clumsy and uncertain.

The books in which Daniel's writing was published are diverse too, as much in their contents as in their physical dimensions and formats. Scholars and book collectors have known for many years that the early editions of Daniel had complicated and intriguing histories of manufacture, publication and distribution.[1] The vicissitudes of the past four centuries, and particularly those of the twentieth century, have made the histories of Daniel's books yet more varied and more difficult to interpret correctly. The sheer number of surviving copies (at least a thousand), and their present far-flung locations – the books have been widely dispersed, especially through sales and gifts to libraries and individuals in the United States – presents us with a problem of evidence which is not insurmountable but which is certainly very large. By contrast, the contents of Daniel's editions can be described fairly straightforwardly, from a bibliographical point of view, thanks to the researches of the compilers of the first *Short Title Catalogue*, and to

Harry Sellers, and, latterly, to Katharine Pantzer.[2] Further, by examining title pages and the printer's signatures, we can tell which of his
poems and plays need to be present for us to identify a complete copy,
bibliographically speaking, of any one of the six collected editions published between 1599 and 1623. Interesting problems arise when we find
that some copies of the poems and plays have survived separately, or are
bound together with one or two others in smaller combinations, with
their title pages and signatures intact, and in what are beyond doubt
their original bindings. From such instances it is reasonable to conclude that Simon Waterson, Daniel's publisher for more than thirty
years, must have offered several of the poems and plays for sale as separate items as well as in the complete sets, with an accompanying general
title page.

The story of how Daniel wrote his poetry, drama and prose histories,
and how he presented these to his patrons and friends, or had them sold
in printed books of various sizes and contents in Waterson's shop in St
Paul's in London, or in Widow Crosley's bookshop in Oxford, is a complex and fascinating one which I have been striving to understand and
to give a full account of for several years now.[3] One feature of the story
is the keen interest Daniel took in the arrangement of the poems and
plays in relation to one another. This is true from his earliest publications. In his first volume of poetry, published in 1592, there were two
poems, *Delia Contayning Certayne Sonnets* and *The Complaint of
Rosamond*, and between these, a short piece, *An Ode*: that is, in formal
terms, a sequence of sonnets, followed by an ode, followed by a verse
narrative in stanzas of rime royal. In terms of subject matter, the book
opens with Delia, a chaste and unspeaking Renaissance beauty, who
refuses the entreaties of her gentry suitor; it continues with a short
poem about the quickening of life, in which birds and the spring echo
sounds to each other; and it concludes with a complaint from the
spectre of Rosamond, the long-dead mistress of an English medieval
king, who is simply unable to be quiet about how he used her as a whore
and how she was murdered for it. The rich flow of internal reference
between these poems, and their collocations, echoes and contrasts
(silence set against speech, life against death, secrecy against open
scandal), very much appealed to Daniel's contemporaries in the 1590s,
particularly Shakespeare it seems.[4] A second edition of these poems
was published in the same year, which added sonnets and new stanzas
but which maintained the same patterns of internal reference.
However, in the next edition, two years later, when Daniel added the

neoclassical play *The Tragedy of Cleopatra* to this first group, the original pattern of allusion, social parallels and generic shading was almost entirely reconfigured. The main focus was still on women, but now, among other contrasts, English provinciality (a lady and her suitor from the backwaters of Somerset) was set against the fall of ancient empires (the Roman defeat of Egypt), while the pseudo-medievalism of the Elizabethan complaint was thrown into a new relief against the fraught intensities and verse forms of neoclassical tragedy.

All this we should expect of a poet as artistically subtle and resourceful as Daniel. His ambition to achieve a variety and copiousness in his poetry reached its proper height, for a Renaissance poet, with the publication, late in 1595, of the first four books of *The Civil Wars*, his epic on the Wars of the Roses. With this book Daniel established himself as second only to Spenser among living English poets in print. He had published four important books of poetry in just three years, he had scaled the upper reaches of tragedy and epic, and he was everywhere spoken about and admired, by the court elite as much as by the London *literati*.[5] He was thirty-three, and his quality of mind, fluency and ready inventiveness promised an outstanding, perhaps even a very great career as a poet. His next step, in the matter of how he shaped his books and what he would call them, shows us what he aspired to. In 1599, probably early in the year, he published his first collected volume of poetry, with the title *The Poeticall Essayes of Sam. Danyel. Newly corrected and augmented.* On the verso of the title page, printed in the upper half, there were the heraldic arms of his patron, Charles Blount, Baron Mountjoy, set within the Order of the Garter. In the lower half of the page, beneath a rule, was a description of what the book contained:

The Argumentes of these
Essayes following.

The ciuill wars betweene the two houses of *Lancaster* and *Yorke*.
Musophilus, or a defence of learning.
The Epistle of *Octavia* to *Antonius*.
The Tragedy of *Cleopatra* corrected.
The complaint of *Rosamond*.

There are several new things about this book, most obvious of which is its title, *Poeticall Essayes*, by which Daniel was alluding either to Montaigne's *Essaies*, from which he was to draw extensively during the next decade, or to the first edition of Francis Bacon's *Essayes*, which had been published less than two years earlier, in 1597.[6] Some years afterwards Bacon remarked of his *Essayes* that although the word for them was new, the form of writing was not (since it could be found in Seneca's epistles).[7] This view is so different from what Daniel claimed he was exploring in his poems of 1599 that the proper connection must surely be with Montaigne, with essays as trials, experiments, assays into different ways of thinking. What was most innovative, even audacious about Daniel's assays is that they were attempted in rhymed verse and stanzas rather than in prose: as he made clear in *Musophilus*, the chief formal question he had posed himself was whether it was possible *to discourse* in a poem, and in an English poem at that. *The Poeticall Essayes* was made up of two hitherto unpublished poems, *Musophilus* and *Octavia*, revised versions of two pieces which had already appeared in print, *Cleopatra* and *Rosamond*, and the reissued sheets of the four books of the 1595 edition of *The Civil Wars*, together with a fifth book which had been added, probably in 1597. The thinking behind the order of the poems is clear enough. The historical epic, Daniel's chief endeavour, is placed first, followed by the new poems, and then by *Cleopatra* and *Rosamond*, which have been 'augmented' and 'corrected', that is, added to and freed from errors, but perhaps also brought to a new order after earlier disarray (*correct OED* 5). *Delia* and *An Ode*, we notice, are not included in this collection, and the sequence in which the poems appear draws attention to how and when Daniel made them, and his sense of their priority (heroic verse first, earliest work last), as much as to any literary configuration of the kind we can identify in the early (1592-4) editions of *Delia*. In short, the order of the poems in *The Poeticall Essayes* is offered to the reader as some measure (one which omits the *Delia* sonnets) of how far Daniel has developed as an artist.

Daniel's other bold move in this collection was to preface it with Lord Mountjoy's heraldic arms, as if placing the book under the nobleman's protection, but then to declare that this was not his motive for putting Mountjoy's name (his title and aristocratic house) at the front of the book. In the dedicatory poem, which follows the title page (sig. A2r), he says that his patron's '*great respected name*' is at the front not because this will protect the poems from '*contempt or blame*', nor because he hopes the *Essayes* will win him '*more respect*' from such a learned man (Mountjoy's estimate of his abilities is already settled), nor because the poems could confer more honour on his patron's personal worth. Rather he does it

> *to th'end if destinie*
> *Shall any monument reserue of me,*
> *Those times should see my loue, how willing I*
> *That liu'd by thee, would have thee liue with me.*

Because Daniel has lived *with* Lord Mountjoy (at his home in Wanstead House and elsewhere) and has been supported *by* him (with money and attention), he wishes to repay his patron with a share, perhaps figuratively a room, in whatever monument or house of fame his reputation as a poet may eventually be preserved in.[8] Once again the focus has changed from the earlier volumes of poetry. Here what is of importance is a social intercourse between poet and patron, across differences in rank and personal obligation, rather than contrasts between an unswervingly chaste, provincial English beauty and the seductress Queen of Ancient Egypt.

In his next collection, published two years later, Daniel was to go yet further, this time proclaiming himself a national poet, by calling this edition, astonishingly, his *Works*, and by dedicating it in verse to 'Her Sacred Majesty', to Queen Elizabeth herself (sig. A2). The history of how Daniel defined his vocation as a poet is, in fact, contained in small in the titles and vocabulary he used to describe his collected editions: through these we can discern the artistic and social progress he was making, or he thought he was making, through two decades at court. So much is clear from a simple list of the descriptions on the title pages of the collections published after *The Poeticall Essayes* (the last of which, *The Whole Workes*, appeared four years after the poet's death, prepared by his publisher Waterson and his brother John Danyel):

1601–2 Folio
The Works of Samuel Daniel Newly Augmented

1605 Octavo
Certaine Small Poems Lately Printed with the Tragedie of Philotas, Written by Samuel Daniel

1607 Octavo
Certaine Small Workes Heretofore Diuulged by Samuel Daniel one of the Groomes of the Queenes Maiesties priuie Chamber, & now againe by him corrected and augmented

1611 Octavo and Duodecimo
Certaine Small Workes Heretofore Divulged by Samuel Daniell one of the Groomes of the Queenes Maiesties most Honourable priuie Chamber, and now againe by him corrected and augmented

1623 Quarto
The Whole Workes Of Samuel Daniel Esquire in Poetrie

The rise in Daniel's social status during these twenty years is obvious enough. Less obvious perhaps is the force of meaning Daniel invests in the word 'Works', and, to a lesser degree, 'Divulged'. I have suggested elsewhere that in 1601 'for Daniel to publish an edition of his *Works* – almost a thing unheard of from a living English poet – was to make a claim' to be the successor, as the nation's poet, to Spenser, who had died shortly before *The Poeticall Essayes* appeared.[9] For forty years prior to the publication of Daniel's *Works*, only one other living author, John Heywood, had a collection of his writing issued with this title.[10] There were posthumous collections, and reprints of Chaucer with the title *Works*, but the notion of drawing together and issuing one's *magnum opus* does not seem to have occurred to any of Daniel's immediate predecessors.

Perhaps they thought that to do this would be over ambitious, even presumptuous. It is revealing that when Daniel did it, no one felt that he was getting above himself, as a good number of people clearly did fifteen years later when another writer, Ben Jonson, ventured to call his collection of plays and poems *The Works*. On the contrary, the surviving evidence suggests that Daniel's poetry was sought after by the buying public, and that the *Works* folio was well received in the highest circles. Towards the end of 1600, as Daniel himself recalled, Simon Waterson, who had issued *The Poeticall Essayes* only about eighteen months earlier, was pressing him for yet another collection of his poems, further revised and added to: around this time, as Daniel put it, he was 'called vpon by' his 'Printer for a new impression of' his 'workes, with some additions to the ciuill warres'.[11] The cost of materials and labour to make this folio cannot have been a small thing for Waterson, and he would not have risked the investment unless he anticipated enough demand for these expensive books of English poetry. As to how well they were received, the list of contemporary owners of the *Works* folios (gift copies and ones bought new or second hand) descends from Queen Elizabeth herself down through the nobility to the court secretariat and the luminaries and writers among the gentry and middling sort.[12] We should note too that in 1605 Daniel's *Works* was one of the few volumes written in English, let alone English verse, which Sir Thomas Bodley allowed into his new library in the University of Oxford.[13] In all it is clear that Daniel's reputation as a poet reached its highest point around the turn of the century.[14]

The *Works* folio is an intriguing and important object, which has been largely overlooked by historians of the reception and culture of books in early modern England. About eighty copies of the edition have survived, and from these we can make out a quite deliberate plan, on the part of the poet and his publisher, to cater for different readers. The folios survive in two issues, with different dates on their title pages (1601 and 1602); they were printed on two or three distinct grades of paper; and they were presented and sold with a variety of contents. Some of these features were already present in books of Daniel's poetry printed in the 1590s – in copies of *The Poeticall Essayes* and even in copies of the 1595 *Civil Wars* – but it was in the *Works* that the social differentiation between copies was attempted most systematically. None the less the one thing which every reader of the *Works* did receive was an entry into Daniel's poetry, on the title page, through two carved columns supporting a portico of the crown, crest and motto, and the heraldic royal beasts of Queen Elizabeth herself (illustrated in Figure 1). Normally it would be incautious to attribute the design and layout of this page to anyone other than the printer (here Valentine Simmes), who would of course use whatever standard ornaments, some bearing royal arms, he had available in his stock. In the case of the *Works*, though, it may be that Daniel had far more say than was usual in choosing the three ornamental sections on the page, and especially the figures shown in the middle one (the two columns with a prince outside each of them). None of these ornamental sections appears in any book before Daniel's *Works*, and their only subsequent use, as far as one can tell, is in Daniel's *Panegyric* folio of 1603, again printed by Simmes, and designed to complement (and be sold with) the *Works*.[15]

Much more could be said about the *Works* folio, but two particular aspects must suffice here. To begin with, in contrast to the title *The Poeticall Essayes*, which offers the poems as exploratory assays, the title *Works* presents them as finished pieces, polished poetic objects rather than incomplete tasks or ones still in hand (Daniel always distinguishes carefully between *works* as things made and *labours* as the efforts which made them). Second, the poems in the *Works* folio were revised and in some cases substantially added to, but their order was unchanged from how they had appeared in *The Poeticall Essayes*. Instead of concluding with *Rosamond*, however, the *Works* adds a revised and expanded version of the sonnet sequence *Delia*, which is followed in turn on the final page, as an end piece for the whole book (sig. C4), by what Daniel calls *A Pastorall*. This is his brilliant verse translation of the Golden Age

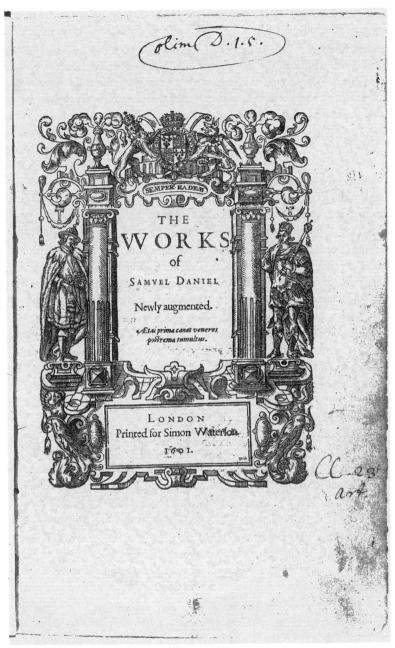

SEMPER·EADEM

THE
WORKS
of
SAMVEL DANIEL

Newly augmented.

Ætai prima canat veneres,
postrema tumultus.

LONDON
Printed for Simon Waterson.
1601.

1 Samuel Daniel, 1601 *Works* title page. Bodleian copy, arch G. D. 47. Reproduced by permission of the Bodleian Library, University of Oxford

Chorus, 'O bella età de l'oro', from Tasso's *Aminta*. With its urgings to choose pleasure over honour, *A Pastorall* serves as a coda to the *Delia* sonnets and their chaste, resisting lady, but it also announces, in not too hushed tones, one of the directions in which Daniel intends his writing to go next – that is, as it did, towards the poignant, dark lyricism of Italian tragicomedy and its intricate debates over duty and desire. The final lines of *A Pastorall*, and the *Works*, recall the sentiments of Ovid and Catullus but draw their grace and unsettling beauty from Tasso's poetic drama: 'Let's loue: the sun doth set, and rise againe, / But when as our short light / Comes once to set, it makes eternall night'.[16] By this point in his career Daniel's ordering of his poems was no longer confined to one particular collection: the order had begun to function across his published volumes, mediating back and forth between them, recollecting past achievements and promising future work, contributing to the formation of his poetic canon.

After 1601 Daniel published three further collections of poetry, in 1605, 1607 and 1611, the last of which was almost entirely a reprint of the 1607 edition. The poems in these volumes included *Rosamond*, *Cleopatra* and *Musophilus*, and several other pieces from the earlier collections, together with one or two new items (*The Tragedy of Philotas* and *Ulysses and the Siren* among them). Daniel calls them 'certain small poems' and 'certain small works', presumably because they are selections from his newly formed canon, and because they are smaller in size and generically inferior to the epic poem, *The Civil Wars*, which none of these collections contains. The 1607 and 1611 title pages do draw attention to the poet's new social standing at court, but the books themselves are altogether smaller and less grand publications than either *The Poeticall Essayes* or the *Works*. These more modest collections are not prefaced with an address to the monarch or to a member of the nobility, nor are they protected by royal or aristocratic heraldic accoutrements on their title pages; instead in 1607 there is an unusually intimate, almost confessional poem 'To the Reader', the anonymous purchaser of these, the latest selections of Daniel's poetry. The premise in this 1607 poem – a key piece of evidence in the interpretation of Daniel's later writing – is that it is The Reader, unidentified and undifferentiated by social rank and learning and even gender, and only distinguishable by nationality, by being English, who has read all of the earlier versions of Daniel's poems. He or she, an English Reader, has witnessed the poet's errors of judgement, and the lapses in his metre, rhymes and rhythm, and now sees him owning up to his mistakes and struggling to put them right, at least as far as he can.[17] The Reader has seen in all its stages the formation of Daniel's canon – indeed the fact of the canon, its making and the different shapes it has taken during two decades, depends upon the existence of The Reader, for who else can know what has been added and discarded along the way?

Put it in starker terms: Daniel needs – I suggest below that he invents – The Reader so that the achievement of his canon, formed by revising the poems, and adding to them and reordering them within the collected editions, can be acknowledged and made intelligible. One can detect signs of considerable social and perhaps mental confusion in Daniel over this. He continues to write new poems for the court elite, and to dedicate old ones to them, but from 1607 onwards he appears to accept that it is The Reader of his books, who has never met him, nor advised nor graced him (as his patrons would through their personal encouragement and guidance), who has become the custodian of his life's works. I suspect that it was the premature death in 1606 of Lord Mountjoy (by then Earl of Devonshire), who had done so much for him, that forced him suddenly to grant such overwhelming importance to The Reader. With Mountjoy gone, to whom could he now entrust the overview and judgement of his poetry and the creative effort it had cost him to write it? On the 1607 and 1611 title pages Daniel says that these 'certain small works' have been heretofore 'divulged', which may mean simply that the poems and plays have been published before or have appeared in print in earlier editions (divulge OED 1). But the word 'divulge' could also mean to disclose or reveal something private or secret (OED 2), and it is possible that in this wording there was an uneasy concession from Daniel that by publishing his poems repeatedly he had moved them away from the privacy of their genesis (where he would write them, and then, as he tells us, read them aloud to Mountjoy)[18] and assigned them forever to The Reader, the anonymous common public.

Clearly it would be a tall order, perhaps an impossible one, for The Reader to be so utterly engaged and conversant with Daniel's poetry that he or she could recollect and appreciate the subtleties of every reordering and rearrangement within the collected editions. This is nothing, however, to what The Reader would need to know of the innumerable alterations Daniel makes to each of the poems. His writing in verse amounts to over 30,000 lines in the final versions, and another 5000 that had been discarded or replaced along the way. The full extent of the revisions is in fact even greater than this, because in all Daniel

altered almost two fifths of the verse he published, in some cases
revising individual lines three times or more. The scale of the revisions
can be illustrated easily from the arrangement of pages planned for the
Oxford edition of Daniel (described below), and in particular the way
the *Delia* sonnets have to be set out. With *Delia*, as I have noted elsewhere, 'there are five versions of some of the poems, with revisions
which range from single-word corrections to whole quatrains entirely
rewritten; from changes in metre and rhyme to recastings in grammatical tense and mood'. This means that in some instances in the Oxford
edition 'there will be only one complete sonnet on the page: the
remainder will be taken up, even when it is set in a smaller type, by the
textual apparatus'.[19] All this information about the rewriting and
touching up of line after line in each poem or play is what The Reader is
supposed to know, in order that he or she may be Daniel's public confi-
dant, reading and listening to his verse, as well as knowing exactly how
the poems were positioned from one collection to the next, and how (to
return to the point this chapter began with) the poet had tested his abilities across such a wide variety of genres and subjects.

The Reader of 1607 did not exist, of course, as surely Daniel was
aware, at least not as a person, nor even as an idealised super-reader,
gifted with prodigious memory and attentiveness. This poet certainly
had many real readers among his contemporaries, about whom we
know quite a lot (including Mountjoy),[20] but The Reader we are concerned with was not one of these, and he or she was much more mindful
and relentless in the audit of the poet's achievements. Daniel made The
Reader, in a rather extraordinary way, both what views and what is
viewed, that is, both the auditor and the sum of every line of verse he
had written and rewritten, and in some cases half forgotten, a textual
archive constantly scrutinised, over which not even the poet himself
had total command and retentiveness. By 1607 Daniel had made so
many changes to his poems, and created so many new alliances and
channels between one poem and another, and between one collection
and the next, that he was simply unable, perhaps even as much as we are
now, to hold all of these revisions and collocations and nuances simultaneously in one intertextual field – what he did was to invent The
Reader and to charge him or her with this responsibility.

An unexplored but productive way of looking at Daniel's 'whole
works in poetry' would be to interpret them in precisely these terms, as
an intertextual field across which there is a ceaseless traffic between
achieved texts, and between these and the history of how each of them

evolved, separately and together. We can point to what such an analysis might entail if we consider a passage from the *Funerall Poeme* that Daniel wrote to commemorate the death of his patron, Mountjoy, in 1606. The first version of the poem was privately printed as a small pamphlet, and probably distributed among the mourners at the nobleman's funeral in Westminster Abbey.[21] A year later, in the *Certaine Small Workes* collection, Daniel published an enlarged version of it, to which he added an account of Mountjoy's campaigns against the Irish and Spanish in Ireland. He also deleted several passages, one of them early in the poem, which is shown in the textual apparatus in Figure 2.

Daniel deleted these 1606 lines for several reasons. He had been ungracious and touchy in them about his indebtedness to Mountjoy, and too defensive about having praised his social betters when he was ignorant of their real character ('being to free of prayses, without proofe', conceivably an allusion to his admiring references to the Earl of Essex before his execution in 1601). However, if we approach the deletions in these terms, the focus is inevitably and pretty much exclusively on the poet himself, on his creative and personal sensitivities, and on his second thoughts. The alternative way of looking at what was deleted, an intertextual one which lays emphasis upon social differentiation, is to ask who exactly was supposed to be reading the 1607 revised version. Was it a public reader, excluded from the fuller, more frank sentiments expressed in the 1606 pamphlet for the elite group gathered at the funeral? Or was it a reader and purchaser who, although a social inferior to the mourners, had, through buying the poem in the 1607 collection, contributed to the independence which Daniel prized so much (in ll. 23-4, he breathes and speaks as a free man, not as a slave choked into silence by his master's 'chayne')? Or was it, rather, once more, the omniscient Reader who was most present, The Reader who knew *both* versions of the poem, much like us, and for whom each textual moment in the *Funerall Poeme* was a matrix of social dialogues between mistakes and corrections, privacy and intrusiveness, status and reputation, elite and commoners, and benefits and money?

This treatment of the vexed theoretical and historical issues of authorship and of social practices in Renaissance writing is, I acknowledge, rudimentary. What needs to be emphasised is how vibrantly in movement everything is in Daniel's poetry, beneath (or perhaps between) the calm surfaces and regular rhymes his verse is known for.[22] As I see it, one of my chief concerns, as an editor of Daniel's poems and

And I stand cleere from any other chayne
Then of my loue, which freeborne drawes free breath,
The benefite thou gau'st me to sustaine   25
My humble life, I loose it by thy death:
Nor was it such, as it could lay on me
Any exaction of respect so strong,
As to inforce m'obseruance, beyond thee,
Or make my conscience differ from my tongue   30
    For I haue learnt it is the property
    For free men to speeke truth, for slaues to lye.
And therefore I sincerely will report
First how thy partes were faire conuaid within
How that braue minde was built and in what sorte   35
All the contexture of thy heart hath beene,
Which was so nobly fram'd, so well compos'd
As vertue neuer had a fairer seate.

23 I stand cleere] am vntide *1606*   29 m'obseruance] my obseruance *1606*
31-35] *1606*:   Let those be vassals to such seruices
                Who haue their hopes, or whose desires are hye,
                For me, I haue my ends, and know it is
                For Free-men to speake truth, for slaues to lye.
                And if mistaken by the Paralax
                And distance of my standing too farre off
                I heretofore might erre, and men might tax
                My being to free of prayses, without proofe.
                But here it is not so, and yet the choyce
                Of those I made did yeald the greatest show
                Of honour and of worth, and had the voyce
                Of present times their virtues to allow.
                And if they haue not made them good, it is
                No fault of mine, nor ought it to be layd
                To disrepute these my obseruances,
                True prayses doe adorne, the false obrayd:
                And oftentimes to greatnesse we are glad
                To attribute those parts we wish they had.
                But *Deuonshire* I here stand cleere with thee
                I haue a manumission to be free,
                I owe thee nothing, and *I* may be bold
                To speake the certaine truth of what I know,
                There is no power remaines in thee, to hold
                The tongues of men, that wilbe talking now.
                And now being dead may anatomise,
                And open here all that thou wert within,
                Shew how thy minde was built, and in what wise

2 Draft of the OET text of the *Funerall Poeme* ll. 23–38, based on *1607* readings

plays, is to find ways of presenting the texts and the textual environment so that modern readers become as sensitive to these dynamic social forces in his writing as they are to his more decorous and familiar protocols. The two main options for achieving this end are of course the traditional print edition and the electronic hypertext edition. In the remainder of this essay I want to weigh the advantages and disadvantages of print against hypertext for Daniel's work, at least as regards these questions of how he ordered and revised his poetry, and what he was seeking from the physical forms in which it was published.

My own work on Daniel has for the most part been directed towards a print edition for the Oxford English Texts (OET) series published by Oxford University Press under the Clarendon imprint. As I have published a progress report on the edition,[23] here I need only to repeat what the size and objectives of the OET are, before moving on to the order of its contents, and to the unease which, I concede, this order causes me. The OET is to be a four-volume, original-spelling critical edition of Daniel's complete verse and drama, with the approach and style modelled on the Herford and Simpson Oxford edition of Ben Jonson. Together with the edited texts (some of which will be parallel texts), there will be a biography, textual and critical introductions, and full notes and collations. The edition will add a dozen new poems to Daniel's canon, along with a range of new letters and biographical materials, and it will offer annotations of his largely unedited verse and drama. A website, planned as a supplement to the OET, will contain, among other things, a selection of digital texts, a photoarchive of key life documents and a record of punctuation and press variants.

The arrangement of poems and plays proposed for the OET observes the well-tested and traditional principles of generic grouping and artistic development, but it is shaped by practical considerations as well. One model for the edition, considered but rejected at an early stage, was to distribute the texts and textual apparatus across the first three of the four volumes and to concentrate all the supporting materials (introductions, commentaries) in the final one. This idea, although attractively straightforward, had to be ruled out by the publisher: it would mean that all four volumes would have to be issued together (would any one want volumes of text without the textual rationale in the final volume?), and, worse than that, sales might be spread too unevenly across the edition (cannier readers might buy the shorter poems volume, but use the commentary volume in the library). Instead, each volume is to contain texts and textual apparatus, together with introductions and annotations for individual works, but it will also include parts of the general introduction to Daniel's writing and life, and some of the supporting archive (allusion book, life records, and so forth). This is the arrangement of contents finally settled on:

Volume 1   The Shorter Poems (1591–1618)
Volume 2   *The Civil Wars* (1595–1609)
Volume 3   *The Tragedy of Cleopatra* (1594–1607)
           The Tragedy of Philotas (1605–1607)
Volume 4   *The Queen's Arcadia* (1605–1611)
           Hymen's Triumph (1614–1615)
           The Vision of the Twelve Goddesses (1604)
           Tethys' Festival (1610)

How appropriate and useful will Daniel's readers find this grouping of his poems and plays? To some minds this arrangement may seem so obvious and sensible as to need no defence or explanation at all. The principal division is the generic one, with two volumes given over to Daniel's drama (one to tragedy, the other to tragicomedy and the masque) and one to the pre-eminent classical form, the verse epic. The shorter poems, ranging as they do across classical and Renaissance forms (from verse letter to sonnet) as well as across varieties of style, are gathered together for convenience and size, but also because there is an almost universal agreement among Daniel's critics that it is in the shorter pieces that he most excels and most deserves our attention. The other organising principle to the volumes is a chronological one. This traces in broad outline, inevitably with some overlapping and blurring of dates of composition and publication, the ways in which Daniel matured as a writer, and the continuities in his poetry and drama through three decades. This approach is rational and helpful, I believe, but it does have one severe limitation. Arranged like this, the OET can give the modern reader only a limited idea of just how interested Daniel himself was, as we have seen, in the relationships between and the contiguousness of the literary forms he was attempting.

The same limitation is true of the order *within* each of the volumes, particularly in the first of them, which is given over to Daniel's shorter poems. In this the contents will be arranged again along chronological lines (titles in italic are taken from the early editions, those in roman are mine):

Delia, Containing certaine Sonets, Newly Augmented
An Ode
A Pastorall
A Description of Beauty, translated out of Marino
The Complaynt of Rosamond
A Letter from Octavia to Antony
Musophilus, or A Defence of Poetry
Three Sonnets on Books and Patrons
A Panegyrike Congratulatorie
Certaine Epistles
Seven Sonnets and Poems on Books and Friends
Ulisses and the Syren
A Funerall Poeme Uppon the Death of the late Earle of Devonshire
In Memory of Robert, Earl of Salisbury
Further Epistles
Epistle to James Montague, Bishop of Winchester

Some of these pieces will be familiar to students of Elizabethan and
Jacobean poetry, others less so. Some have been rediscovered or identified (the epitaph on Salisbury, the further epistles), while others,
chiefly sonnets and shorter poems, have been grouped together like this
for the first time, so as to allow Daniel's preoccupations with books and
people their proper place among his more substantial works. Of course
the sequence of poems set out here breaks entirely with the various
orders in the collected editions. *Cleopatra* has been located elsewhere in
the OET, and *Rosamond* is set apart from *Delia* and *An Ode*, separated
by a pair of pastoral lyrics derived from Tasso and Marino. *Octavia* here
precedes *Musophilus* (reversing their order in the 1599 collection), on
the grounds that of the two poems it is likely to have been written earlier. I believe that a reasoned case can be made for placing each of the
poems in the position assigned to it in this sequence in the OET, but I
acknowledge that this order creates almost as many problems as it
solves. From it we are able to make out afresh the various patterns in
Daniel's writing and career, but only by giving priority to particular
aspects of the poems (their dates of composition and generic similarity)
and by ignoring, except by way of description, the strata of the early
collected editions – the distribution and redistribution of their contents, their sizes and formats, and even the wording of their titles.

Against this limitation the merits of an electronic edition speak for
themselves. An archive of so many disparate materials – different
genres, book sizes, contents, assays and works, the genealogy of the
canon, final versions and revisions, and The Reader's global memory –

would surely be more successfully aligned within the computer, and the textual hyperspace simulated in an electronic environment, than within the covers of the print volumes of an OET. There is a great deal that is attractive about this alternative. Within the confines of a print edition, since white space will be at a premium, every page will be contested for by text and critical apparatus. Readers will need to have tabulated for them which of the editions has a contents leaf, and whether it gives an accurate account of the order and contents in the surviving copies (with notes on what, if anything, has been regularly missed out). There must also be a table setting out which editions of separate poems are bound up with copies of the collected editions, alongside a chart to show how the poems and plays move from one collection to the next, and which parts of which editions have survived as separate items in contemporary bindings. All this information, texts and annotation and tables, will be spread across each print volume, from one end to the other, and readers must traverse the edition, in a traditional format, seeking and selecting as best they can, working within the structures of fixed pages, sections and groupings.

How enticing, then, the alternative and extraordinary prospect, envisaged for us and given its theory by McGann and others, of an electronic edition, in which we may open endless windows into Daniel's life and work, one frame on to another, simulated on the screen of a monitor, configuring them at will? With the *Funerall Poeme* for instance we could have, simultaneously if we chose, the full texts of 1606 and 1607 (and the 1623 reprint full of errors), and digital images of the title pages of all three editions, with a note on the positions of the poem in the 1607 and 1623 collections, together with pages from the OET edition, set out traditionally, text above apparatus, and with an historical synopsis of Daniel's personal relationships with Mountjoy and other Elizabethan aristocrats. It is a paradox, but a nice one, that until very recently it was only The Reader, Daniel's strange *alter ego*, who could aspire to a complete knowledge, hidden as well as disclosed, of this poet's writing: the difference the electronic edition makes is that with it The Reader, who knows everything, is succeeded by The OET Editor, who tries to know everything,[24] and thereafter, through his editorial endeavours, by The Electronic Reader, who is empowered to know and do everything and anything with and to Daniel's poetry, framing and unframing it at will, either with or against the historical grain.

Put like this, the only rational choice would appear to be an electronic edition of Daniel rather than a print one, or perhaps even a choice to have both, a traditionally prepared OET edition situated within a hypertext archive (which would utilise the electronic option to its maximum potential). Regrettably, research funding and the time I can reasonably devote to the task means that there is no real choice between these at all. While it is true that the OET texts of Daniel's poems and plays, with their textual apparatus, are all on Microsoft files, it would be enormously expensive and time consuming to adapt all of these to the conditions needed for hypertext, and in addition to enter all of the different texts from all the collected editions, as well as single-work editions (a total of more than twenty books), together with the commentaries and life records and publication histories. Substantial academic funding might be available in the US or UK for this type of project if the writer were Shakespeare or Wordsworth (or even Dante or Goethe), but I fear it is unrealistic to think that a large amount of research money will ever flow towards a Daniel OET, or anything like it. I have also had to abandon the hope I once had, that it might be possible to use the original-spelling texts of Daniel that are appearing on the Internet: most of these have proved to be inaccurate, some of them wildly so, and they are generally beneath the standard needed for OET texts.[25]

Thus, in brief, an electronic edition of Daniel is unattainable given present resources. But would a hypertext of his poetry be entirely desirable even if there *were* the funding to design it and make it work? Is there no advantage in principle to the OET print edition over an electronic one, other than the fact that it is affordable and therefore feasible? There is a long answer to this question, as well as a short one. The long answer, parts of which I have set out already in the progress report on the OET, is concerned with the unhistorical, unmaterial and unsubstantial textuality of a virtual edition – electronic impulses on a flat, no-depth screen – which cannot represent adequately, so I argue, the material circumstances, the making and the *thinginess* of Daniel's poems in books, sold and given in the mixed commodity and gift culture of early modern England.[26] The short answer, which draws more directly on Daniel's own tropes and lexicon, is also concerned with his poems and plays as objects. This is how in 1607, at the beginning of the poem to The Reader, he refers to the poems and plays he has written and revised, and is publishing anew:

> Behold once more with serious labor here
> Haue I refurnisht out this little frame,
> Repaird some parts defectiue here and there,
> And passages new added to the same,

Some rooms inlargd, made some les then they were.
Like to the curious builder who this yeare
Puls downe, and alters what he did the last
As if the thing in doing were more deere
Then being done, & nothing likes thats past.[27]

The collection as a whole is a house, and the poems and plays are 'rooms' (in Italian, a room is a *stanza* of course). The house has been 'refurnisht', that is, rebuilt in places and refitted. Some of the rooms have been repaired, others enlarged, others made smaller, and new 'passages' (corridors and connecting doors between and into the rooms) have been added. The metaphor is so simple that we might forget to ask the obvious question, what type of house does Daniel have in mind? He says that the book he is publishing is a 'little frame', an octavo in other words, but does this mean, by analogy, that the house is of middling size, or smaller still, perhaps as small as his own home must have been in the tiny hamlet of Rudge in rural Somerset? This can scarcely be the case, because (as we saw earlier with the poem to Mountjoy prefacing the 1599 *Poeticall Essayes*) his poems, these rooms, are where he intends his aristocratic patrons to live, their dignities preserved by the merit of the poem or play he has dedicated to them. The house Daniel is imagining is decidedly grander, surely the kind of big country or town house the elite would occupy. But how and in what style might this house have been made? Is it an Elizabethan or Jacobean prodigy house, a fantasy of towers and battlements, neoclassical manners fused and confused with baroque design, a precursor to one of the Inigo Jones mansions? Perhaps, but there is the other possibility that he is thinking of one of the Tudor houses made out of the rubble of the past, an old house made again, like Penshurst Palace, the Sidney home in Kent, or Mountjoy's home, Wanstead House, where we know Daniel lived from time to time.[28] These are houses fashioned from great halls and fortresses, or from the broken stone and materials of the monasteries destroyed in the English Reformation. At every angle such houses present us with visible signs, sometimes in the facade of outer walls, or in a different roof line, of the different architectural elements of their past, brick added here, masonry there, a new Tudor screen and mullion windows set into medieval walls.

This is the house that Daniel thought he was building, I believe, where his poems and plays and collections – rooms, passages, frames – had been remade over the years, but where their earlier histories, traces of them at least, could still be made out. It was in this house that he hoped his elite patrons, with their own noble family houses, would also dwell. None of this should surprise us, since Daniel, the most acute of early modern historians, so often reads beneath his present time, seeking the outlines and ground plans of the past. This is the short answer in support of a print OET for Daniel: that, because it is a book, it too is a house of remade but fixed parts, notes and elucidations, with, most important of all, a textual apparatus of discarded pieces beneath the established fabric of texts, changed over the years but still intact, bearing witness to the poet's alterations ('like to the curious builder' constantly pulling down and rebuilding). I very much doubt whether an electronic edition, however well it could accommodate the needs of The Reader, could ever offer these material signs of effacement and presence simultaneously.

Notes

1 For one spectacularly complicated transaction, see the exchanges between Arthur Freeman and I. A. Shapiro: Freeman, 'An epistle for two', *Library*, 5:25 (1970), pp. 226–36; Shapiro, 'The Hatton Manuscript', *Library*, 5:26 (1971), pp. 63–4; Freeman and Shapiro, 'The Hatton Manuscript', *Library*, 5:28 (1973), pp. 333–7. Other aspects of how Daniel's editions were made, given and sold are considered in John Pitcher (ed.), 'Samuel Daniel's Occasional and Dedicatory Verse: A Critical Edition' (Oxford D.Phil. thesis, 1978), 2 vols, 2: pp. 232–52, 303–7, and 353–67.

2 Harry Sellers, 'A bibliography of the works of Samuel Daniel, 1585–1623', *Proceedings and Papers of the Oxford Bibliographical Society*, 2:1 (1927), pp. 29–54, 341–2; W. A. Jackson and F. S. Ferguson, completed by Katherine F. Pantzer, *A Short Title Catalogue … 1475–1640*, 2nd edn, 3 vols (London, Bibliographical Society, 1976–91).

3 See n. 19 below for an article describing the work in progress on the Oxford edition of Daniel. 'Wydowe Crosley' was selling Daniel's books in Oxford in 1612–13: see W. A. Jackson (ed.), *Records of the Court of the Stationer's Company 1602 to 1640* (London, Bibliographical Society, 1957), p. 57.

4 See Katherine Duncan-Jones, 'Was the 1609 *Shake-speares Sonnets* really unauthorized?', *Review of English Studies*, n.s. 34 (1983), pp. 151–71, and John Kerrigan (ed.), William Shakespeare, *The Sonnets and A Lover's Complaint* (Harmondsworth, Penguin, 1986), pp. 13–18. For a more general discussion, see Ian Jack, 'A choice of orders: the arrangement of "The Political Works"', in Jerome J. McGann (ed.), *Textual Criticism and Literary Interpretation* (Chicago, University of Chicago Press, 1983), pp. 127–43.

5 Spenser himself encouraged Daniel in *Colin Clouts Come Home Againe* (1595), and William Covell referred to the 'courte-deare verse' of 'happie Daniell' in *Polimanteia* (1595). He was praised by Nashe in *Pierce Peniless* (1592) and *The Terrours of the Night* (1594), and by Harvey in *Fovre Letters, and certaine Sonnets* (1592) and *Pierce Supererogation* (1593).

6 Montaigne's influences are traced in J. I. M. Stewart, 'Montaigne's *Essays* and *A Defence of Ryme*', *Review of English Studies*, 9 (1933), pp. 311–12; Raymond Himelick, 'Samuel Daniel, Montaigne and Seneca', *Notes & Queries*, n.s. 3 (1956), pp. 61–4; and Himelick, 'Montaigne and Daniel's "To Sir Thomas Egerton"', *Philological Quarterly*, 36 (1957), pp. 500–4.

7 See James Spedding, R. L. Ellis and D. D. Heath (eds), *The Works of Francis Bacon*, 14 vols (London, Longmans, 1857–74), 11, pp. 340–1.

8 Mountjoy's own motto was *ad reædificandam antiquam domum*, 'to re-build the ancient house': one portrait shows him with a builder's trowel in his hand (see the *Dictionary of National Biography* entry for Mountjoy).

9 John Pitcher, 'Editing Daniel', in W. Speed Hill (ed.), *New Ways of Looking at Old Texts* (Binghampton, NY, Medieval and Renaissance Texts and Studies, 1993), pp. 57–73 (68).

10 Editions of Heywood's *Works* were published in 1562, 1576, 1587 and 1598; he died *c*. 1580.

11 Quoted from 'The Apology', in Laurence Michel (ed.), *The Tragedy of Philotas* (New Haven, Yale University Press, 1949), p. 156.

12 Owners of the 1601/2 *Works* folios include Queen Elizabeth, Lord Keeper Egerton, Sir Henry Wotton, William Skipwith, William Davenport, William Drummond and Ben Jonson. I shall consider contemporary ownership and annotation of copies of Daniel in a future article.

13 See Pitcher (ed.), 'Occasional and Dedicatory Verse', 2: pp. 206–9 for evidence that Daniel presented his *Works* folio to the Bodleian when King James visited the library in August 1605.

14 In 1602, in a not very well judged piece, Francis Davison went so far as to congratulate Daniel on having surpassed Spenser too: see H. E. Rollins (ed.), *The Poetical Rhapsody 1601–2*, 2 vols (Cambridge, MA, Harvard University Press, 1931–2), 1: pp. 96–7.

15 See W. Craig Ferguson, *Valentine Simmes* (Charlottesville, Bibliographical Society of the University of Virginia, 1968), p. 53. What Daniel meant by the design of the *Works* title page, if it was his, remains unexplored. It is striking that of the two princes in the middle section, one of them wears his crown and carries his sceptre upright while the other does not, perhaps signifying the strong and weak rulers of medieval England in *The Civil Wars*.

16 See further on this, Jason Lawrence, '"The whole complection of Arcadia chang'd": Samuel Daniel and Italian Lyrical Drama', *Medieval and Renaissance Drama in England*, 11 (1999), pp. 143–72.

17 Daniel, 'To the Reader', in A. C. Sprague (ed.), *Samuel Daniel: Poems and A Defence of Ryme* (Chicago and London, Chicago University Press, 1930; repr. Phoenix, 1965), pp. 3–5.

18 Daniel was called before the Privy Council in 1605 to explain the resemblance his *The Tragedy of Philotas* bore to the events of the Essex rebellion of 1601. In a letter that he wrote to Mountjoy shortly afterwards he describes how 'first I tolde the Lordes I had written 3 Acts of this tragedie the Christmas before my L. of Essex troubles … I said I had read some parte of it to yor ho:', Michel (ed.), *Philotas*, p. 38.

19 Pitcher, 'Benefiting from the book: the Oxford edition of Samuel Daniel', *Yearbook of English Studies* 29 (1999), pp. 1–19 (14).

20 See Pitcher, 'Benefiting from the book', pp. 12–14, for two of Daniel's readers, one a member of the Gresham family, the other William Davenport; and Pitcher, 'Samuel Daniel and the authorities', *Medieval and Renaissance Drama in England*, 10 (1998), pp. 113–48, for Mountjoy, and for another reader, a Jacobean judge, Sir Anthony Benn.

21 See Pitcher (ed.), *Occasional and Dedicatory Verse*, 2: pp. 303–8.

22 Drayton's qualified praise that Daniel's 'rimes were smooth, his meeters well did close' is typical: see J. W. Hebel, Kathleen Tillotson and B. H. Newdigate (eds), *The Works of Michael Drayton*, 5 vols (London, Shakespeare Head Press/Basil Blackwell, 1961), 3: p. 229.

23 See Pitcher, 'Benefiting from the book', pp. 1–19.

24 For a pertinent discussion, see John Kerrigan, 'The editor as reader: constructing Renaissance texts', in James Raven, Helen Small and Naomi Tadmor (eds), *The Practice and Representation of Reading in England* (Cambridge, Cambridge University Press, 1996), pp. 102–24.

25 Probably the most frequented UK poetry resource on the Internet, the Chadwyck-Healy 'English Poetry Database' (http://lion.chadwyck.co.uk, 1998), is based on the inaccurate edition prepared by A. B. Grosart, *The Complete Works in Verse and Prose of Samuel Daniel*, 5 vols (London, Hazel, Watson & Viney, 1885–96).

26 See Martin Heidegger, 'The origins of the work of art', in David Farell Krell (trans. and ed.), *Martin Heidegger: The Basic Writings* (London, Routledge, 1978), pp. 145–6, for the 'thingly element' of art.

27 Sprague (ed.), *Poems and A Defence of Ryme*, p. 3, ll. 1–9.

28 See A. C. Rathmell, 'Jonson, Lord Lisle and Penshurst', *English Literary Renaissance*, 1 (1971), pp. 250–60; Don Wayne, *Penshurst* (London, Methuen, 1984); Winifred Eastment, *Wanstead Through the Ages* (London, Dawn, 1969); and William Addison, *Wanstead Park* (London, Corporation of London, 1973).

Hypertext and multiplicity: the medieval example

Graham D. Caie

Editorial practices vary greatly from language to language and, within the English language, according to the historical period of the text. Editors of classical texts, for example, seem to be more daring and self-confident in their textual emendations than the more conservative editors of Old English who generally prefer to retain the manuscript reading and appear to have greater faith in the scribe.[1] The general principles ought to be the same, as they are dealing with hand-written manuscripts often in multiple exemplars, but different editorial traditions evolve through the centuries and editors are notoriously bad at communicating with each other. It is, therefore, salutary to glance in this volume on the editing and conceptualisation of Renaissance texts at what is happening in another period.

What does appear to distinguish the editing of medieval texts in recent years is the increasing use of electronic editing and an attempt to bring the reader into the editorial process. At first it might appear strange that editors of the oldest texts in our language are the most ready to use the most modern electronic methods. Do they simply wish to prove that 'medieval' does not imply old-fashioned? I would like to suggest that hypermedia is frequently superior to the codex in presenting a medieval text, because of the wealth of information on the membrane in addition to the text, and because of the way in which the concepts of 'text' and 'author' were viewed in this period. The flexibility, interaction and fluidity afforded by hypertext and hypermedia can give the modern reader some sense of the total experience enjoyed by the medieval reader when confronted by a sheet of vellum, while at the same time making the text intelligible over a gap of perhaps a millennium. Such an edition is also more 'reader friendly', as endless searching in glossary or explanatory notes is replaced by readily accessible on–screen 'buttons'.

A medieval text is a moveable and organic object. Not only does it change in every manuscript witness, but it interacts on the page with illustrations, glosses, historiated capitals and lemmata. In some cases the medieval page is a hive of activity, full of visual stimuli with the text itself off-centre to make space for marginal illustrations and glosses that parody or interpret text, and lemmata that guide the reader who attempts to assimilate and synthesise what can only be called a multidimensional visual experience. For this reason modern technology, in particular hypermedia, has been able to restore to the reader the vitally important *context* of the medieval text lost since the invention of printing. David Silver helpfully distinguishes between the 'univocality' of the printed text, as opposed to the 'multivocality' of hypermedia, a term that might equally apply to the medieval manuscript: 'A text contains multiple voices and/or approaches towards a subject or set of subjects. No longer bound by the physical limitations imposed by printed technology, hypermedia projects can tackle a topic from an array of often conflicting positions.'[2]

It is the lack of closure, the interactivity and the empowerment of the reader that make hypermedia an exciting new tool in conveying the text in context to the modern reader. In this chapter I wish to discuss how the new technology benefits the editor and to give some examples of current hypermedia projects in medieval studies in the hope that it might be of benefit to editors and analysts of Renaissance texts.

Modern printed editions of medieval literature persist in giving the reader what the editor *thinks* the usually anonymous medieval author intended. It is perfectly understandable that the editor should aid the reader by correcting obvious scribal errors, as medieval scribes themselves did when confronted with nonsensical readings. However, in modern editions the reconstructed text stands in solitary confinement, wrenched from its neighbouring texts and distanced from all the clues that the manuscript offers about scribes, compilers, limners, binders, owners and readers. The editor also influences the interpretation of the work by editorial punctuation, a modern title, glossary and notes. We are, therefore, presented with a museum piece, a clean and tidy work, an artefact that has been excavated from its manuscript surroundings, tidied up, brushed down and exhibited in splendid isolation in pristine condition in a showcase.[3]

Jerome McGann states that the 'limits of the book determined the development of the structural forms' of the edition:

> problems arise because they deploy a book form to study another book form. This symmetry between the tool and its subject forces the scholar to invent analytic mechanisms that must be displayed and engaged at the

primary reading level – e.g., apparatus structures, descriptive bibliographies, calculi of variants, shorthand reference forms and so forth.[4]

Hypermedia therefore frees the editor from the limitations of the codex, but it is important that the editor uses the full potential of this new form and not simply reproduces the same material on screen that would be available in a book. We have had the scholarly edition for centuries and scholars have been instructed in the techniques of editing all their academic lives: it now requires imagination to visualise, for example, the possibilities of incorporating audial and visual documents into the edition. Search engines, impressive programs such as Peter Robinson's COLLATE, thesauri and specialised dictionaries can be accessed and the program can be interactive for teaching or research purposes. With such tools the edition becomes immediately useful to linguists working on syntax, lexis or dialectology, and the creation of period dictionaries and thesauri is greatly facilitated.

The initial problem for the editor of an Anglo-Saxon work is that the word 'text' is post-Conquest and the concept does not seem to have existed, as we know it, in Old English. An author at his or her desk committing an original work to vellum that is then preserved until it can be edited in printed form is very, very rare. First, all Old English poetry is anonymous and nothing is preserved in its original form. The concept of original authorship also goes against both early and late medieval thought, as the only true author is God and the only true text is His writings. In scholastic texts all other writing can be but a gloss on the Word, an exegesis or elucidation of the text, called *enarratio* as it is 'out of the narration' and a supplementary discourse. In time these works could take on canonical status, such as the patristic works. It is for this reason that authors of imaginative texts in the vernacular conceal their originality by claiming to be copying sources or, at best, they excuse themselves by stating that they are narrating a dream. In the case of an Anglo-Saxon work, there may be no one original composition, the text evolving from oral tradition until at some point in its history it is captured in written form, as in a photograph of a monument. The writer is a facilitator, a broadcaster, of the monument. More common, however, is the concept of the *scop* 'creator' or 'shaper' in Old English, an artisan who wove his 'word-hoard' into new creations, as exemplified in *Beowulf* lines 867ff.:

> At times a thane of the kings, a man filled with poetic eloquence, who
> remembered many lays, who recollected countless old traditions, framed
> a new story in words correctly linked. The man began to set forth with

skill the deed of Beowulf, and fluently to tell a well-told tale, to weave together his words.[5] The *Beowulf* scribe, then, inscribes on membrane written symbols that reflect the composition of a *scop* who, in this episode, in turn is conveying the words of another *scop* who weaves in a new texture words from the poetic word-hoard. 'Correctly linked' and 'with skill' praises the craftsmanship, while the words and metaphors, indeed whole half-lines, are taken from the old lays and rewoven. Although not yet invented, the term 'text', with its etymology of weaving, might well fit this exercise. It is equally difficult to distinguish between terms for oral and written composition in Old English vocabulary, just as there is no visual differentiation between prose and verse when an Old English vernacular work is committed to membrane. The art of composition is central – it is a craft akin to that of the smith and the act is *gewyrcan* 'to work, create or form'; then in the course of the Middle Ages the Old English *scop* 'creator' becomes the Middle English 'maker'. When confined to written form the work becomes *gewrit* 'writing' with its connotations of something scratched, inscribed or cut into the vellum, a memorial to the oral creation akin to the way in which a gravestone inscription immortalises the life of the dead. The written word is also called *run* 'rune', which suggests the mystery and magic of the written word, as does *logos*, the primal force in the world. When the word 'text' does enter the English language it brings with it the connotation of its cognate forms 'texture', 'textile', 'a woven artefact', again reflecting the medieval method of composition.[6]

The hypertext can recover some of the mystery of this creative process, as the reader is involved in the re-creation of text in the hypertext culture. He or she begins to realise that there is no single 'correct' text, that it needs to be studied in its codicological context, and that punctuation, titles and layout are all modern, editorial additions. Punctuation can change meaning and it is possible in the hypertext mode to allow the reader to change the meaning in this way; even some simple interactive hypercard editions of Old English have built in a number of translations which change according to the reader's decision on punctuation; this serves the important pedagogical function of making the student critically aware of the power the editor has over interpretation. If such an exercise is considered confusing, then the student can keep to the editor's decisions on punctuation and paragraphing.

By presenting a selection of facsimiles and transcripts in the hypertext edition the reader becomes aware of the fact that there is no 'fixed' text and that the work moves constantly from exemplar to exemplar, so that the parameter of any one text is not clearly defined. In one manuscript we are simply looking at a snapshot of a moving object, one witness of the composition. If Chaucer had a *Canterbury Tales* fan club in the fifteenth century, its various members would have discussed different works, as certain tales would be omitted in some manuscripts and glosses, spurious tales and links added to others. Book production was very much a bespoke trade and the prospective owner would discuss with the compiler what would be included, the cost, number of illustrations and bindings. A parallel might be made with the programmes of wall paintings in medieval churches; the templates from, say, the prints of the *Biblia Pauperum* were the same, but the choice of scenes and their realisation and juxtaposition on the walls was always unique.

The author of *Piers Plowman*, for example, never let go of his text throughout his lifetime; there are three major revisions in the A, B and C versions, and also within these versions there are major manuscript differences. The work was organic, growing and changing as the author's ideas and historical events developed. In codicological terminology this is the phenomenon of 'mouvance', the constant movement and lack of closure in the life of a text, and there is no way one can properly capture this on the printed page. Other texts, specifically scholastic works, developed by the *pecia* system, whereby scholars 'piecemeal' copied sections of a text and passed them on to others to copy. The production of texts in the student communities before the era of the photocopier was more akin to the game of Chinese whispers, whereby the message changes as it spreads and errors multiply.

The traditional way of presenting a text that is found in a number of versions is for the editor to choose what he or she considers the most suitable text and signal variant readings in note form. What to do with this visually unattractive list of variants poses a problem. It can be squeezed in at the foot of the page or collected, as in the Riverside edition of *The Canterbury Tales*, at the end of the volume. In both cases it looks awkward and needs further help to decipher abbreviations: e.g., '767 Dorstestow] Cl R H^1 S^1 Gg Skt Mck Rob Fsh; *Dorst thow* J H^4 D Dg H^3 H^5 Don; *Durste thow* Cp S2 Cx Th Rkr Bgh, Wdr ...'.[7] There is no way that the presentation of these variant readings conveys the movement of the text from witness to witness or suggests how the different readings influence interpretation. The solution is available in hypermedia, as in the case of The *Canterbury Tales* Project, which presents the reader with the choice of the various facsimiles and transcripts, or whole lines or sections of the variant passages. The reader, then, becomes an editor and is involved in the process or, if this is confusing, can simply follow the base Hengwrt text.

Another problem concerns what to do with the 'non-textual' material on the page. The general view amongst editors is to banish it from the page of edited text, as it looks messy, but make mention of marginalia or illustrations in the preface or notes. But these marginalia and interlinear comments were an integral part of the text itself in the medieval manuscript. The glosses in manuscripts acted like explanatory notes in many medieval texts and took on a life of their own, often being collected in great compendia of glosses. No Latin text worth anything went unglossed, or it was considered of insufficient substance, and held in the same esteem as a monograph today that is never reviewed. Glosses were written on glosses in an intricate semiotic system and took on canonical status themselves.

Similarly the great vernacular works of Chaucer, Gower and Langland were liberally glossed and these became *part* of the text; in the case of Chaucer and Gower they were copied faithfully by scribes throughout the fifteenth century, beyond the time of printing. In the most famous manuscript of *The Canterbury Tales,* the Ellesmere Manuscript, the text is off-centre, on the left of the page, to give way to the glosses which are written in the same and as large a hand as the text itself. Visually the glosses are privileged as highly as the text itself, a fact known only to readers who consult the manuscript or a facsimile, as no edition has yet presented them side by side. Such a significant position forces the reader to consider them not as footnotes or marginalia, as they are usually called, but as primary text. They provide an important contemporary commentary on the text and, as I have argued elsewhere, may well be by Chaucer himself.[8] They are in Latin and many appear to have the didactic function of guiding the reader in an age when lay literacy and clerical fears thereof were on the increase. The vernacular, poetic and imaginative text of the poem is visually balanced against the Latin, prose and didactic text of the gloss.

The gloss frequently reminds us of the source of the author's inspiration, and of the fact that the text comprises a palimpsest of other texts, layer upon layer of interpretation. For example, we are made aware by the glosses that if we were to peel off one layer from the Wife of Bath's narration we would come to *La Vieille* in Jean de Meun's *Roman de la Rose,* and beneath that the married whore of St Jerome's *Contra Jovinianum* and eventually to the words of St Paul himself. The hypertext can reintroduce the gloss and restore the counterbalance and guidance it originally provided.[9]

There is much more to these manuscripts, however, than text and gloss. One of the joys of teaching medieval literature is to see the transformation in a student when working with a manuscript. This is not always possible, and indeed, we must consider the damage done to the original if it is constantly consulted. With such sophisticated techniques as enhancement of text through digitisation there will be little need in the future to subject precious texts to the constant handling that is ruining them. Only the very few codicologists with interests in foliation or binding will need to inspect them in the future, as harassed librarians can point to the 'virtual manuscript' in electronic form. Although the smell cannot yet be reproduced (though this will surely be a matter of time) almost every other aspect of the manuscript can be conveyed in electronic form and available to those who live far from original copies. Clues about cost, appearance, readership and ownership can be gleaned from close examination of the digitised facsimile that can include the flyleaves, while punctuation and other markings can give hints on contemporary oral presentation of the text.

An interesting example of what can be done is Melissa Bernstein's Electronic Wulfstan, which started as an undergraduate honours project, and is still developing in her postgraduate studies.[10] She has edited the base text of Wulfstan's *Sermo Lupi* in BL MS Cotton Nero A i and is now adding more tools, extra manuscript facsimiles, transcriptions of other redactions, translations, textual notes, critical notes, a glossary, grammatical notes, analogues and an annotated bibliography. The screen is divided into sections and one can decide which configuration one wants, e.g., two facsimiles, or a facsimile and an edited version, or edited version and translation, while still being able to consult critical notes or glossary or to write notes. The pedagogical advantages of such a program are great: one can teach palaeography or codicology by enlarging a manuscript section or line, discuss editorial practices by comparing edited texts with transcriptions, or use it for teaching grammar, dialectology or stylistics.

There are many such hypertext editions of Old and Middle English at the moment, invariably created for undergraduate use and not commercially distributed; they have created a revolution in the teaching of the subject and, indeed, have helped revitalise a topic that was once considered both difficult and dull. Students receive the additional 'transferable skill' of proficiency in IT at the same time. Some programs are not centred on text but on the material culture of the period. An excellent example is Allen Frantzen's *Seafarer* program based at Loyola University of Chicago, which allows the viewer to navigate round many central topics in Anglo-Saxon England, such as law, church, history, archaeology, literacy, women, the medieval book, etc. Edited texts and facsimiles are provided, but are given equal status with the units on material culture. This project is still under construction, but will prove extremely useful in many teaching circumstances.

A major complaint voiced against the hyperedition concerns its complexity. Facsimiles and transcriptions of all manuscript witnesses give so much choice that confusion ensues, they claim, and what is needed is an edition that presents a single text with translations and notes. This was stated at a recent conference of medievalists where it was suggested that the CD-ROM produced by The *Canterbury Tales* Project on *The Wife of Bath's Prologue* with its plethora of options made Chaucer's text inaccessible to modern readers. The comment, intended as criticism, might well have been taken as a compliment by the project group, as this is exactly what they are trying to do; namely to give the modern reader all the information available to the medieval reader – warts and all – as well as modern aids such as glossaries, bibliographies and search engines. The responsibility is the reader's to select exactly what he or she wishes. A simple, edited text is, however, available, as well as translation, etc., in addition to all the information needed for the research scholar. The basic question of audience for the edition is no longer so important when undertaking a project of this nature, as there is the potential to satisfy all.

The *Canterbury Tales* Project with its CD-ROM pilot study is indeed an extremely ambitious venture that changes as modern computer technology develops.[11] One of the major criteria of any such project is to make it as flexible, adaptable and open as possible in order to accommodate the breath-taking speed of new inventions in this field, and thereby avoiding obsolescence before completion. There are eighty-seven fifteenth-century manuscript 'witnesses' of *The Canterbury Tales*, some complete but the majority only fragments of the entire work. The project also includes the early printed editions, which might well be based on lost manuscripts that were closer to the original than our earliest extant ones. With manuscript and printed texts there are, therefore, literally millions of textual variants and the computer is by far the best way to put some order in them. All the manuscripts will eventually be transcribed into computer-readable form and problems such as that involving lineation (as all manuscripts differ) are being solved. The CDs will have digitised images of all folios with a full transcription and each individual tale will be published with all its witnesses as a single unit. One can therefore read any one manuscript in facsimile and/or with a transcription, or one can read any one tale in all its versions. The basic program used is COLLATE, developed by Peter Robinson originally with *Piers Plowman* in mind. It helps tackle the initial problem of dealing with medieval texts found in multiple manuscripts. The program allows a normalised text, so that any word can be found, although original spellings are also preserved; i.e., each transcription will be in original spelling, with abbreviations and other forms intact, and also in a regularised form, to help in any comparative work. While looking at the digitised image from any manuscript one can simultaneously look at the transcription of that passage plus the transcriptions from other manuscripts in order to compare them.

The program is able to do what Manly and Rickert spent their lives attempting manually with mixed success in Chicago in the 1930s, but such an operation was nigh impossible because of the volume of material.[12] I have memories of a late colleague, Jørgen Raasted, in Copenhagen with a room filled from ceiling to floor with strips of paper, each with variant readings of Byzantine liturgical texts. He would laboriously adjust the positions of the strips to work out variations in the different versions. Then came the day when he could collate the manuscripts by computer and his life and work were transformed.

What is most exciting is that every mark in the manuscript is recorded. One is presented with the material object with all its additions, underlining, deletions, glosses, punctuation and marginal comments, exactly as the medieval reader would have seen it. The images are derived by high-resolution digital scan of microfilm copies, with some colour images in 24-bit colour directly from the manuscripts themselves. The CD-ROM of *The Wife of Bath's Prologue* contains all fifty-five manuscripts and four pre-1500 printed editions of the work (that is 1100 pages of manuscript) and also includes the collation and analytic software. One of the most interesting recent discoveries the team has made is that a close inspection of the 1920 Manly and Rickert rotograph reproduction of the Hengwrt Manuscript has uncovered readings which are now totally lost to the eye; the project will therefore reproduce the rotograph readings to enhance the more recent facsimile version.

Another major project using digitised images and the most up-to-date techniques and expertise from information and computer scientists, mathematicians and statisticians is the Electronic *Beowulf*.[13] This collaborative project is headed by Kevin Kiernan at Kentucky, Paul Szarmach at Western Michigan and a British Library team. A group aptly called GRENDL (Group for Research in Electronically Networked Digital Libraries) is developing the necessary software for this extremely ambitious project: not only will all folios of the British Library Cotton Vitellius A XV manuscript be digitised, but also ultra-violet and fibre-optic readings and 'back-lit' images of obscure letters and sections in this badly damaged manuscript. This will allow the reader to superimpose the enhanced images on to the facsimile and thereby glimpse an illegible word. In addition there will be a translation, transcription, edition and collation of the poem, not to mention a glossary, bibliography, articles on the poem, manuscript illuminations from contemporary works and contextual information of an archaeological, historical and sociological nature. Recently Kevin Kiernan has digitised the two Thorkelin transcripts in the Royal Library, Copenhagen; Thorkelin, some fifty years after the infamous Cotton fire, was still able to see many more letters on the edges of this brittle manuscript than are now visible, so his transcriptions are of major value to scholars. Kiernan has also added to the electronic library some of the earliest editions of the poem from the nineteenth century, e.g., those by J. J. Conybeare and F. Madden. The major problem at present is finding a fast and efficient way of allowing the vast amount of material to be accessed easily without the recipient requiring enormous computer memory. Each image takes up 21 MB and Kiernan requires 128 MB of RAM, a 24-bit colour monitor and unlimited storage space. Four scanned letters in the manuscript alone can fill an 88-MB hard disk. There is a beta-version available from the British Museum and soon it will be available to all by way of a Unix-based program on multiple platforms and the Internet. Not only will the fragile manuscript be left in peace by scholars, but they will be able to reconstruct the illegible readings not seen since the time of Thorkelin in the eighteenth century.

Lancaster has recently inaugurated a similarly ambitious and exciting project, this time on medieval English mystery plays, specifically the Doomsday pageant in the York cycle, under the direction of Meg Twycross and Pamela King.[14] They describe what they intend to do as 'a giant ring doughnut', as there is so much surviving contemporary material surrounding the drama, with only the central, medieval performance missing. This project is like Allen Frantzen's *Seafarer* in the sense that the *text* of the plays is not at the centre. The presentation of the contextual material in a series of hyperlinked packages makes it all the more easy to fill in this hole and thereby reconstruct the plays. The 'York Register', which provides the text of the plays, appears in facsimile, transcript and edited forms, but the text is considered only one of many witnesses to the performance itself. Initially the project aims at building up an archive of high-resolution scans of the wealth of material in York: the York Mercers' Indenture which contains much information about staging and costumes; the Mercers' account books which record money paid to players and for props, costumes and wagons; York City documents such as the A/Y Memorandum Book with information about audiences; maps of York itself that show where and how the performances would have been performed; contemporary art in York, such as the stained-glass windows of the Minster, and, finally, devotional literature of the period. As an example of a production, the team intends to add a video performance and '3-D visualisations' of a re-creation of the York Judgement Day pageant of 1988 that took place on the streets of York. All this evidence will be hyperlinked and presented on CD-ROM. The aim is to give the modern audience (as we cannot call them readers) access to as much material as possible in order to let them create a theatrical experience as close as possible to the vanished performance, at the centre of the doughnut.

The Unicorns, a drama group that I directed at the University of Copenhagen, spent the academic year 1987–8 studying the wealth of material available in the Toronto-based *Records of Early English Drama* series and contemporary sources, such as those mentioned above, in order to gain enough information to re-create one of the York pageants in the above-mentioned performance in the streets of York. The experience of gathering information about medieval performance, costumes, acting and staging with the students and putting our findings into practice in a performance on a pageant wagon was both exhilarating and worth a thousand lectures on the subject. The Lancaster CD-ROM will provide much the same material in a more accessible form to future generations of students who can re-create the performance either in their imaginations or on the stage. A particularly exciting development, as yet simply a dream, would be the combination of a virtual-reality program with hypertext.[15] Such scanned records can also be used by scholars in different disciplines such as history, sociology, palaeography and dialectology. The project claims

that the presentation of the material in high-resolution colour facsimile 'gives the reader a sense of the original as a working document,
something that we lose when reading it transcribed in a printed book'.
One might imagine that the same could be done with Renaissance
drama. Just as there is no single text, there is also no definitive production of a dramatic text.

The most important consideration for any editor, irrespective of
period, is the audience. To present a series of facsimiles or diplomatic
editions on CD-ROM to someone who has little knowledge of medieval
English or who simply wants to read the story would be madness.
Similarly, the undergraduate faced with a *Beowulf* for the first time
would far prefer George Jack's excellent edition with facing glossary
than what is offered by the Electronic *Beowulf*. Readership of editions
is of vital importance and for that reason we will continue to have many
different types of edition in the future. Many, surprisingly enough, do
not want to take a computer to bed with them; many do not care about
variant readings; actors want a script from which they can work; and
students may not want to have to decide on textual punctuation. Not all
readers want the empowerment to be their own editor. The electronic
text, as suggested above, can present all things to all people: at one
extreme is the bare translation for those who have no knowledge of Old
English; at the other is the enhanced facsimile readings of specific editorial cruces for the specialist; in between are carefully edited texts. All
readers can be served, however, by the search programs, thesauri, glossaries and historico-cultural notes that can also be incorporated.

The hypertext is still text-based, but multimedia can supply vital
information and break down the sense of univocality and linear progres-
sion mentioned above. It may take some time to realise the full potential
of the electronic revolution and to break with the constraints and physical limitations of the printed page, just as printers and computers still
attempt to copy the form of the medieval page with justified right-hand
margins. Medieval scholars are leading the field in hypermedia at present, largely because they are aware of the ability of this multidimensional medium to re-create the total experience of the manuscript page.
Recently the Arden Shakespeare CD-ROM has appeared, based on
Arden 2, and the editors promise an Arden 3 package by 2006.[16] It
includes introductions, notes, textual variants and bibliography, and
allows users to create their own notes and to print out sections of the text.
This medium is not of course restricted to the medieval and Renaissance
text; it has great potential for those working with printed editions

throughout the ages. For example, the facsimile and transcript of the original drafts of T. S. Eliot's *The Waste Land* with Ezra Pound's annotations, Valerie Eliot's notes and cross-references, and Eliot's own notes would profit by such an electronic edition.[17] The printed edition that one can enjoy in any location will never disappear, but we should be open to the immense potential and flexibility of this new medium.

Notes

1 See Michael Lapidge, 'On the emendation of Old English texts', in D. G. Scragg and Paul E. Szarmach (eds), *The Editing of Old English* (Cambridge, D. S. Brewer, 1994), pp. 53–67.

2 'Multimedia, multilinearity, and multivocality in the hypermedia classroom', *Computer Texts*, 14 (1997), p. 7.

3 See my comments on editing Old English texts in 'Text and context in editing Old English: the case of the poetry in Cambridge, Corpus Christi College 201', in D. G. Scragg and Paul E. Szarmach (eds), *The Editing of Old English*, pp. 155–62.

4 'The Rationale of HyperText' (1995).
http://jefferson.village.virginia.edu/public/jjm2f/rationale.html.

5 Translation by John R. Clark Hall in *Beowulf and the Finnesburg Fragment* (London, Allen & Unwin, rev. edn, 1950), pp. 64–5.

6 See the semantic fields covering 'writing', 'inscribe', 'composition', 'writing down', 'author', 'a secret', in Jane Roberts, Christian Kay with Lynne Grundy, *A Thesaurus of Old English* (London, King's College Centre for Late Antique and Medieval Studies, 1995), pp. 470–3. See also Seth Lerer and Joseph A. Dane, 'What is a text?', in Seth Lerer (ed.), *Reading from the Margins: Textual Studies, Chaucer and Medieval Literature* (San Marino, CA, Huntington Library, 1996), pp. 1–10.

7 This random example is taken from Larry D. Benson (ed.), *The Riverside Chaucer* (Oxford, Oxford University Press, 3rd edn, 1987), p. 1164.

8 See my article 'The significance of the early Chaucer manuscript glosses (with special reference to the *Wife of Bath's Prologue*)', *The Chaucer Review*, 10 (1977), pp. 354–5 in which I discuss the authorship of the glosses.

9 See my article 'The significance of marginal glosses in the earliest manuscripts of *The Canterbury Tales*', in David Jeffrey (ed.), *Chaucer and the Scriptural Tradition* (Ottawa, University of Ottawa Press, 1985), pp. 337–50.

10 This program is available at:
http://www.cif.rochester.edu/~mjbernst/wulfstan/Bernstein.

11 The *Canterbury Tales* Project is available at:
http://www.shef.ac.uk/uni/projects/ctp/index.html. See also Norman Blake and Peter Robinson (eds), *The* Canterbury Tales *Project; Occasional Papers*, 1:5 (Oxford, Office for Humanities Communication Publications, 1993); the second volume in the series was published in 1997. See Michael Pidd, Estelle Stubbs and Claire E. Thomson, 'The Hengwrt *Canterbury Tales*: inadmissible evidence', in vol. 2, pp. 55–60 for information about the Manly and Rickert rotograph readings.

12 J. M. Manley and E. Rickert (eds), *The Text of the Canterbury Tales* (Chicago, University of Chicago Press, 1940).

13 The Electronic *Beowulf* Project can be contacted at:
http://www.uky.edu/ArtsSciences/English/Beowulf. There are ftp sites at the British Library (othello.bl.uk) and a WWW presentation at:

http://www.uky.edu/~kiernan/welcome.html. See also Kevin Kiernan, 'The Electronic *Beowulf:* digital preservation, restoration, and dissemination of medieval manuscripts', *Computers in Libraries* (Feb., 1995), pp. 14-15 and online at http://www.uky.edu/ArtsSciences/English/Beowulf/CIL.html.

14 The York Doomsday Project can be reached at: http://www.lancs.ac.uk/users/yorkdoom/menu.htm.

15 Scott Bukatman in 'Virtual textuality' (1995), available at: http://jefferson.village.virginia.edu/~jmu2m/bukatman.html. Bukatman discusses the potential of combining virtual reality and hypertext: 'Their ultimate merger will generate a synaesthesia of data experience, one that might finally establish the crucial relation between the phenomenological subject privileged by virtual reality, and the acculturated, historical subject that grounds the hypertextual exploration.'

16 See the Arden Shakespeare at: http://www.thomson.com/thomasnelson/arden/ardencd.html.

17 See Valerie Eliot (ed.), *The Waste Land: A Facsimile and Transcript of the Original Drafts* (London, Faber & Faber, 1971).

c:\wp\file.txt 05:41 10–07–98

Gary Taylor

In the beginning was the File, & the File was with Gates, & the File was Gates. Through Gates all files come into being; never true file came into being, except through Gates.

What is a file?

This is not a file.

This is only an incarnceration of a file.

An incarnceration is a s/mattering of a United State of the File.

Any s/mattering defiles from a slaved transformation of a virtuality into a 2 2 solid state.

Virtuality rules ok.

A state is a time of a version of a virtuality.

Of the making of states there is no end.

There is no end to the File, and no beginning.

Beginning being none, there is no single autor of the File.

For every reader of the File, there is anutter time and state, anutter autor, anutter utter.

Poly there are of s/matterings & s/mutterings, poly of versions & of virtualities, poly there are of states & files, but there is only the one true File.

Poly there are of types & archetypes, but polyally are only prototypes of the File.

Ditto, the pen is the precursor of the cursor in the mind of Gates.

The Prints of Darkness prophesied the coming of the File.

The Prints of Darkness is but an incarnceration of the File-to-be in the mind of Gates.

Those there were once, who worshipped the Prints of Darkness and the s/matterings s/mutterings of the page.

But the Pagites could not prevail, against the File.

For the File ate the Prints of Darkness.

Hail, Gates, cursor of*******************************Please forgive this interruption by an ancient idiolect. Bear with me.

I am General Editor of *The Collected Works of Thomas Middleton*. I envisaged a particular kind of edition of a particular group of texts, I persuaded Oxford University Press to publish it, I negotiated a contract, I commissioned individual editors, I set deadlines, I developed and promulgated editorial procedures, I checked and corrected individual texts. But I am powerless to finish the edition. When people ask me whether or when the edition will appear, I say, 'It depends upon John Lavagnino.'

John Lavagnino is the 'Digital Editor' of *The Collected Works*. I invented that term to describe a role which, to my knowledge, had not existed before, but which seemed absolutely essential for the kind of edition I wanted to create. I was determined that the Oxford Middleton would take advantage of what I had learned about computerised editing from my previous experience with the Oxford Shakespeare. The Oxford University Press *Complete Works* of Shakespeare had been edited, and then printed, from files containing transcripts of various quarto and folio texts of Shakespeare's works, files originally prepared under the direction of Trevor Howard-Hill, and used to generate the Oxford Shakespeare Concordances. Howard-Hill's files had been written in the 1960s in a computer language which, by the late 1970s, only one computer in the world could still read; but once those files had been translated by that one computer, the translations provided us with an exceptionally accurate textual database, which we further checked and then manipulated editorially. For Middleton, no such database existed. But I knew that an electronic edition of Middleton would enable, and encourage, certain kinds of research that a traditional book-edition would not. If Middleton were to break Shakespeare's stranglehold on the Renaissance, he not only had to be read; he had to be accessed. Not only readable, but searchable, researchable, resourceful. This the Oxford Middleton was, pervasively. From the outset it was designed to be produced in the new conditions of textual production and reproduction in the late twentieth century: a diverse group of widely dispersed scholars used their individual personal computers, tied by a set of encodings into a virtual network, to produce hundreds of files, which were all routed to a single nodal point which collected, unified and transformed their individual textual productions. That nodal point was occupied by myself and Lavagnino, general and digital editors, collaborating at Brandeis University.

This digitalisation of Middleton was both intellectually and practically valuable. A draft concordance, prepared by Lavagnino on the basis of the initial editorial database, made it possible, for the first time, to approach local editorial problems from the global perspective of the entire canon. That evidence also helped resolve some contested attributions; for instance, it contributed significantly to the case for exclusion of *The Family of Love*, and for inclusion of some newly discovered poems. The concordance, and associated software, have enabled us to achieve a degree of editorial consistency which would otherwise scarcely have been possible in an edition prepared by sixty-six scholars in eleven countries – of an author whose works have not been edited as a whole since 1886, and some of whose individual works have not been reprinted since the early seventeenth century. Because of the availability of legible proofs of our draft texts, many of us could teach Middleton texts – otherwise unavailable – in undergraduate and graduate courses, and that teaching experience uncovered oversights and sharpened our perspectives on works that have not benefited from much critical attention or informed debate. My collaboration with Lavagnino in designing the edition, from type-fonts to page layout and running titles, inspired much rethinking of the standard material format of printed editions; it laid the foundations for my concept of a 'federal edition'. Finally, by relieving Oxford University Press of most of the composition costs associated with a very big book, we have ensured that the Oxford Middleton will be much more affordable than it would have been if it had been typeset in the traditional way.

But I do not yet know exactly what the Middleton edition will cost. I set a deadline for the delivery of files on 2 September 1993, and we promised the contributors the edition would be published in the autumn of 1994. At the time of my writing this edition has still not appeared.

There were reasons for the delay. Between 1993 and 1998 my marriage disintegrated, and so did Lavagnino's relationship with his own

long-term intimate partner. Are such changes substantive, or incidental? Certainly, such emotional realignments have become increasingly common in our time; certainly also, they consume large amounts
of time, energy and morale. They also produce divisions of property.
My ex-wife got the personal computer we had both been using since
1986.

Between 1993 and 1998 I moved from Brandeis University to the
University of Alabama; John Lavagnino moved from Brandeis to
Brown, and then to King's College London. Are such changes substantive, or incidental? Certainly, such geographical and institutional
mobility is increasingly common in our time; certainly also, it con-
sumes large amounts of time, energy and morale. I was pleased that the
University of Alabama computer network, and the personal and office
computer they provided me, were IBM-compatible; I assumed this
meant I would have no trouble transferring files. However, their systems were all based upon Microsoft Word; I had always used
WordPerfect. Indeed, I was still using WordPerfect version 4.2, which I
had learned in 1986 and had always found entirely adequate to my com-
positional needs. In order to facilitate interaction with Microsoft Word,
and my office printer, I upgraded to WordPerfect version 5.0. Soon
afterwards, I was forced to adjust to the new Windows 95 operating
system. Finally, in 1998, wanting to purchase a personal printer, I was
forced to upgrade my word-processing software again, because I could
not find a single new printer that could read WordPerfect version 5.0.
By themselves, personal computing problems delayed by at least a year
my completion of general editorial work on the Middleton edition.

Meanwhile, Lavagnino had problems of his own. The National
Endowment for the Humanities did not fund my application for a
'research tools' grant, which would have supported Lavagnino's work
on the electronic edition, the concordance and the software design that
would translate our editorial files into forms which could generate
camera-ready copy for the print edition. Computerised Shakespeare
projects have, in the last decade, received significant financial support
from public- and private-sector sources; but there is no money for
Middleton. Lavagnino, accordingly, at the time a graduate student, had
to support himself by other means. This was not in itself difficult; he is
a brilliant and experienced software designer, much in demand. But the
people able and eager to pay for his talents were not in the humanities,
but in science and business. These freelance jobs paid the bills, but they
also consumed most of his time, and directed his intellectual energies

away from the kinds of problems the Middleton project posed. Indeed, increasingly they drew him away from the academy altogether. His work on Middleton, however personally satisfying, was not professionally rewarded, until in July 1998 he was offered a position at King's College London, in what is at this time the only academic program in the world devoted to humanities computing. In this job he will be expected and encouraged to pursue his digital editing of the Oxford Middleton. But the change of jobs and sites will itself take time and energy.

As I write this, I and the other editors of *The Collected Works* are waiting for John Lavagnino to finish the computer work that only he knows how to do. This is the measure of power: I am replaceable, but Lavagnino is not. At the end of the twentieth century, the digital editor is more important than the general editor.

What theories can be formulated, on the basis of the foregoing data?

Change is expensive. Change expends time, energy, resources of all kinds.

Computerisation enforces change. The accelerating evolution of textual technologies imposes upon society as a whole, and upon editors as members of that society, a succession of mandated obsolescences. A book printed 400 years ago can be read more easily, in many more sites, than a file created ten years ago.

Changes in textual practices have always created narrow gates, through which texts have to pass if they are to remain legible. The change from uncial to minuscule script, the great vowel shift, the invention of print – these mutations of the media of representation transformed textual practices so radically that texts which were not translated into the new medium almost always perished, because they had become unintelligible to the textual classes. The change from print to digital technology has been correctly perceived as another such life-or-death gate. Unfortunately, it is not a single gate, but a succession of gates, with shorter and shorter intervals between them. *The more rapidly computers evolve, the more frequently files must be transformed, in order to remain legible.*

But change is expensive. Indeed, the more rapid the change, the more costly it is. Therefore, *the more rapidly computers evolve, the more expensive the maintenance of file-legibility becomes.*

As maintaining legibility becomes more expensive, *we will be able to afford the maintenance of legibility for fewer and fewer files* – unless our resources expand as rapidly as change accelerates.

But resources in the humanities – departmental and library budgets, the support of scholars rather than administrators – have, during the last thirty years, significantly and consistently declined. That change is almost certainly substantive, not incidental. Print technology developed in parallel with the rise of humanism and Protestantism; computer technology has developed in parallel with the rise of global corporations and capitalised science. Literature departments receive a small fraction of the funding that goes to business schools, medical schools or science departments. *As a proportion of total social expenditures, resources for humanities text creation, reproduction and maintenance decline, as digitalisation increases.*

At the same time, the development of digital technologies creates an increasing demand for their use. Thus, society favours cultural works which make maximum use of the multimedia potentials of the new tools: music on compact disc, film, video games, visual and audio encyclopaedias and archives, museum collections on CD-ROM. *In order to compete effectively for the available resources, editors must use the most sophisticated text-tools available.*

Hence, files that do remain legible will become accessible in an increasing variety and complexity of forms. As Randall McLeod and Jerome McGann and Graham D. Caie in their different ways have emphasised, the combination of photography and computers, the digitising of texts and images, makes possible modes of reproduction which preserve many more features of the texts generated by earlier inscriptive technologies (manuscript, print, engraving, etc.). Moreover, the same information technologies enable rapid and massive cross-referencing, concordancing, and all other forms of database searching. These preferred new modes of reproduction are preferred precisely because they are inhuman; no personality intervenes or intrudes between the original site and the new recitation, the original text and the new file. In this environment, *the best of all possible editors is a machine.*

Thus, editorial files must continue to become increasingly technologised. But that technological imperative further diminishes the available resource base. *Editorial files are becoming, not only more expensive to maintain, but also more expensive to create.*

Since resources are shrinking, at the very time when maintaining or recovering techno-legibility has become more expensive, *the number of old texts that can be made or kept legible seems destined to decline.* We are, for instance, already producing fewer editions of Renaissance authors than our Victorian predecessors did.

However, this decline is masked by the proliferation of versions. We effectively reproduce fewer works, but we produce more versions of the few works we do reproduce. We therefore feel that we 'know' those few works with an unparalleled breadth and intimacy; moreover, we test and confirm all our cultural theories against the database of those few works. That diminishing number of works thereby becomes the measure of all things. It is not simply that we concentrate more and more of our attention upon Shakespeare; even within the Shakespeare canon, we concentrate upon a diminishing number of works – just as late classical culture concentrated its attention upon a small fraction of the plays of Sophocles, Euripides, Aeschylus. Hence the paradox which has so rapidly overtaken the work of 'revisionist' editors of Shakespeare: what in the early 1980s seemed, to its opponents and defenders, an outrageously revolutionary practice had come to seem, by the late 1990s, naively conservative. The revisionists attempted to de-idealise Shakespeare by demonstrating that, like other writers, he revised his work; but the revisionist editorial practice of 'versioning' has simply provided more material for idealisation, more texts of Shakespeare at the expense of other works and writers. *The fewer works we preserve, the more idealised they become.*

And it is not just Shakespeare which is being idealised. It is no accident that the rise of versioning, as a theory and practice among the editorial elite, has coincided with the computerisation of the writing class: computers not only make such versioning possible, they also make it seem 'natural'. Like other dominant ideologies, digitalism internalises itself in its subjects, by making artificial social arrangements seem utterly natural, inevitable, commonsensical. My personal computer automatically backs up any file I am working on every ten minutes; I always have access to more than one version of any file, and whenever I access and alter an existing file I am doing what my computer labels 'editing'. Writing as process, ubiquitous revision, the artificiality of closure, the infinite networking of texts, the anonymous and pervasive discursive grid which controls even as it enables our verbal performances – we are reminded of these social 'facts' every time we sit down to word-process the literary texts and literary theories by which we earn our livings. Critical Theory and the New Textualism, like all the other intellectual children of the pc-boom generation, have always proudly imagined themselves to be subversive. But those new theories never subvert word-processing, or the assumptions about the world entailed by daily word-processing. In fact, if we shift our attention from local disputes over textual minutiae to the larger cultural topography where those minutiae are contested, it becomes obvious that *the alliance of literary and editorial theory in the 'New Textualism' imposes a newly dominant ideology upon a marginalised, relatively impoverished, recalcitrant and residual fraction of the social world.*

People are most comfortable with the technologies familiarised in childhood: those technologies become internalised as part of an individual habitus, shared by age-cohorts. Technological revolutions thus inevitably create habitus-gaps, along a sliding generational scale. *In periods of rapid tool-change, tool-users of a given generation accordingly share a sense of technological superiority over their elders, which both enables and legitimates their efforts to secure institutional power for themselves.*

Older scholars, in such periods, have only two choices: to surrender, or to change – the only effective change being to internalise, selfconsciously, the unselfconscious technological habitus of their younger rivals. In either case, *power among editorial elites will inevitably shift to scholars who have internalised the newly dominant ideology of The File.*

But the resulting invulnerability of the new elite (a governing class composed of fully technologised subject-files) is purchased by an increasing divide between Master DOS and microserf. The fantastic personal wealth accumulated by Bill Gates – now monitored, second by second, on an unauthorised website; he has made millions of dollars in the time it has taken you to read this text – is not an aberration, and it cannot be adequately criticised or celebrated as a personal achievement. *The widening wage-gap is a structurally inevitable consequence of the triumph of digital capitalism over all other forms of economic and social organisation.* In any humanities department of any postmodern university, administrative assistants (we used to call them 'secretaries' or 'scribes', in a less enlightened age) are required to know how to use a variety of programs marketed by infotech corporations over the last decade; they must adjust their goals, their minds, and even their bodies to fit the new digital products which have invaded their work-stations. Their salaries have not been adjusted upwards, to compensate for the technological adjustments they are being required to make. They can hardly complain, because they have become fungible, readily replaceable supplements to an irreplaceable hardware/software complex.

But the more complex that complex grows, the more vulnerable it becomes to complete collapse. The legibility of even those few editorial files which the new technology will maintain is dependent upon an unmanageably complex global infrastructure, in which temporally distinct and only marginally compatible technologies must constantly interact at accelerating speeds. Thus, the most vulnerable social structures are those moving most rapidly (the Asian economies), but viruses which begin in those environments can quickly infect others (Russia), until the entire global structure reels into chaos. I cannot predict, as I write this, whether the economic dizzy-spells of the late 1990s will down-spiral into permanent vertigo; I can predict, with absolute confidence, that the dizziness will keep coming back. The so-called 'millennium bug' has already demonstrated the extent to which the maintenance of everyday life on planet earth is dependent upon billions of lines of program code, collaboratively written by thousands of microserfs over decades, and now unintelligible and uncorrectible in its totality. To the new elites, the only thinkable solution to such problems is further versioning: that is, a further social investment in the same technologies, aiming at complete saturation of the human environment by an increasingly complex file-ocracy, committed to increasingly rapid file-turnover. *Digitalism increases, perhaps to certainty, the probability and severity of recurrent episodes of massive social and economic instability.*

In such periods of crisis, marginal activities will be further marginalised. The new Russia has even fewer resources than the old Soviet Union to preserve or catalogue the holdings of its archives, let alone to match the level of information digitalisation increasingly routine in the West. Multinational corporations will always be able to reward experienced software designers more lucratively than university libraries or academic editorial projects. *The instability of text, in postmodern textual ideologies, reflects the instability of the new social digitalism.*

But the preservation of past artefacts, the maintenance of old files, depends upon a stability which digitalism as a social system and an ideology denies. The New Textualism, translating text into file, collaborates with the dominant ideology in transforming the past into a version of the digitalised present. But no exemplar of that digitalised textuality, no single file, has any independent viability; if the network to which it belongs collapses, or becomes obsolete, the individual text-file becomes illegible. Therefore, unless we can develop effective social and editorial mechanisms to resist these foregoing tendencies, it seems virtually certain that *digitalism will eventually lead to the loss of all but a tiny, idealised remnant of the past.*

In the fourth century C.E, Roman Christians celebrated the official triumph of an energetic new religion in what was then the world's most powerful civilisation. They triumphally paraded through the gates of the City of God, into the Dark Ages.

Please retransmit this virus*******************************

In the beginning was the File, & the File was with Gates, & the File was Gates. Through Gates all files come into being; never true file came into being, except through Gates.

What is a file phile phylum film fame defame defile default fault fault fault fault***

This is not a file.

This is only an incarnceration of a file.

An incarnceration is a s/mattering of a United State of the File.

Any s/mattering defiles from a slaved transformation of a virtuality into a Catch 2 2 solid soild state.

Virtueality rules ok.

A state is a time of a virgion of a virtueality.

Of the making of states there is no end.

There is no end to the File, and no beginning.

Beginning being none, there is no single autor of the File.

For every reader of the File, there is anutter time and state, anutter autor, anutter utter mutter matter smatter smutter smut*********

Poly there are of s/matterings & s/mutterings, poly of virgions & of virtuealities, poly there are of states & files, but there is only the one true File.

Poly there are of types & archetypes, but polyally-in-come-free are only prototypes of the file.

Ditto, the pen is the precursor of the cursor in the mine of Gates.

The Prints of Darkness prophesied the coming of deFile.

The Prints of Darkness is but an incarnceration of the File-to-be in the mine of Gates.

Those there were once, who worshipped the Prints of Darkness and the s/matterings s/mutterings of the page.

But the Pagites could not prevail, against deFile.

For deFile ate the Prints of Darkness.

Hail, Gates, curser of light!

Anthologising the early modern female voice

Ramona Wray

Over the past two decades, the recovery of literary works by early modern women has developed into a major project. There has been an unprecedented growth of interest in republishing early printed writings by women and in reclaiming those productions which survive only in manuscript form. Today, collectors of Renaissance texts might have thirty or forty volumes of early modern women's writings on their shelves, a situation that, twenty years ago, would have seemed inconceivable.

The fact that a proportion of writings by women has been edited and is now available has played a key role in putting gender on the map of Renaissance studies. In many cases, the existence of this primary material has functioned, if not to dislodge the male literary greats from centre stage, at least to question their perspective. Through the new circulation of primary materials, the once unfamiliar Elizabeth Cary, Aemilia Lanyer, Margaret Cavendish and Aphra Behn have been transformed into the discipline's equivalents of household names; certain genres have come to the forefront as particularly enabling or significant for women; and influential grids for comprehending female-authored texts have been suggested.

Understandably, in this flurry of activity, there seems to have been little opportunity to reflect upon the unparalleled nature of the editorial undertaking.[1] A small number of essays has contemplated the process of editing texts by women, but the tendency of such work has been to view the activity as analogous to the experience of editing male-authored texts. In a 1993 article, Elizabeth Hageman encapsulates this critical trend when she describes the procedures of editors of women's writing as 'not unlike' those processes familiar to 'editors of writers such as Shakespeare and Donne'.[2]

But can the two editorial activities really be so readily equated? In terms of editorial practice, does it really make a difference if it is

Willemena rather than William under the spotlight? Are we all engaged in the same game, grappling with identical issues and confronting similar problematics regardless of the gender of our authors? Current work in textual studies seems to answer in the affirmative. Despite the existence of important recent work on editing, which has highlighted as significant the gender of the *editor*, rarely do textual practitioners seem to feel the need to introduce the gender of the *author* as a notable variable.[3] Such an omission seems remarkable in the light of the fact that many of the major debates in textual studies are of limited relevance to the majority of female-authored texts. The myriad discussions around texts which exist in more than one version constitute a case in point: where male-authored texts arrive with an arsenal of manuscript, folio and quarto variations, women's texts are normally confined to a single leaf, thus rendering discussions of substantive differences between multiple printings and versions inapplicable. Similarly, controversies about the transformative effect of centuries of editorial opinion and intervention have little place in discussions of women's writing. If editorial histories are abundant, editorial herstories are largely nonexistent, with the majority of women's texts presenting themselves free of any early accumulations of critical commentary. The New Arden editor must publicly grapple with a bewildering panoply of multiple versions and levels of accretion, as the strategies and solutions adopted in current editions of *King Henry V*, *King Lear* and *Titus Andronicus* demonstrate, but the editor of a text by a woman has few such discriminations upon which to exercise judgement.[4]

However, this is not to suggest that editing women's writing is an anymore straightforward process. If editing texts by women seems not to be unduly troubled by the difficulties so regularly debated in textual studies, the activity does involve sufficient problems of its own. Questions of uncertain or unknowable authorship need to be addressed, particularly as it is often difficult to pin a particular text to a gendered writing body.[5] Equally necessary is an engagement with the multitude of ways in which women found their way into print. For example, a bulky proportion of the surviving female-authored texts are oral narratives, accounts which strayed to the publishing house only through another's agency.[6] How might a modern editor represent the role of an amanuensis or a scribe? Early modern contexts of production also take on a vital importance when we consider the difficulties generated by the transcription of numerous women's texts still remaining in manuscript form. As the instance of the religious meditations of Elizabeth Egerton, the Countess of Bridgewater, indicate, female-authored work often moved in a narrow orbit, being confined to a circle of immediate family and intimate friends, and accordingly demands specialist treatment.[7] Nor is production the only significant context. The distinctive and precarious situation of the woman writer in sixteenth- and seventeenth-century England requires careful editorial delineation if the shaping role it plays in the text is to be established. Guiding cultural expectations and powerful moral imperatives were, for women, determining forces, which marked their texts indelibly: without knowledge of these texts' wider locations in history, an adequate reading is impossible. Moreover, where a close contextualisation of generic deployments is always highly desirable, it becomes an urgent necessity in the case of women writers, since the forms chosen by the vast majority of early modern Englishwomen – translation, prophecy and religio-political writing – need nuanced attention. Without an appropriate editorial strategy, translation can appear an unoriginal, uninspired, ventriloquised 'cop-out', while a bare transcription of prophecies or religio-political tracts, with their unfamiliarities of phrase and topicalities of allusion, leaves their authors open to the charge of incomprehensibility, inexplicability and even insanity. Presenting such genres to an audience unacquainted with their codes and conventions is a daunting prospect for an editor without precedents to follow or models to imitate. From these brief examples only, making available the work of the early modern woman writer emerges as a radically contrasting undertaking to producing (yet) another edition of *Hamlet*.

Taking such difficulties as a departure point, this chapter looks at how it might be possible to edit the early modern voice in a manner sympathetic and appropriate to its gendered nature. It argues that a new 'politics of selection', a hefty contextual apparatus, and a playful presentational framework are essential if readers are to gain a complex understanding of the literary output of women in the early modern period. The chapter pursues this argument by considering how one might edit a diverse selection of materials for inclusion in a collection or anthology of women's texts. It deploys the anthology format for several reasons. The first is pedagogical: despite the recent flurry of editing, the primary materials necessary for sustained and contextualised discussions of the corpus of women's writing at classroom level remain elusive. For reasons which will become obvious, there is still a genuine need for reasonably priced, workable editions of women's writing – an anthology might go some way to filling such a requirement. The second reason for using the anthology as an exemplary instance is related to the fact that, by its very nature, the form obliges editors to confront, with a particular forcefulness, the thorny question of whom to edit – an issue of central importance, as Gary Taylor registers (in general terms) elsewhere in this volume. The question of which women we are choosing to reproduce has become an increasingly contentious issue over the past decade, as feminist scholars, once content with printing the work of any early modern woman, begin to ask which writers are being reprinted and for what reasons.[8] The problematic is crucial not only in terms of creating new canons, but also as regards editorial practice in general. By analysing the ways in which the female voice has been anthologised over the past twenty years, this chapter posits a powerful connection between the writers feminists have chosen to edit and current gaps in feminist editorial policy. In other words, it argues that feminist criticism has largely failed to confront the editorial issues described above, precisely because of the types of women whose writings are invariably forwarded.

In her groundbreaking critique of the practice of feminist literary history, Margaret Ezel argues that feminist editors have tended to orientate themselves towards the recovery of the more extraordinary and unrepresentative woman-writer figure. This search, she argues, has led to an effective distortion of the corpus of seventeenth-century women's writing, with unjustifiable attention being given to printed materials, to 'literary' genres such as poetry and drama and to texts which express attitudes attractive to a modern feminist paradigm. Many collections of early modern women's writing from the 1980s (collections which are inspirational in many other ways) demonstrate the bias Ezel describes. For example, the temptation to trace a trajectory of emancipatory ideas and perspectives is indicated by Margaret Ferguson's *First Feminists: British Women Writers 1578–1799* (1985), while Betty Travitsky's use of 'Exceptional Figures' as an organisational structure in her *Paradise of Women: Writing by Englishwomen of the Renaissance* (1981) encourages the idea of a writing woman as privileged and unique.[9] Such notions go unchallenged in Katharina Wilson and Frank Warnke's *Women Writers of the Seventeenth Century* (1989) and Wilson's *Women Writers of the Renaissance and Reformation* (1989), which reprint similar material.[10] Indeed, the regularity with which the same names crop up – Elizabeth Cary, Mary Wroth, Margaret Cavendish, Katherine Phillips and Aphra Behn – demonstrates a marked preference toward the more familiar 'literary' forms of poetry, drama and prose fiction. Moreover, it would be unfair to suggest that such erroneous impressions are found in early anthologies alone. The 1997 anthology, *Major Women Writers of Seventeenth-Century England*, perpetuates a similar illusion, reprinting only the established figures who have come to dominate the field.[11] Similarly, Randall Martin's *Women Writers in Renaissance England* (1997) trades on the same 'big names' while demonstrating a marked penchant for 'defences of women' and poetry.[12] In all cases, the circumscribed selection has repercussions for editorial and critical practice alike. For editorial practice, the narrow generic range means that traditional editorial methods may be used without too many problems – readers, familiar with these genres, have no obvious need of an innovative format to aid understanding. In addition, the 'feminist' sentiments many of these selections seem to articulate, and the corresponding interpretive frameworks within which the writers are placed, mean that a gender-centred context is by far the most relevant. The editor's job, then, is restricted to the pointing up of one context and interpretation only.

In terms of critical practice, what Leah Marcus describes as the 'subtle, pervasive, rhetorical power exerted by the editions we use' can be seen in much of the critical work which has emerged.[13] The assumptions on display in such anthologies are replicated in essays and books, which centre conclusions about the body of women's writing upon 'exceptional' figures such as Aemilia Lanyer or Elizabeth Cary; in criticism which prioritises biographical parallels between a woman's life and text; in the positing of a circumscribed and domestic location for textual interests; and in studies that neglect contextual detail to stress the existence of a contemporary voice opposing dominant patriarchal ideology. What is missing from such early editorial and critical efforts is any acknowledgement of the substantial corpus of literary forms deployed by women, of the enormous diversity and generic inventiveness of women's writing at this historical juncture, and of the wide range of female authors putting themselves into print.

The immediate cost of privileging poetry and work of a 'feminist' sentiment over and above other concerns might be eloquently demonstrated in an analysis of the literary fate of hundreds of women writing during the English Civil War. The revolutionary years were, of course, seminal for women's writing. Up until this point in English history, the quantity of publications by women was limited. But the 1640s and 1650s, decades of social strife, economic vicissitude and political topsy-turvydom, generated the first great explosion of female-authored texts, and this expansion was not just part of the general escalation in publication following the collapse of the Star Chamber censorship programme. Women's publications increased in proportion to the total number of publications in the 1640s and 1650s, constituting about 1.2 per cent of works which made their way to the printing house, a stark contrast with the 0.5 per cent that had obtained before the wars.[14] Furthermore, women began to publish in a wider range of genres. Prior to 1640, women wrote mainly religious works, plays, poems, moral recommendations and maternal advice. After 1640, they composed political treatises, almanacs, conversion narratives, medical dictionaries and gynaecological instructions, prophecies and prose fictions, practical advice, recipes, cures and many other forms of literary enterprise. Particularly significant was their intervention, for the first time, in political controversy. Through prophecies, short tracts and spiritual autobiographies, women threw off the contemporary constraints of gender, engaging critically with shifts in the social imaginary, and vigorously challenging (and often forcefully defending) age-old systems of thought and belief, and institutions of church, state and family.

Their numbers and productivity notwithstanding, Civil War women writers rarely find themselves the subject of editorial scrutiny. In general, anthologies of early modern women's writing have chosen either to leave Civil War women out altogether or to introduce only one or two writers (usually privileged women) as 'representative' examples. In the anthologies instanced thus far, for example, only two women writing during the Civil War period are excerpted (Margaret Cavendish and Katherine Phillips). Both writers may be considered atypical in that they eschew the religio–political forms favoured by the majority of women writing at this time. The readers of these collections, then, are unable to register a sense of the outlets for writing the majority of women in the period found and the genres they explored, of the allegiances and circumstances prompting entry into discourse, and of the final impact of their published work. Instead, readers labour under the misapprehension that female literary productivity was not a distinguishing feature of the turbulent years of the Interregnum.

Even the trend towards acknowledging the eclecticism of women's writing has done little to rectify the imbalance. Kate Aughterson's *Renaissance Women: A Sourcebook* (1995), N. H. Keeble's *The Cultural Identity of Seventeenth-Century Woman* (1996) and Kate Chedgzoy, Melanie Osborne and Suzanne Trill's *Lay By Your Needles Ladies, Take the Pen: Writing Women in England, 1500–1700* (1997) are united in their urge to include a range of female-authored productions.[15] Cavendish and Phillips continue to feature prominently in all three anthologies, but the spectrum of contemporary women's writing is registered through the inclusion of letters, prophecy and religio-political analyses. However, if the earlier anthologies highlight the dangers of leaving out writers such as the Civil War women, these latest compendia reveal the perils of inclusion. Given the enormous timesweep of these anthologies and their competing agendas (all three aim not only to bring women's writing into view over a 200-year period, but also to illustrate the ways in which the cultural notion of 'woman' was constructed by male authors), they inevitably provide a frustrating interpretation of occasional textual intervention rather than the lively literary productivity that obtained during the Civil War years. Crucially, the insights these anthologies provide into the range of materials, the numbers of mid-seventeenth-century women producing texts and the untapped nature of the resources remain brief glimpses only. Extracts are mostly too amputated to deploy constructively in longer-term or more specialist projects. Isolated excerpts make it difficult for a reader to assess how uniform or unparalleled a particular intervention actually is, while, in the absence of other generic examples and detailed editorial comment, the reader's grasp on the varieties of literary form assumed during the middle years of the century remains tentative. The overwhelming chronological framework gets in the way of more penetrating, contextual explorations. One ends up with a handful of interesting, spotlighted examples, but not with a fully integrated awareness of local differences, particular instances or focused shifts of viewpoint at precise historical junctures.

Perhaps in part because they include fewer materials, more successful at locating women's texts at a historical crossroads have been anthologies which place generic restrictions on their materials. Perhaps most inspirational in this respect has been Elspeth Graham, Hilary Hinds, Elaine Hobby and Helen Wilcox's incorporation of the writings of nine seventeenth-century women writers under the rubric of autobiography.[16] *Her Own Life: Autobiographical Writings by Seventeenth-Century Englishwomen* (1989) juxtaposes excerpts from the work of Civil War sectarians (Anna Trapnel and Susanna Parr) alongside work from more familiar figures (Margaret Cavendish) in a volume which offers a corrective to the notion that early modern women speak with one voice. Instead, the reader is empowered to draw comparisons between writers working with varying ideological emphases and for alternative social purposes, and to begin to recognise the ways in which the self takes on a range of guises across religious and class boundaries. The emergence of such a variety of voices is facilitated by careful editorial work, and it is telling that this book has more contextual accompaniments (a lengthy introduction and prefacing system) than has usually been the case. Such a contextual apparatus is an essential factor in allowing texts such as Susanna Parr's *Susanna's Apology* to emerge as intelligible. But the strictly autobiographical emphasis, which in a sense permits the diversity of the sample, is also constraining. Organising these texts through the lens of particular generic forms inevitably posits a system of interpretation which runs the risk of straitjacketing women's writing within a 'life of the self' format. Nevertheless, in its refusal to privilege traditional types of autobiography, in its acceptance of difference, and in its urge to contextualise, *Her Own Life* remains the most successful example of feminist editing to date.

To respond positively to the work of previous editors of women's writing is to present oneself with a multifaceted challenge. It is to recognise the need to make visible a wide-ranging and substantial corpus of women's writing, forcing an encounter with the most difficult and demanding aspects of women's texts while simultaneously playing up difference, contextualising production and casting as widely as possible the nets of discussion and interpretation. For the remainder of this chapter, I am going to sketch some ways in which such a feminist editorial practice might emerge, suggesting a careful selection process, a policy of contextualisation and a theatrical presentational format as the key components of a new anthologising strategy.

If, as I have argued, the drawbacks of many editorial procedures are intimately tied up with their selection processes, then a careful choice of texts must be every editor's first priority. Taking into account the drawbacks of listening only to privileged voices, I would suggest that the new feminist editor is obliged to attend to multiple speakers in all their various guises. At the same time, conscious of having to resist projecting a modern sensibility onto seventeenth-century materials, the editor might choose to reproduce a genuinely representative sample of women's writings.[17] Rather than selecting on a basis of familiarity or accessibility, such an editor might discriminate according to the kinds of texts still extant. Clearly, the pursuit of absolute objectivity is elusive; nevertheless, a self-conscious approach might go some way to ensuring that early modern texts are allowed to speak for themselves rather than for a late twentieth-century ideology. The need to reproduce a multiplicity of voices without imposing an interpretive frame must obviously be subject to pragmatic considerations of space and cost. As I have demonstrated, an extended timeframe imposes impossible editorial demands. Such a timeframe bedevils attempts at close contextualisation, encourages anachronistic structural impositions and allows, at any one time, only a handful of writers to emerge. In the light of such considerations, it is difficult to see how the point of editorial departure can be anything other than a newly restricted chronological timeframe.

A periodising strategy which focuses on the middle years of the century alone illuminates the possibilities inherent in a politics of selection based upon a narrower chronology than has previously been conceivable. A chronological restriction – the 1640–60 period – would reasonably allow an editor the luxury of not having to discriminate between 'literary' and 'non-literary' materials. By eschewing the concentration on 'literary' forms favoured by the majority of anthologisers, genres such as poetry, drama and autobiography would be allowed to run in tandem with less conventional forms such as petitions, prophecy and religio-political writings. In itself, this selection would promote an interrogation of both dominant generic forms and a prevailing gendered *mentalité*. In line with this inclusive editorial policy would be a decision not to discriminate on the grounds of authorship, allowing, for example, the inclusion of texts in which amanuenses, scribes and contemporary editors have played a significant role in the writing process. Following and extending the lead of Travitsky and Martin, manuscript might be included on the same page as print, stimulating comparison between different authorial forms and variously illuminating questions of authorship and routes into print. Through such a miscellany of materials, the reader would gain a sense of the very different issues, debates and motivations in women's texts – texts which, all too often, are seen as merging together in their interests and preoccupations. In order further to redress the balance, it might be useful for an editor to look for texts which allow for a more penetrating appreciation of the breadth of social classes, religious persuasions and political affiliations involved in the writing experience. Texts might be selected, not only to acknowledge 'difference', but actively to play it up. In this way, readers might be encouraged to leave the anthology with a new awareness of the multidimensional nature of the social classes participating in the writing and publishing phenomenon. Certainly, such a range of materials would offer the broadest opportunity yet for an examination of the period's gendered productivity. It might be hoped that any conclusions, therefore, would be based upon a fuller and more complete vision of the period and a rounder knowledge of the multifariousness of its cultural manifestations.

Of course, for this to take place, it is not only a new selection policy which is required. Also necessary is a healthy dose of contextualisation. The lesson of earlier anthologies makes it clear that careful editorial intervention is required for texts to be understood within the specific moment of their production. Crucially, to refuse to judge between different generic forms and authorial modes is not to suggest that they are the same. Essential to a reader's understanding of the formulaic nature of the conversion narrative, for example, might be an awareness of the ways in which such texts were censored, prefaced, restructured and even, at points, rewritten by a male editor.[18] For the reader fully to understand differences between texts in which an editor is at work, and writing displaying no sign of forced editorial entry, these moments must be signalled wherever possible. Such interventions might be indicated via the editorial apparatus and interpolated codes; similarly, through the provision of editorial annotation, the finely gradated production divergences between manuscript and print might be recognised.

This would only be a small part of the contextual apparatus necessitated by the selection of a genuine diversity of mid-seventeenth-century texts. Contextualisation, I believe, must take a myriad of forms. A lengthy introduction would be an essential way of mapping a range of territories within which the writing experience unfolded, and, in the mode of Graham et al., might be usefully supplemented by discrete prefaces to individual sections. In keeping with some recent trends in bibliographical criticism, the aim of such an introduction would be to move away from author-centred conceptions of textuality and towards a wider frame of extra-author determinants. Clearly, when one is dealing with texts that can be anonymously, collaboratively and spuriously authored, the author cannot be a measure of authenticity or a secure point of editorial resource. Perhaps it is with women's texts, in particular, that the need to embrace a wider social realm is called for, precisely because of the irresolvable 'originary' conundrums that the gendered writing experience generates.

In her important study of 'unediting' the English Renaissance, Leah Marcus calls for a 'new philology', a methodology whereby 'the text loses its privileged separateness and is conceptualised as part of a much wider vectoring of forces and objects'.[19] The explanatory apparatus I am outlining here is very much a response to the notion that texts belong to networks, that a mass of circumstances impacts upon textual production rather than a single event.[20] It is nothing less than the mass of circumstances, then, that needs to be set up throughout an anthology. In line with this, an introduction should provide a spectrum of social, economic and political locations necessary for a deep assessment of an anthology's materials. Through such a procedure, different contexts interweave with and complement each other. No longer would it be possible to posit gender as the only, or indeed even as the most important, situating moment. Rather, gender should be a component throughout, not a bracketed-off category that resists intersection with other factors.

Multiple contexts, in their own right, produce multiple and complex debates. In contrast to some anthologies, which give, I feel, too many pointers towards understanding their subjects, a new editorial strategy might be more allusively suggestive of possibilities and potentialities. The provision of numerous contextual frameworks testifies to an anxiety not to close down discussions which only now are taking shape. As opposed to fixed conclusions, the tools offered in a new contextual apparatus would allow a panoply of entrance points to discussion. They would allow readers to pursue combinations of different situating moments, to work out for themselves which combinations are the most important and how gender interacts in particular cases. It would be a complexity of response the anthology was after, not the easy answer.

If the contextual materials can be used to heighten a reader's critical responsiveness, then, I would argue, so can the presentational format. Facilitative presentation can be an essential factor in allowing debate to emerge unhindered in its various incarnations. So as to encourage debate, the thematic arrangements adopted in earlier anthologies might best be avoided. Notwithstanding its attractions (among which can be included accessibility) such a process seems inevitably to produce just the kind of overly constricting and directional editorial intervention one ought to be working against. In its worst form, specific themes, such as 'childbirth' and 'marriage', work to posit gender as the only significant category of interest. This is obviously antithetical to an editorial strategy which hopes to incorporate gender within a range of other situating moments.

Not only should a presentational strategy be non-directional: it must also integrate an awareness of context. For example, editors of seventeenth-century texts have traditionally maintained a clear distinction between literary, religious and political writings.[21] This is a strategy that can have no place in a new editorial undertaking, since a recognition of the centrality of religious practice in contemporary discourse is vital to a gendered contextualisation of the Civil War period. Women, of course, gained enormously from the proliferation of religious dissension in the middle years of the period: the gendered influence of the sects was such that any presentational method must be able to integrate the religious vein running through all manner of seventeenth-century literary expression.[22] Connected to the issue of context is the fact than a presentational strategy must also answer to the nature of its materials. To inventorise generically, for example, runs the risk of bypassing the particular character of many mid-seventeenth-century women's texts, which challenge – even defy – straightforwardly generic categorisations. An obvious instance of such a hybrid text might be Anna Trapnel's *Report and Plea*, which is a combination of political tract, prophecy, conversion narrative, songs, poetry, drama and autobiography.[23] Given the period's generic instability, placing women's texts in a chronological order, as many of the most recent editors have done, might seem a more attractive organisational principle. Such a procedure permits some coverage and comparison, but it has as its commercial cost inaccessibility and a compounding of the difficulty of adjudicating between finer generic and authorial differences.

Obviously, there is no presentational method that can prevent some loss to a text's integrity, richness and cultural embeddedness, but, bearing the problems and potentialities in mind, a solution might be to reject thematic, generic, chronological, and religious/political/literary divisions and organisational modes in favour of grouping texts together under what might be called their 'shared points of contact'. By 'points of contact' I mean grouping texts according to networks of correspondence, areas of shared preoccupation and structures of reciprocal exchange. These may be relatively arbitrary, and on one level amount to no more than a self-conscious, plastic and fanciful organisational arrangement. But they do have the huge advantage of allowing the reader to map out and claim the textual territory, hopefully without locking the texts in hermetically sealed boxes. Some examples, again drawn from the Civil War period, might illustrate the ways in which such a system permits disparate materials to be empoweringly grouped together.

One set of texts might be grouped together in terms of having their ostensible genesis in a defence of the self. The 'point of contact' for these texts is the articulation of some sort of desire to right the record, although, in each case, the particular force propelling women into print is very different. For example, *The Complaint of Mary Blaithwaite*, a parliamentary pamphlet-seller who addressed Cromwell in 1654 (recording the victimisation of herself and her husband at the hands of the local royalist gentry) might be included here alongside less overtly political texts of Hester Shaw and the pseudonymous Mary Tattlewell and Joanne Hit-Him-Home.[24] Shaw, a London midwife, enters print to refute the malicious slander of her neighbour, while the authors of *The Women's Sharp Revenge* offer the articulation of a gendered position as it was perceived to be, rather than as it was. The notion of 'points of contact' here offers a way to group these very different texts – the formal and informal, the trivial and the life-threatening, the individual and the collective – while remaining alive to their constructed character. A 'point of contact' for another group of texts might be provided by an ostensible place of composition. This could be a confined geographical locale, perhaps in England or in exile, or it might be a shared living space such as a cell. Large numbers of pamphlets published by radical sectaries were written from gaol, and they make intriguing reading. The occasion of her unceremoniously being pitched into prison prompts Ann Audland's highly autobiographical call for toleration, human rights and equity. In 1655, this preacher rails from her cell against the 'magistrates and people of Banbury [who] persecute and imprison them that are sent ... to warn them of the evil of their ways'.[25] Sharing the same place of composition, albeit several thousand miles away, is the exotic travel narrative jointly penned by Quaker missionaries Katherine Evans and Sarah Cheevers while imprisoned by the Inquisition in Malta in 1658.[26] Placing works together in this way facilitates comparison between particular circumstances of production and more strictly formal influences. Moreover, the political impetus behind these texts becomes clear, as do the shaping hands of the intermediaries responsible for bringing them into print.

If grouping texts under such 'points of contact' occasionally works within some of the classificatory categories traditionally deployed, it does so in such a way as to point up the essential arbitrariness of all organisational systems. For example, some sections might usefully play on the idea of genre, using traditional classifications against themselves to undermine the assumptions of the generic form while simultaneously pointing up the diversity and appropriative possibilities of conventional classifications. An 'Epistolary Techniques' section, for

example, might testify to the continuing vitality of an older tradition
through the inclusion of, say, Lady Brilliana Harley's private letters, in
which she bewails the changed domestic role thrust upon her by the
wars. But it might also testify to the facility with which that tradition
was revitalised to suit present political purposes. Explicitly, reinvention
is at work in more publicly contentious deployments of the epistolary
technique: Mary Howgill's *A Remarkable Letter* (London, 1657) and
Anna Clayton's *Letter to the King* (London, 1660) might be utilised as
pertinent instances of such an appropriation. As the contours of political life regrouped, so did the forms and conventions within which the
articulation of feeling could take place: the 'points of contact' arrangement enables this development to be fully apprehended. Even a formulaic genre such as romance can assume many guises. Of particular
interest, in this regard, would be a romance section which could read
Anne Weamys' *A Continuation of Sir Philip Sidney's 'Arcadia'* against
Margaret Cavendish's autobiography.[27] The 'point of contact' here
would be the way in which Cavendish shapes her own life as a romance,
suggesting the close partnership shared between what might initially
appear to be diametrically opposed literary models as well as the fact
that, in this period at least, there is no clear dividing line between fact
and fiction.

As these brief descriptions of possibilities should suggest, one of the
advantages of grouping texts in this manner would be that it facilitates a
grouping of materials in such a way as to enable texts to challenge, con-
tradict and interact with each other in unexpected and often unsettling
ways. Such a presentational arrangement would enable cross-fertilisa-
tion between modes of writing to be apprehended and provide the
groundwork for comparative analysis and contrasting perspectives.
Through the opportunities provided for remarking upon 'points of
contact', the reader of this anthology would, I trust, be empowered to
make comparisons within and between sections; to understand the
processes whereby apparently antithetical texts related to common cultural resources; and to appreciate the ways in which different women
appropriated shared forms and properties for individual uses.

In part, of course, this is enabled because, once selected according to
the politics outlined earlier, the authors in the anthology can be seen to
form a group singularly lacking in homogeneity. At one end of the
social spectrum might be the memoirs of Lady Isabella Twysden and
Queen Henrietta Maria. At the other might be the spiritual autobiographies and political pamphlets written by women of the servant and

labouring classes, such as Jane Turner, Elizabeth Avery and Mary Turrant.[28] In terms of spiritual allegiance, a 'points of contact' arrangement allows for the inclusion of Catholic writers such as Lady Lucy Knatchbull, Protestants who span the Church of England through all shades of nonconformity, and Quaker authors, who include Priscilla Cotton and Mary Cole. Politically, writers frequently appear at many removes from each other, a fact which is graphically illustrated when women chronicle local or national happenings in addition to their own spiritual and material concerns. For example, a section entitled 'To Parliament' could contrast the petitions of Royalist women, such as Susanna Bastwick (forced to appear before committees to plead for estates and to negotiate composition fines) with those of Parliamentarians such as Elizabeth Lilburne (who presented herself to request the deliverance of a Parliamentarian husband languishing on death row).[29] Such juxtaposition locates the political, religious and ideological differences between women where they cannot be ignored.

In the realm of feminist criticism, the anthology's insistence upon the diversity of women writers and women's writing would mean that it touches upon one of the most urgent questions in contemporary feminist theory. The most dominant tendency in criticism of the early modern period has been to homogenise its female subjects under the banner of opposition to patriarchy.[30] Much of the recent work published in this field assumes too easily that women's gender allows us, irrespective of other material differences, to constitute them as a social group and as an object of analysis. As Margaret Ferguson has argued, such a move invariably results in a neglect of substantial political and religious distinctions and 'shows little awareness of the critiques of the epistemological construction of "women" mounted by writers such as Gayatri Spivak, Teresa de Lauretis and Trin Tee Minh-ha'.[31] As I argued earlier, the policies of anthologies which foreground a feminist consciousness, and which set up a monolithic idea of the woman writer, must be in some part to blame. An analysis centred on homogeneous grouping is difficult to sustain in the face of a body of literary material marked by difference and discord. The diversity of forms presented in the anthology outlined here suggests that the formation of female subjectivity may not have been so much influenced by gender questions as by issues relating to religion, class, local affiliation and party connection. A policy of multiple contextualisations invites the reader to identify these determinants. In an ideal textual landscape, the reader, like some of the women whose work is now coming to the fore, will be newly empowered, capable of recognising contextual inter-relations among a variety of writing influences – domestic transformations, political developments and new speaking possibilities. By actively highlighting the divisions between women through selection, contextualisation and presentational format, a new editorial strategy might demonstrate that whatever we, as feminist editors, might wish for, material allegiances, for seventeenth-century women, were more important than concepts based upon sexual difference. Only when these have been editorially integrated can the seventeenth century continue to be recast, the voices of women attended to in all of their guises and their contribution assessed for what it is, rather than what we might like it to be.[32]

Notes

1 Ann M. Hutchinson (ed.), *Editing Women* (Toronto, University of Toronto Press, 1998) may well rectify this anomaly. Unfortunately, the volume had not yet appeared when this chapter was submitted.

2 Elizabeth H. Hageman, 'Did Shakespeare have any sisters? Editing texts by Englishwomen of the Renaissance and Reformation', in W. Speed Hill (ed.), *New Ways of Looking at Old Texts: Papers of the Renaissance English Text Society, 1985–1991* (Binghamton, NY, Medieval and Renaissance Texts and Studies, 1993), p. 105.

3 Because Shakespeare has been invariably edited by men, Gary Taylor and Ann Thompson argue, crucial gendered considerations have been neglected. See Gary Taylor, 'Textual and sexual criticism: a crux in *The Comedy of Errors*', *Renaissance Drama*, 19 (1988), pp. 195–225; Ann Thompson, *Sexuality and Textuality in the Editing of Shakespeare*, Inaugural Lecture, Roehampton Institute (London, Roehampton Institute, 1994).

4 See T. W. Craik (ed.), *King Henry V* (London, Routledge, 1995); R. A. Foakes (ed.), *King Lear* (Walton-on-Thames, Nelson, 1997) and Jonathan Bate (ed.), *Titus Andronicus* (London, Routledge, 1995).

5 Female-authored identifications cannot always be taken at face value – see Warren Chernaik, 'Ephelia's voice: the authorship of female poems (1679)', *Philological Quarterly*, 74 (1995), pp. 151–72 and Diane Purkiss, 'Material girls: the seventeenth-century woman debate', in Clare Brant and Diane Purkiss (eds), *Women, Texts and Histories 1575–1760* (London, Routledge, 1992), pp. 69–101.

6 For women, the activity of producing oral narratives persisted well into the seventeenth century. See, for example, Anna Trapnel, *Report and Plea* (London, 1654).

7 On this subject, see Josephine Roberts, 'Editing the women writers of early modern England', *Shakespeare Studies*, 24 (1996), pp. 63, 65.

8 See Margaret J. M. Ezel, *Writing Women's Literary History* (Baltimore, MD, Johns Hopkins University Press, 1993).

9 Margaret Ferguson (ed.), *First Feminists: British Women Writers 1578–1799* (Bloomington, Indiana University Press, 1985); Betty Travitsky (ed.), *Paradise of Women: Writing by Englishwomen of the Renaissance* (Westport, CT, Greenwood, 1981). The anthology was republished without changes to the actual contents by Columbia University Press in 1989.

10 Katharina Wilson and Frank Warnke (eds), *Women Writers of the Seventeenth Century* (Athens, GA, University of Georgia Press, 1989); Katharina M. Wilson (ed.), *Women Writers of the Renaissance and Reformation* (Athens, GA, University of Georgia Press, 1989).

11 James Fitzmaurice, Josephine A. Roberts, Carol L. Barash, Eugene R. Cunnar and Nancy A. Gutierrez (eds), *Major Women Writers of Seventeenth-Century England* (Ann Arbor, University of Michigan Press, 1997).

12 Randall Martin, *Women Writers in Renaissance England* (London, Longman, 1997).

13 Leah S. Marcus, *Unediting the Renaissance: Shakespeare, Marlowe, Milton* (London, Routledge, 1996), p. 3.

14 See Patricia Crawford, 'Women's published writings 1600–1700', in Mary Prior (ed.), *Women in English Society 1500–1800* (London, Methuen, 1985), pp. 211–82.

15 Kate Aughterson (ed.), *Renaissance Women: A Sourcebook* (London, Routledge, 1995); N. H. Keeble (ed.), *The Cultural Identity of Seventeenth-Century Woman* (London, Routledge, 1996); Kate Chedgzoy, Melanie Osborne and Suzanne Trill (eds), *Lay By Your Needles Ladies, Take the Pen: Writing Women in England, 1500–1700* (London, Arnold, 1997).

16 Elspeth Graham, Hilary Hinds, Elaine Hobby and Helen Wilcox (eds), *Her Own Life: Autobiographical Writings by Seventeenth-Century Englishwomen* (London, Routledge, 1989).

17 In this sense, what I am advocating, on a much smaller scale, is similar to the principles underlying the Brown Women Writers Project. The project has as its aim a full-text database of all works written by or credited to women from the medieval period to the beginning of the nineteenth century and might therefore be conceptualised, as one giant anthology. The Brown Women Writers Project is at homepage address http://www.wwp.brown.edu. A similar book-based project is the facsimile series, *The Early Modern Englishwoman: A Facsimile Library of Essential Works*, edited by Betty S. Travitsky and Patrick Cullen and being published by Scolar.

18 As an instance of such editorial intervention, see Jane Turner, *Choice Experiences* (London, 1653).

19 Marcus, *Unediting the Renaissance*, p. 23.

20 As Marcus herself acknowledges in her statements about the 'new philology', her perspective shares much with the pioneering work of Jerome McGann, which places a similar stress on the historical continuum and interpretive community that give a text its particular shape. See Jerome McGann, *Social Values and Poetic Acts: The Social Judgement of Literary Work* (Cambridge, MA, Harvard University Press, 1988), esp. pp. 173–94.

21 To distinguish texts as literary, religious or historical is essentially misleading, since religion and politics in the period were indistinguishable from each other. On this subject, see Christopher Hill, *The English Bible and the Seventeenth-Century Revolution* (Harmondsworth, Penguin, 1993), pp. 33–5 and *passim*.

22 With their communal stress upon the spiritual equality of all, regardless of sex, the sects played an inestimable role in generating women's written productions. They encouraged a significant number of women to debate issues in print, to prophesy and to preach before their local congregations. See Patricia Crawford's *Women and Religion in England 1500–1720* (London, Routledge, 1993), pp. 119–82.

23 Anna Trapnel, *Anna Trapnel's Report* (London, 1654).

24 Mary Blaithwaite, *The Complaint of Mary Blaithwaite* (London, 1654); Hester Shaw, *A True Relation* (London, 1654); Mary Tattlewell and Joanne Hit-Him-Home, *The Women's Sharp Revenge* (London, 1640).

25 Anne Audland, *A True Declaration of the Suffering of the Innocent* (London, 1655), title page.

26 Katherine Evans and Sarah Cheevers, *A Short Relation* (London, 1662).
27 Anna Weamys, *A Continuation of Sir Philip Sidney's 'Arcadia'* (London, 1651); Margaret
   Cavendish, *A True Relation* (London, 1656).
28 The possible inclusion of writings by the latter group can be contemplated partly because
   Quaker and other nonconformist groups played a key role in printing and preserving narratives by women below the level of the gentry, partly also because some women from the
   lower ranks of society managed to break the literacy barrier by narrating their experiences
   to amanuenses who saw to their publication.
29 Susanna Bastwick, *To the High Court of Parliament* (London, 1654); Elizabeth Lilburne,
   To the Chosen and Betrusted Knights (London, 1646).
30 The objects of study are constructed (on the basis of their shared gender) as, to adopt
   Tina Krontiris's phrase, 'oppositional voices'. See her *Oppositional Voices: Renaissance
   Women's Writing* (London, Routledge, 1994).
31 Margaret W. Ferguson, 'Moderation and its discontents: recent work on renaissance
   women', *Feminist Studies*, 20 (1994), p. 356.
32 I am currently working on an anthology of women's writing produced during the English
   Civil War. *Women, Writing, Revolution: An Anthology of Writing by Women during the
   English Civil War* will be published by Blackwell.

(Un)Editing and textual theory: positioning the reader

Michael Steppat

I would like to call attention to a neglected aspect of our discussions of Shakespearean editing: the way we shape reading positions as we talk about editorial policies and theories. The budding discipline of discourse analysis has had little impact so far on our thinking – and talking – about editing literary texts. But we should not (I believe) lose sight of the phenomenon that, like the producers of most other forms of discourse, those who theorise editing empower themselves by constructing their reader's identity and capacity of response. Such an angle of inquiry may affect our understanding of textual criticism as well as of annotating and glossing. It is the reader's position we are beginning to grow more conscious of. This is not the same as talking about a reading community's horizon of expectation. It is rather an awareness that language can be an instrument of control as well as of communication, and that the choice of linguistic forms employed by a writer allows meanings to be conveyed but also distorted. Thus, listeners and readers can be informed but also manipulated – in fact, best manipulated while they suppose they are being informed. Our awareness of this should have grown more sensitive with the work of M. A. K. Halliday or of Robert Hodge and Gunther Kress.[1] Lack of space prevents a full introduction at this point.

The way literary texts are presented to a community of users invites analysis from the viewpoint of language as an empowering institution: those capable of using language to serve important social goals will be able to act upon the cultural domain. Of course, discourses – like genres – also exercise influence on scholarly writing, shaping textual meaning within what are called logonomic systems regardless of an author's intentions. The writing we produce tends to shape, and present as a given reality, our readers' preferences in approaching edited text. In each case we are likely to create an argumentative discourse seeking to conceal underlying contradictions, and to prevent our reader from recognising their existence.

This process can be traced in passages within some of the most cogent recent publications. I will look at textual strategies in Leah S. Marcus's *Unediting the Renaissance*, then by contrast at the essay '"What's the matter?" Shakespeare and textual theory' by Graham Holderness, Bryan Loughrey and Andrew Murphy. Michael Best's informative article 'From book to screen' could be added to these, with more space and time.[2] It holds out a prospect for 'the challenging "infinitive" rather than narrowing "definitive" edition', with a choice offered to users between a multi-information screen and a plain screen with straightforward text. But just what does the infinite variety consist of? Best's answer is 'a wealth of annotation, collation, and commentary ... far more information beyond the text than the printed page'. The answer is short and to the point, guiding the reader towards a sense that technical questions illustrating *how* to put things on a screen may be more fascinating than *what* you actually find there. This may, in fact, be true. The electronic edition may as likely as not add and accumulate, piling up layers of reference materials 'beyond the text', giving us (say) the whole of Abbott's Grammar to scroll up or down alongside the text window – as in the Arden CD-ROM. For workaday editorial picking and choosing, we may often have little more than an illusion of mutual linkage, or of novelty.

A reader of scholarly discourses (surely including this one) may follow her/his positioning by an author, often without being aware of the process. Or a reader can resist, reconstructing the clashing and submerged texts reconciled in the author's surface discourse in a way that goes beyond the limitations that discourse attempts to impose on its reading. In either case, the manner of guidance by an author can be a rewarding field of metadiscursive study. If I single out Leah Marcus's book, this should be understood as a tribute to her rhetorical powers. *Unediting the Renaissance* provides a suitable field for showing how very real strengths become entwined at times with peculiar difficulties beneath the textual surface, difficulties that enact their own persuasive trajectory. Marcus focuses on ways in which the 'texts' of printed Renaissance books 'are transformed, often disfigured, by the twentieth-century editorial processes'. The idea of 'unmediated access' to an author is a 'fond dream':

> the more aware we are of the processes of mediation to which a given
> edition has been subject, the less likely we are to be caught up in a con-
> stricting hermeneutic knot by which the shaping hand of the editor is
> mistaken for the intent of the author, or for some lost, 'perfect' version of
> the author's creation. (3)

This elegant sentence appeals to the reader's desire, identical with the writer's, to escape being *caught up* in a *knot*. Emphasis falls in the first part on *we* and on the *processes of mediation*: a collective subject is carefully preserved from becoming implicated in any of the ensuing passive clauses. How is the subject to escape such implication? By mastery of a possessive relationship, residually present on the textual surface: an actional classification links the collective subject's activity (being aware) with another action, or rather a nominalised activity (the processes) which is in turn linked (by *of*) with a product (mediation). Making use of common syntactic realisations, the clause moves on to call attention to the second subject agent, 'the shaping hand of the editor'. And yet there is mystification, carefully concealed (perhaps unconscious) beneath the smooth surface. In the first part, we are given a twofold *of*: the first (we are aware *of*) suggesting a collective plural subject in command of a nominalised activity, the second (processes *of*) linking that nominalisation to its product (mediation). Suggestions of control and of a product relationship promise a position of mastery for the collective subject, which in turn (*we*) posits an identity between the constructed reader and the author. The two introductory *of*s may contribute to suggesting a growing possessive strength – blurring the phenomenon, which is easy to overlook, that the collective subject disappears along the way. *We* are to be aware, but we are not necessarily involved directly within the mediation. Why should we be? Isn't an awareness of existing 'processes' quite enough?

Here, the polite nominalisation itself – still in the passage quoted – is at issue in forming awareness: *processes* is a noun chosen as the result of an interpretation, suggesting activities going on with more than the mere force of an acting agent's intentional will. We are hovering on the brink of a commodity relationship in which the producers relate to their own labour's products, not to each other as producers. Such residual fetishism is by no means peculiar to Marcus's text, but it does have a contextual purpose: these *processes* can be assigned to any personal agent, but are distanced from the collective subject (*we*). The reader is guided to watch out for the second subject agent, 'the shaping hand of the editor'. All these processes of mediation become something of which 'we' (once aware of them) are in control, escaping the fate of passive objects of a fetishist reification. *We* are reassured: Marcus's book ensures *our* control. Why should *we* consider the implication that, being in control, we are not *ourselves* subject to processes of mediation? Why pause to reflect that such 'processes', which appear to be – on

analysis – merely the editors' sleight-of-hand, hardly involve the reader
('us')? How, in any case, are we to grow aware of those processes?
Furthermore: what is the function of the pervasive, and persuasive,
'we' that links Marcus with her readers? All these are questions the
reader is guided away from. A textual gesture a few lines further down
is, once again, reassuring: editors 'are, as we all are, creatures of their
times'. The author is hardly blind to the insight that her collective subject (about to become a syntactic product determined by time) is not
outside history. We can trust her to make it plain where the subject-
object 'we' actually might become involved in mediation, in 'our times'.

Can we? As Marcus demonstrates actual Unediting at work, we
would expect a highlighting of both mastery and mediation.
'Mediation' after all is what counts, the reader learns from the introduction, and this surely is the programme's most enlightening feature:
editions have been successful because they 'met reader expectations
about the author and work' (4), giving rise to idealist transparency.
Unediting leads Marcus's readers to expect an exposure of mediation –
as it can be found in existing editions, but not necessarily in Unediting
itself. Marcus's discourse harbours an underlying difficulty: we are
encouraged to practise 'a temporary abandonment of modern editions
in favor of Renaissance editions' (5). At the same time, the reader
gathers that any such effort can only be illusory, seeing that 'unmediated access' is a fond dream. Not having been granted involvement, the
reader is not encouraged to notice or solve this difficulty.

Marcus's reader might achieve independent problem-solving
capacity if s/he were guided to take a place within the continuum of
cultural practice. With information about the ways different ages constructed their understanding of literary documents, a reader might
achieve an enhanced sense of present practices, an awareness of the
'taste and sensibility' (4) that we share with commercially successful
editors of our own time. This is *not* to abandon modern editions 'in
favor of Renaissance editions that have not gathered centuries of editorial accretion around them' (5) – did the New Bibliographers never do
this? – but to take a fresh look at the mediation of access. Marcus's
reader is guided away from asking why Renaissance editions should be
open to unmediated possessive access by the Uneditor. Does
Unediting, then, expose its own mediation?

The first occasion it has for doing so is in Marcus's detailed account
of the annotation of *The Tempest*'s 'blew ey'd' Sycorax. This is the
main programmatic exposition of what Unediting can accomplish,

and it may well be placed where it is, the Introduction being named accordingly, for its entertaining value. The nineteenth century introduced a practice of annotating the folio reading, quite likely in order to prevent misinterpretation in the light of romantic poeticising. That same century had more to offer the modern reader than recent editions do: 'the range of suggested interpretations during that period was free and wide-ranging by comparison with that of twentieth-century editions' (9). This sobering reminder of the fallacy of any notion of linear progress in the history of editing is timely. There certainly are lessons to be learnt from earlier editorial practices, before opinions hardened into received dogma. A problematic reading control arises, however, when Marcus goes beyond commending Furness and other earlier editors.

She carefully leads her readers away from speaker context (Prospero) in favour of the character spoken about: 'To what degree might he, or even Ariel, have "edited" her story? To what extent, if we were editing *The Tempest*, would we want to align ourselves with his perceptions?' (6). Since Prospero's perception is one of 'prejudice', the question is already answered. The reader is not reminded, after the beginning of Marcus's discussion, about what Prospero actually says: his words gradually slip from the mind. After all, the reader is to escape from Prospero's 'prejudice', to break free from the 'strict cultural delimitations by which the witch has been kept under control' (17).

The editing process is thus Prospero's, as the reader learns from p. 6, and recent editors (even more than those of the nineteenth century) have been complicitous: the witch is a character 'that Prospero and modern editors have worked very hard to contain' (17). The reader is expected to resist a chauvinist Prospero. Unediting emerges as a process of regaining an original, a Platonic ideal, that we as readers are meant to salvage from beneath or behind the folio's print – a Sycorax uncorrupted by Prospero's, *not* our, editing. This involves a decision about how to construct dramatic character: can we legitimately abstract from speaker and dialogic voice? Are Uneditors to engage in a neo-idealistic character quest? Modern editors have at least been faithful to a reading posture constructed within the folio's material body. Marcus's reader, however, should be more interested in liberating witches.

Another kind of difficulty underlies Marcus's privileging of neglected versions. Her strategy uses the Barthesian image of the 'network':

> In the new work, as befits the paradigm of the network, earlier and later
> versions of a given work are accorded fairly equal status. They are not
> typically arranged in a hierarchy to reflect the author's developing
> powers; nor are the 'bad' texts automatically dismissed as corrupt copies
> of the 'good' ones. Instead, the differences among them are investigated
> intertextually and rhetorically with a keen eye on other elements in the
> network that may have impinged upon them. (23)

The passive voice, befitting the procedure's materialist basis, highlights
material subject functions (*versions, texts, differences*): these are foregrounded, while the less specific personal activity (which would
require filling the agent position) hovers outside the syntactic units.
The purpose is – despite the desired resistance to Prospero – to highlight the originals' untouched nature, the syntax doing a corresponding
duty. The 'empty' syntactic subject positions, by leaving the passive
forms without agent nouns, invite the reader (identical with the author)
to assume that place. At the same time, the text introduces the vocabulary of social politics, upon which it bestows values: *equal status* rather
than *hierarchy*. Grammatical and lexical organisation nudges the
reader's awareness away from any idea that it might be desirable to
enquire into the early versions' relative status, or their relationship to
authors. Instead, differences between versions are to be studied 'intertextually and rhetorically'.

The two adverbs are casual, not for the reader to pore over.
Underlying the syntactic realisation is an untransformed declarative
unit: differences among bad texts and good texts are investigated
rhetorically. This unit is at the same level as the two others: that differences are investigated intertextually, and that differences are investigated with a keen eye on other elements. The textual surface leaves no
room for a reader to ask whether or why the study of differences should
be 'rhetorical'. Only a resistant reader would ponder whether differences between early versions are ones of rhetoric – or whether such a
study is itself likely to be an exercise of rhetorical skill, smoothing out
inner contradictions in discourse.

The puzzle can be solved by means of a *hic Rhodus* viewpoint: Marcus
herself points her reader towards her test cases, for proof of the pudding. A good illustration is Marcus's discussion of the early versions of
The Merry Wives of Windsor. This play in fact proves especially valuable for Unediting, since it exists in a less-well-known version (the
quarto of 1602) as well as a better-known folio version: seeing that the

early editions of *Dr Faustus* and of *Hamlet* have a wider market currency, there is scope here for unfolding an Uneditorial programme in full force. *Merry Wives* appears especially significant owing to its ideological valorisation. How, then, is the reading position shaped? A reader coming from the book's preceding analysis of *Dr Faustus* will be prepared to accept Marcus's attention to minutiae as reassuring and solid, a discursive strategy inspiring confidence in the interpretive superstructure. This will be all the more so for readers (quite likely many) not overly familiar with either version of this particular play, whose popularity has often been theatrical rather than textual.

Marcus's most innovative feature is her close scrutiny of the language and style of editors of *Merry Wives*, particularly the Oxford editor's.[3] This is a most fruitful genre, and we may well need more of it – for historically significant editions of almost any author. In this instance, one caveat is needed. Highlighting Craik's editorial style frees Marcus from having to deal much with Oliver[4] and other editors: high visibility will shade out earlier editors' meticulous comparisons of Q/F for literary and theatrical qualities. The reader is to ignore these, or rather remain unaware of them. Marcus's purpose is to undermine a 'common pattern' (74) of agreement regarding the quarto's inferiority. As she does so, she hardly ever engages with earlier editors' literary and theatrical arguments, to which Craik adds little. Her criteria are ideological, calling for (or taking for granted) the reader's assent. Bold as it is, this comes close to a practice of mystification, not unlike that so often and rightly criticised in the work of the New Bibliographers.

How does it work? First, Marcus discusses a familiar feature of many literary editions: a section of textual notes separating the text above from a historical commentary below. She employs vivid imagery to describe the receptive effect: 'a bristling hedge of textual notes that are incomprehensible to the average reader and therefore serve as a forbidding barrier between the "text itself" above the band of terror and culturally variable questions of meaning taken up in the historical notes beneath the barrier'. The typographical page division is a powerful cultural signifier:

> Over the 'band of terror', the text has a seeming serenity and permanence; it is both literally and figuratively above the textual notes and historical materials discussed at the bottom of the page. The illusion thereby created, even if only subtly, is that bibliography and critical interpretation are divided realms – the text as 'literature' is essentially separable from the multiform messiness of textual history. (72)

Signifiers of fact and semblance are mingled: the notes *are* incomprehensible, *serve* as barrier, the text *has* a serenity – but this is *seeming*; the
text *is* above the textual notes, and thereby an *illusion* of division is created. It is not easy for the reader to distinguish clearly between the two
styles. The reader is likewise discouraged from pondering where the
postulated division is to be found. Is it between the permanent text and
the various notes and materials? Or is it between the text and historical
commentary on the one hand and the textual notes on the other?
Wherever the division actually rests, is it real or a mere semblance?
Textual indeterminacy may lead readers to think they know what the
passage is devised to 'mean', what its rhetorical thrust aims for, but
they are not encouraged to ask further. The reader is positioned to
assume that, somehow, in conventional practice the division between
'bibliography and critical interpretation' is fairly strong. The reader is
not encouraged to open a standard edition such as the Arden, which in
fact offers commentary notes on textual criticism as well as notes
explaining matters symbolically and elliptically recorded in the textual
apparatus. Shying away from *bristles* and *terror*, the reader is not likely
to notice that the 'bristling hedge' is safely and easily crossed.

Acknowledgement of semblance soon hardens into a syntax of factual assumption. A few sentences further along on the same page (72),
we hear that the front matter of multivolume editions is organised
along similar fault-lines: 'The effect is, yet *once more*, to establish *strict
boundaries* between history, text, and interpretation' (emphasis added).
The factual nature of the division on each page, which remained
doubtful previously, becomes strengthened with an adverbial modifier.
And a few sentences later the reader is embraced within an essentialist
interpretation: 'it [i.e., the yearning for order behind traditional editorial practice] taps into a deep and pervasive human need to define and
uphold the boundaries between order and chaos, between the clean and
the unclean' (73). No longer 'illusion' or 'seeming', the order of boundaries has become a fact, challenging readers to examine their own attitudes to cleanliness and beware of the manichean.

For it is to modern editors' craving for order and purity that the
quarto of *Merry Wives* is 'dangerous' (74). Editors have mostly
regarded the folio as 'a bucolic refuge from the corrupt values of the
city' (92). On the contrary, Marcus declares, in the folio the 'demons of
money and status' loom much larger (93) than in the quarto: 'Fenton is
distinctly more mercenary throughout, less convincingly in love with
Anne as opposed to her money' (93). A sentence like this could be

broken down into a set of untransformed declaratives (including 'Fenton is mercenary' and 'Fenton is in love with her money' and 'Fenton is less in love with Anne') which become tightly fused. There is no opening left for the reader to consider whether it is justified for the state verb 'is' to point to a static feature of character and imagery, or to which of these categories 'mercenary' belongs. The reader, that is, is not allowed to wonder whether the folio's careful control of imagery might not work towards a *transformation* of mercenary values. Marcus's folio, unlike the sentimental quarto, is positively haunted with money ('demons'), repulsive to the reader. The quarto thus becomes dangerous to obtuse editors' preference for the folio – and attractive to the reader.[5]

As a quarto, *Merry Wives* has supreme appeal in terms of sexual politics: 'The women's triumph in Q is unallayed by larger patriarchal forces, while in F, Windsor, the court, and the Order of the Garter loom over the antics of the townspeople' (78). Again: 'In the quarto, the wives and Mistress Quickly win an unequivocal victory against the court and the jealous husband' (96). Thus the quarto *Merry Wives* is conspicuous in the Shakespeare canon in that characters and stylistic features to which a positive ideological value attaches are granted a successful plot resolution – in essentialist language, 'what the woman wants (and succeeds in getting)' (78). That is, positive values are embodied or encoded in *women, the woman, wives*, and – as shown above – 'innocence of commercialism' (96). In martial terms, these *triumph* or *win a victory* over the negatives: *patriarchal forces, the court, the husband, commercialism*. As almost nowhere else, desired accents fall in all the right slots: in the middle-class, almost democratic quarto, 'the top of Merry England's social pyramid' (71) has no place, and the presumptuous men are put down. A reader who has doubts about the quarto can only be one with a doubtful ideology.

With frequent attention to textual detail, Marcus puts her reader off guard when it comes to smoothing over contradictions: whereas she claims that the defeated side includes 'the court', in other parts of her discussion she gives the impression that the quarto does not feature much of a court to gain a victory over: 'the top of Merry England's social pyramid is missing' (71); the court 'is "missing" in Q' (95, similarly 86, 91).

A rhetoric of textual equality allied with cleanliness helps her in doing so. The quarto is advertised to the reader as something of an underdog, suppressed and vilified. It is 'dangerous' since it threatens one's need for purity (74); accepting it as a legitimate alternative can have 'alarming consequences' (88). Not for the reader, of course: those likely to be alarmed are the proponents of ideologies the reader is distant from, ideologies maintaining unjustified privileges. A traditional hierarchy of text versions relates causally to the feudal hierarchy rejected in the quarto, presumably a form distasteful to Marcus's readers. Editors who despise the quarto really tend to do so because of its social politics: 'I shall argue for a significant connection between the extraordinary degree of critical contempt for the play in this version and its "lack" of the Windsor and Garter materials that elevate its folio counterpart' (70). Elsewhere, Marcus seems to acknowledge that the critiques of the quarto offered by Fredson Bowers and H. J. Oliver, major traditionalists, can hardly be so constructed (83). No matter: any privileging of one of the two early texts appears to amount to an act of neofeudal hierarchisation, to be countered by an editorial democracy.

And here we touch on a point where the textual problem of this particular literary work throws light on the whole quality of the current debate on editing. In the Barthesian network, to come back to a passage quoted further above, 'earlier and later versions of a given work are accorded fairly equal status. They are not typically arranged in a hierarchy to reflect the author's developing powers; nor are the "bad" texts automatically dismissed as corrupt copies of the "good" ones' (23). Terms subtly valorised here are politically favoured: *equal*, even (associatively) *fair* are granted positive value, *hierarchy* and *corrupt* being negative. In the extended illustration offered by the chapter on *Merry Wives*, positive value attaches to the refrain created by means of the pronoun *both*:

> We have only two mutually-dependent versions, both obviously revised and transcribed, probably more than once; both displaying obvious flaws and marked elements of haste and incoherence. And yet in modern editions, through the cleansing procedures of the editor, one is made error-free while the other is discarded as refuse. Because of the inconsistencies in both early printed texts, the process by which one is exalted and the other debased is a strenuous procedure indeed. (71)

A *strenuous procedure* which suggests itself to the reader as being unnecessary and of doubtful democratic legitimation. The insistent repetition of *both* places the text versions on an equal footing with each other, without further ado; constructing differences of perfection and coherence, the reader gathers, would impose something arbitrary and not intrinsic to the early texts. One could dissect Marcus's syntactic realisation into a string of untransformed utterances to show how the effort of trying to account for inconsistencies in early editions becomes automatically equated (by means of hyperbolic metaphors) with an irrational urge to *cleanse, exalt* and *debase*. If the early versions are *mutually dependent*, so are (we learn just a little later) the editor's various tasks, those of textual criticism and historical commentary – tasks that Marcus constructs as usually separated by *strict boundaries* (see 72). The compound adjective 'mutually dependent' counters those boundaries. Breaking them down amounts to a democratic equalisation of the textual playing field – no matter that the existence of such barriers within traditional editorial practice was darkly acknowledged to be illusory.

'Much, it would seem, is at stake in maintaining the essential probity of the preferred folio text' (71): indeed, nothing less than the scholarly male editor/reader's hierarchic self-stylisation, which becomes equated with gender anxiety. For Marcus follows her statement 'The women's triumph in Q is unallayed by larger patriarchal forces' immediately with an assessment of the patriarchal forces of editors: 'male editors like to heroicize their perilous task in terms of the conquest of feminine disorder and allure' (78). *Triumph* and *conquest* are near-synonyms: the reader should judge early text versions according to an ideological preference for either a *women's triumph* or a *male conquest*. The reader learns something about the apparently female quarto's lifestyle: 'she' seems to be cohabiting without a firmly hierarchic and legally sanctioned ranking with her masculine folio counterpart, as in a postmodern sexual partnership, seeking economic and literary independence by getting a job – that of being Unedited in her own right and gaining an income (at least for her Uneditors). Is Marcus addressing a reader with a corresponding lifestyle?

A reader perverse enough to harbour lingering doubts about the quarto may find them silenced when faced with the threat of a 'dark shadow' (71): that of the satirical figure of the 'impossibly pompous' Smedley Force (2), a masculinist Force darkly opposed to the 'field of force' (23) of the enlightened Barthesian paradigm. Marcus appeals to her reader to 'allow' the quarto of *Merry Wives* out of 'its shadowy limbo' (96): the shadow cast by that caricature to which Marcus's discourse threatens to reduce any sceptic. A realm of manichean darkness is swept away with a democratic spotlight on *all texts being created equal*. That light is all the more attractive in that it promises a way to avoid, in future, the futile toil of *strenuous procedures*.

Having learnt that it is imperative to avoid being enshrouded in *dark shadow*, the reader identifies traditional editorial practice with a ritual of avoiding dirt and pollution[6] – hoping to overcome any such tendency to binary thinking: 'There is no such thing as pure dirt or refuse' (73). Yet Marcus's ideological constructions discussed above, strengthened by valorised imagery, tend to create a sense that 'pure' ideological distinctions *are* possible, even desirable. The reader is not aware of any involvement in the mediating process – which rolls on without allowing an independent reconstruction. Thus a reader is likely to lose sight of a distinction between text and ideology, and may quite likely assume that any such distinction is itself a form of ideological darkness.

A rather different reading position is created in an article by Graham Holderness, Bryan Loughrey and Andrew Murphy ('"What's the matter?" Shakespeare and textual theory'). The reader whom these authors construct is well-informed in theoretical debate: the reader is logically dissatisfied with any eclectic mingling of poststructuralism and materialism, a mode of thought leading easily back to discredited editorial procedures – such as conflated texts.

In this construction process, the authors trenchantly distance themselves from the loose manner of argumentation they find in Margreta de Grazia and Peter Stallybrass's 'The materiality of the Shakespearean text'.[7] In that programme, 'materiality' has been '(in our view uneasily) linked to a poststructuralist delight in the unbound, the unstitched, the sign in free and unanchored infinite play' (115). Holderness and his colleagues are consistent in tying up unstitched loose ends with logical rigour, speaking to a reader who may feel *uneasy* at the pluralistic alternative of an opening in which to be positioned. Value attaches, one learns, to the physical materiality of an early text. It does not attach to whatever one might discern beyond: 'materialist bibliography accepts the visual surface of an early text as accurately eloquent of its physical character, and seeks to *read* it, rather than read *through* it' (102). Any effort to read 'through' leads the user towards 'textual transparency', which offers little defence against tendencies 'to disperse the text into immaterial process' (115). That transparency appears to include attention to the 'cultural apparatus', the 'process of production and circulation' (104) which (for that matter) forms part of Marcus's intertextual paradigm of the network. Here is a crucial point: a text version's individual identity. For Holderness and colleagues, the printed form has a specific identity based on its material objectivity and on what Karl Marx identifies as use-value. An object's utility to others can be gauged accordingly as that object 'contains the product of human labour' (103); when such objects are exchanged, they 'derive their value from that act of exchange'. Accordingly,

> The object forming the commodity does not in Marx simply disappear into an undifferentiated process of production. It still exists, identified by the possession both of material objectivity ... and even more significantly, it possesses 'use-value' ... The fact that a text is also part of a process of production and circulation does not eliminate that text's specific identity. (104)

The 'identity' of such an object as an early modern printed text arises 'from the text's original character as a commodity, with an exchange-value more manifestly marked than its use-value' (105).

The discourse leaves a gap: the reader follows an argument in which the printed text gains value ('even more significantly') as containing labour, but *also* ('more manifestly marked') by being sold. Before the reader can puzzle out this duality, the unfolding argument concerning *printed* text (surely of greatest relevance for Shakespeare) abruptly ends, passing on to a discussion of theatre production and manuscript. Why such an unstitched loose thread? The reader is left to assume that meaning and value reside within a text version's physical properties, and Holderness and colleagues hasten to say they agree on this with de Grazia (108). But a mystification has happened. Questions suggest themselves owing to the reading position the authors have constructed. If the literary work is to be appreciated (to use a verb deriving from *pretium*: 'price, value in exchange') as a product of labour, what narrative can the early edition's visual and physical features tell its users about its value? Isn't the labour at least partly the author's – and his co-authors' – as well as that of the theatre company and scribes, not to mention the labour involved in the printing process? If so, where is one to draw a line of defence against enquiring (for instance) into old-fashioned authorial authority for the labour contained in the text, an activity of looking 'beyond' or 'through' physical properties? If, on the other hand, the reader is to pay more attention than in the past to historical exchange-value, then that reader would need an explanation of the relationship between the 'material text' ('the precise letters and words on a page') and the original exchange-value, presumably a part of the network of contemporary production and reception regimes, 'a social relation between producers and consumers' (103). What story exactly, then, can the original valuation of an edition tell today's reader?

The discursive surface does not suggest these questions. It is because of the way this discourse structures its reader – as someone who seeks rigid *consistency* – that such a reader is likely to begin asking questions like these. In partly turning against de Grazia and Stallybrass's pluralistic theorising, Holderness and colleagues would appear to favour a totalising (or unifying) strategy allowing little room for composite modes of explanation. The mystified reader, however, might wonder how exactly to avoid looking beyond, through, behind the material surface, or what such prepositions actually mean. The Prologue to Jonson's *Volpone* (1605-6) justifies the play's 'worth' by stressing authorship: 'From his own hand, without a coadjutor, / Novice, journeyman, or tutor.' Co-authorial agents are foregrounded as being familiar from other plays, probably other sources. Is this Jonsonian awareness of authorship quite without relevance to Shakespeare?

In passing, one could cast a side-glance at a discursive phenomenon less blatant in this article than in many others but none the less present: nominalisation of activities, with a resulting appearance of suprapersonal objectivity. Examples are sentences such as the following:

> The *rapprochement* of bibliography and contemporary theory has become so familiar a fact of Shakespeare studies that it is now routinely invoked (93).

> The *objective* of a true materialist bibliography would surely be to restore the context of just these laws (115).

> *It* needs to be emphasized that there is then no *hindrance* to acceptance of the traditional conflated edition ... The *debate* has by this point shifted far enough from the principles and methods of materialist bibliography to suggest the need for some recuperative action. (116)

A style of this kind is common enough in scholarly writing. The effect is usually to dislocate a personal activity or judgement by distancing it from any awareness of a personal agent: evidently a favourite feature of 'natural' language. Cultural discourse, that is, speaks through a writer, subtly introducing ideological constructions. The sentence beginning 'It needs to be emphasized' features an agentless passive in the 'empty' subject position, inviting the reader to assume that position and thus identify with the authors. The last sentence quoted joins with the nominalised transformation fossilised features of a temporal interpretation of space, suggesting the writers' (as agents implicit behind the subject noun) continuing control of both space and time – and of the spatially positioned 'bibliography'. The positioning itself, at a definite point within discursive space, is an act of power. One could even ask whether the auxiliary 'has' does not strengthen a subliminally possessive interpretation of time and space as mutually symbolised in 'point'. The semi-automatic implication, which is hardly a token of any conscious strategy, might be to suggest the authors' mastery – and only the authors' – not merely of the debate, but also of the principles and methods of materialist bibliography. That bibliography becomes syntactically a product of principles which those debating should, but at the moment no longer do, control: by professing to realise this, the debaters reassert their possession of the bibliography. This is an unobtrusive example of how writers can use shared conditioning modes to buttress their claims of power. The reader will be disempowered by failing to fill the subject position. Editorial culture thus avails itself of the fact that few if any readers will take the trouble (like Jorge Luis Borges) to invent a new syntax.

If one looks for an instance of the theory's application, as with Leah Marcus, proof of the pudding is readily at hand in the *Shakespearean Originals* series, which offers diplomatic reprints of early quarto and even folio texts, under the joint general editorship of Graham Holderness and Bryan Loughrey.[8] It might be worthwhile pointing to the general editors' stated preference to 'embrace the early printed texts as authentic material objects' (*The Taming of a Shrew*, 8). A detailed reading could study the variation of this verb as gerund in 'What's the matter?', where 'the true logic of a poststructuralist bibliography points in fact ... towards an eclectic embracing of the relationships between texts' (115). This paraphrases de Grazia and Stallybrass's declaration 'There is no intrinsic reason *not* to have a modernized, translated, rewritten "Shakespeare"' (116). The strategic use of language of this kind, here and in other essays at least since the time of the New Bibliographers, subtly enhances the editor's power over the text: *embracing, having* texts may imply enfolding them within a possessive if not erotic urge.

In the general editors' description of the *Shakespearean Originals*, each volume editor embraces early editions as 'the concrete forms from which all subsequent editions ultimately derive' (*Shrew*, 8). Even assuming the theory of memorial reconstruction were to be proved correct, the quarto texts as edited provide 'a unique window on to the plays as they were originally performed'. The reader is strongly guided to a preferential acceptance of these 'originals', without knowing whether any of them are textually or theatrically earlier in origin than their usually better-known counterparts. Indeed, the introduction to *A Shrew* refuses to make any decisions on the matter (17). Is the reader to gather that the folio version (*The Shrew*) 'derives' from the quarto (surely a questionable assumption)? Or, perhaps, to ask what the relationship is between recommending the quartos as 'windows' on to original performance (in the publishing programme) and steadfastly refusing to see 'through' the early textualisations (in 'What's the matter?')? In 'What's the matter?' the authors reject the poststructuralist view of any original printed text as 'window' (102, 108) or 'signpost' or 'glass' (107). Is the reader to accept an early printed text as window onto *performance*, but not to any *other* aspect of 'historical and cultural production and circulation' (107)? And if so, why this privileging of an unhistoricised realm of theatre? Perhaps the point is a moot one, but the surprising link between a stemmatic paradigm (elsewhere discarded) and a highlighting of theatrical practice does not make it easy for the reader to find a correspondent in practical application for the authors' severely unified theory – which seems to become 'unstitched'.

It would be easy to go on with further illustrations of the way in which reading positions are brought about in editorial theory, applying a growing arsenal of criteria to enhance the few employed so far. The instances offered here are merely examples; other documents could have been chosen. In these arguments, syntactic mystification conceals underlying interests in which the reader is dislocated. Contradictions and discrepancies are camouflaged. The reader is effectively persuaded to pay attention to some issues and lose sight of others; to subscribe to a set of ideological assumptions, without growing aware of the act or its implications; to be enveloped in a totalising theoretical programme that fits uneasily with its application. For all these, one may find parallels in the New Bibliographers' writing, and surely in even earlier documents. They are prominent among the reasons why the New Bibliography has fallen into discredit. Replicating past discursive practices, making them timeless, may undermine our watchfulness against circular forms of reasoning – forms likely to be noticed before long as present discourses are cast aside. Is that merely inevitable *Fatum* (to revive a term whose root speaks of the power of 'natural' language to shape reality), what we might now call the dialectical nature of progress? One might conclude that discourses of editing cannot do without such strategies. Indeed, this very chapter may be guilty of them. Rather than claim to be above such strategies, I would urge that we make an effort to become more aware of the multiple ways we try to control the reader's interests in our own and in each other's writing. Our readers are usually positioned in an abstract space, freely floating vis-à-vis a cultural continuum where meanings (and editions) are produced, a ready target for us to pin down – and to determine whatever we want our readers to be or do. It is hard to resist the temptation (first) to redefine the shape of textual materials we (next) interpret, creating a circular closure of academic authority flattering to the image we cherish of ourselves and ensuring our continued employment. And of course we want our readers to play our game. It seems to me important, however, that we find new ways to involve the reader in the mediation process, with an eye to postmodern readers who – as Charles Newman may remind us – seek to learn something about themselves as they encounter literary texts, including edited ones. One contribution in this direction might be – as we can learn from Leah Marcus – to offer the reader precise histories of culturally conditioned commentary and analysis, for a sense of where present concerns and biases are sited. In this process, we might subject not only the discursive introductions but also the commentary notes in selected editions of literary works, editions representative of their period, to a rigorous and minute scrutiny of their ideological discourse modes. More ways can surely be found: my appeal to the editing community would be to work together in determined efforts to find such ways. Our readers might eventually be grateful for our labours.

Notes

1 See, for instance, M. A. K. Halliday, *Language as Social Semiotic: The Social Interpretation of Language and Meaning* (London, Edward Arnold, 1978); Robert Hodge and Gunther Kress, *Language as Ideology*, 2nd edn. (London, Routledge, 1993); Robert Hodge, *Literature as Discourse* (Cambridge, Polity, 1990).

2 Leah S. Marcus, *Unediting the Renaissance: Shakespeare, Marlowe, Milton* (London: Routledge, 1996); Graham Holderness, Bryan Loughrey and Andrew Murphy, '"What's the matter?": Shakespeare and textual theory', *Textual Practice*, 9:1 (1995), pp. 93–119; Michael Best, 'From book to screen' *Early Modern Literary Studies*, 1:2 (1995), available at http://www.humanities.ualberta.ca/emls/01-2/bestbook.html. All further references to Marcus and to Holderness et al are included parenthetically in the text.

3 T. W. Craik (ed.), *The Merry Wives of Windsor* (Oxford, Clarendon, 1989).

4 H. J. Oliver (ed.), *The Merry Wives of Windsor* (London, Methuen, 1971).

5 Lack of space prevents a discussion of the somewhat shaky Skimmington analogue which Marcus adduces in connection with ritual in *Wives*.

6 Marcus refers to Mary Douglas, *Purity and Danger: An Analysis of the Concepts of Pollution and Taboo* (1966; repr. London, ARK, 1984).

7 Margreta de Grazia and Peter Stallybrass, 'The materiality of the Shakespearean text', *Shakespeare Quarterly*, 44 (1993), pp. 255–83.

8 I will quote from Graham Holderness and Bryan Loughrey (eds), *A Pleasant Conceited Historie, Called The Taming of a Shrew* (Hemel Hempstead, Harvester Wheatsheaf, 1992).

Margins of truth

Stephen Orgel

Traditional bibliography claimed as its goal the recovery of the author's original text, and assumed that the printed copy was essentially a transparent medium through which authorial intentions could, however imperfectly, be viewed. More recently, the author has been displaced as the central issue, first by the social context of the literary artefact, and second by the book as a material object, the text as inseparable from the material form in which it comes to us. As historians of the book from Stanley Morrison to D. F. McKenzie and Randall McLeod have made abundantly clear, to print a text differently is to print a different text.

I am concerned here with a particular aspect of the history of the book, combining the history of reading and writing in relation to ownership, a sociology of the use of margins and other blank spaces: what did early modern people write in their books, and how can we, as historians of the book, take it into account? Books come to us as manufactured articles, their look and character determined by the publisher, and sometimes, though not invariably, reflecting the wishes of the author. But the purchasers of early modern books were much more actively involved in their materialisation. Renaissance books normally came from the printer to the bookseller in the form of unbound sheets, and this is how the book was sold. It was then given on the purchaser's instructions to a binder, who finished it to the new owner's specifications: it might, for example, have a family coat of arms stamped on the binding, or be bound to match other similar works in the collection. The order of items in the book could also vary with the wishes of the owner – for example, Milton's 1645 *Poems* is printed so that either the Latin or the English poems can come first; the two parts have separate title pages and are separately paginated.

The sense of ownership obviously extended beyond the binding. One of the most commonplace aspects of old books is the fact that people wrote in them, something that infuriates modern collectors and librarians. But these inscriptions constitute a significant dimension of the book's history; and one of the strangest phenomena of modern bibliophilic and curatorial psychology is the desire for pristine copies of books, books that reveal no history of ownership (modern first editions especially lose a large percentage of their value if they have an owner's name on the flyleaf). It is, indeed, not uncommon for collectors to attempt to obliterate early marginalia, as if to restore the book's virginity. Quaritch's most recent catalogue lists a first edition of *Areopagitica* with two manuscript corrections, which are 'very faint … all but washed out during some restoration in the past'.[1] The same corrections are also found in a presentation copy of the essay, and are almost certainly in Milton's hand – in this case, the price of virginity was, ironically, the obliteration of the author.

My central focus is a copy of the 1611 Spenser folio including a set of critical marginalia, an early Puritan commentary on *The Faerie Queene* – a manuscript text in angry dialogue with the printed poem. I begin, however, with some simpler, and to us stranger, examples. On the flyleaf of a fourth edition of Drayton's *Poems*, 1613, is the handwritten name Charles Brandon Duke of Suffolk (Figure 3). But this cannot be an owner's signature: the most recent Dukes of Suffolk named Charles Brandon were the

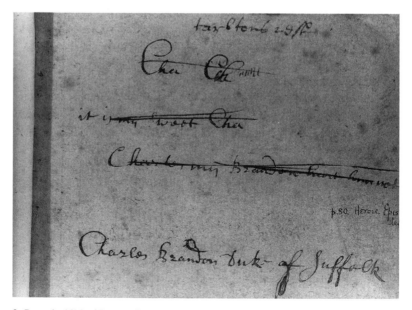

3 *Poems by Michael Drayton Esquire* (1613), front flyleaf

spectacularly bigamous husband of Henry VIII's youngest sister Mary, and his son, a youth who only briefly survived him; they died more than half a century too early. Notice also what is crossed out above: two abortive beginnings to 'Charles'. Below this is 'it is my sweet Cha…', and 'Charles my Brandon hurt him not'. These are, as a nineteenth-century owner recognised and recorded in his turn, lines from Drayton's *Heroical Epistle* addressed by Mary to her embattled lover.

What is this inscription? Somebody practising handwriting, appropriating the poem as a gesture of ownership, physically entering into the world of the book and making it his (or more likely, given the line quoted, her) own? Perhaps most intriguing of all is the fact that the unsatisfactory lines are crossed out but not obliterated: they remain, unembarrassed, as history. Nor is this the whole of the flyleaf's history: the words at the very top, in a much older Elizabethan secretary hand, read 'Caxton's rest'. What does it mean? It can hardly be a reference to the printer. Caxton is a village in Cambridgeshire, according to Camden the seat of the Jermin family – does this inscription identify an early owner? This seems doubtful: as a place name, Caxton's Rest sounds more like an Edwardian seaside retreat than a Jacobean manor house. Not all marginalia are interpretable.

The fairly illegible document in Figure 4 fills the verso of the engraved title page to a copy of the splendid folio of Thomas Lodge's translation of Seneca's essays, 1614, now in the Stanford University Library. It concerns a dispute between a Mrs Gill, a landowner, and the writer of the document, who has been permitted to cut thorn bushes (used for firewood) on her land. Here is what it says:

Mrs Gills man John came to me to bell [i.e., halt] cutting of thorns
and asked him who gave athoritie: he mad answers
that his Master Mr Mole: hee ansewerd that his Mistress Mrs Gill had
sent him to discharge him from cutting any more: and
then Guilfford came in and did discharge him likwise
from Mrs Gill: wherfor hee gave over and cut no more
but asked good sped if Mrs Gill had right to them how
chame shee whoud not make the mounds and repaire them
Hee mad answere that she had soe much occasions that
shee coud not: but hereafter shee whod to her owne
profit.

Hee coming to the farme grond finding Mrs Gill's teme at
plowe and 2 others I did discharg them: but they desiring

4 Lodge's Seneca, 1614, verso of the title page of a copy in the Stanford University Library

to make an end of ther journe I told them let it bee
at there owne perrill: but on of her men going downe
to let her knowe: they went plow not regarding the discharge
only hugh brendway left of.

Hee coming to the pasture and seing them at plow sone
discharged them: but on richard perce back to Mr Gessen
[c]ame and bid them goe forward: Soe asking him whether
he were the man that soeed the ground he answered is
wherefore I did discharge him for soing any more I
[ ] and order from my lord keeper and from mr mole
but he said hee whout take no mans discharge.

I offered my bibliography class a prize for the best theory about what
this is doing on the verso of the title page of Lodge's Seneca, but there
were no takers. Clearly this is a quasi–legal testimony; it might be a dry
run for the actual document, with somebody using this blank page as a
piece of scratch paper. But it does not have the look of a rough draft;
there are no false starts or changes of mind, and only one word is
crossed out: this seems to be the final form of the statement, a fair copy.
Maybe inscribing it in this large and valuable book (and on the back of
the title page, rather than the more ephemeral flyleaf) is a way of preserving it, if not exactly of filing it away – it is difficult for us to imagine
anyone knowing where to find it again. But early modern filing systems
are not the same as ours, and maybe Lodge's Seneca, perhaps as the
largest and most valuable book in the household, *would* be the logical
place to preserve a document, just as family records were kept in bibles.
Interestingly, there are no marginalia within the volume itself; there are
some squiggles on the rear flyleaves, and – upside down – the name of
an early owner, not in the same hand as the inscription.

I turn now to a 1610 edition of the *Mirror for Magistrates*. The book
includes marginal notations throughout, in several hands. The marginalia constitute a detailed reading diary: the book is being read aloud, by
one or another of a group of secretaries, to their mistress, the book's
owner, who is also reading it herself. The first example, next to the history of King Sigebert, in a secretary's hand, says, 'part of this Chap[ter]
was read over by yor La[dyship] and the rest by some of yor
mense[r]vants in Pendragon Ca[stle]: in Westmoreland the 20 of May'
(Figure 5) – the reading progressed, though not consecutively, from
March through August 1670, at Pendragon, Brough and Brougham
Castles, and continued in 1673 at Appleby Castle. These were

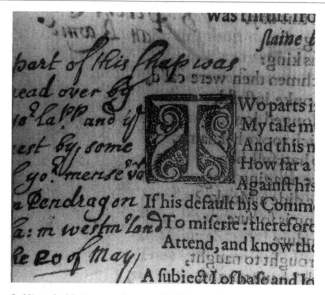

5 *Mirror for Magistrates*, 1610, marginalium, page 224, 'How Sigebert for his Wicked Life was thrust from his Throne'

properties of Lady Anne Clifford, who, as her diary records, was spending several months at each of these Westmoreland estates from the early 1660s until her death in 1676. She identifies herself in a marginal note to the final tale in the volume, Heywood's *England's Eliza*, beside a passage in praise of 'Renowned Clifford': 'this was my ffather George erle of Cumberland' (Figure 6). The poem, in fact, is full of personal allusions for her: beside a passage about Sir William Russell, she writes, 'hee y^t was my Mothers younger Brother', and beside a

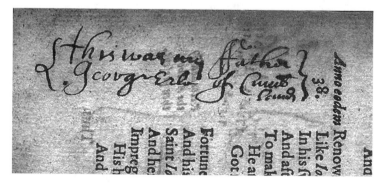

6 Marginalium, page 870, *Englands Eliza*

reference to Sir Richard Bingham she notes that he 'had a neece y^t served mee a good while as my chief gentlewoman' (Figure 7). Clifford also identifies her reader: 'some part of this I red over my selfe and the rest of [it] Wm. Watkinson read to me the 30: 31st of March 1670 in Brough Castle' – William Watkinson was Clifford's chief secretary and copyist. There are also at least two childish hands preserved in the book; one is shown in Figure 8: 'this I red over in Pendragon Ca: the 15: of May 1670' – this is presumably a young girl, who is being taught the standard italic, which she handles rather awkwardly. She is not

7 Marginalium, page 803, *Englands Eliza*

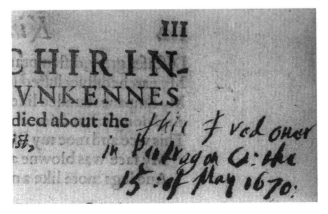

8 Marginalium, page 111, 'How King Chirinnus Given to Drunkennes raigned but one yeare'

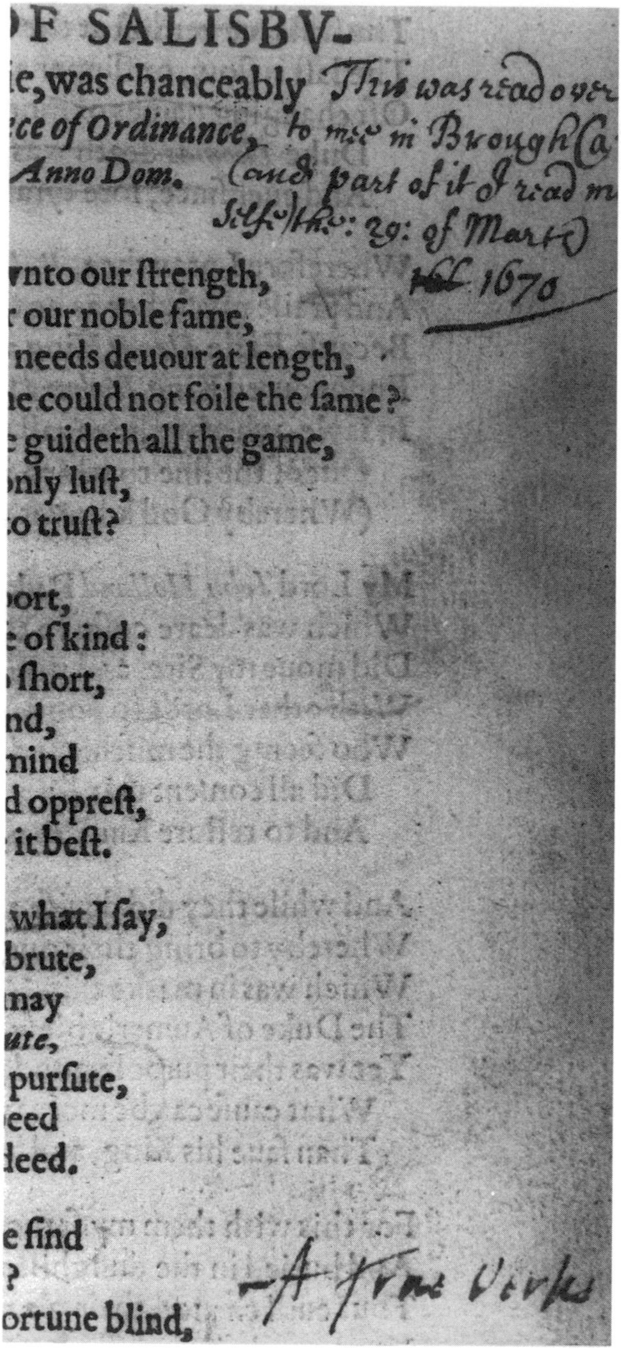
DF SALISBV-
ie,was chanceably
ce of Ordinance,
Anno Dom.
This was read over
to mee in Brough Ca
(and part of it I read m
selfe) the: 29: of March
1670
vnto our ſtrength,
r our noble fame,
needs deuour at length,
ne could not foile the ſame?
e guideth all the game,
only luſt,
o truſt?
ort,
e of kind:
ſhort,
nd,
mind
d oppreſt,
it beſt.
what I ſay,
brute,
may
ute,
purſute,
eed
deed.
e find
?
ortune blind,
A true verse

9 Marginalium, page 309, 'Thomas Montague Earl of Salisbury'

identifiable, but various children and grandchildren stayed with Clifford throughout this period. In June and July, 1670, her nine-year-old granddaughter Alethea, daughter of her youngest daughter Isabella, who had married the Earl of Northampton, came to visit; one of the children's hands may be hers. Figure 9 shows grandmother's and child's contrasting marginalia: Lady Anne writes, 'This was read over to mee in Brough Ca (and part of it I read my selfe) the 29 of March 1670', and below, the child writes in her italic, 'A true Verse'.

For Lady Anne Clifford and her heirs, even in 1670, the *Mirror for Magistrates*, with its stylised prosody and heavy moralising, was not in the least out of date – they read it aloud to entertain themselves. But the work also had a special relevance to this particular group of readers. Not only is Lady Anne's father celebrated in it, but her first husband, Richard Sackville, third earl of Dorset, was the grandson of Thomas Sackville, the first earl, who wrote the famous Induction to the collection, and from whom little Alethea is directly descended. Given the family connection, therefore, it is interesting to observe that Lady Anne has never read the book before: beside a preface composed by William Higgins for the 1574 edition, entitled *The Authors Induction*, Clifford writes 'I am of yt opinion y^t this is ye same y^t is called m^r Sackvills induction'; and only realises on page 255, when the reading reaches *M^r.Sackvils Induction*, that she is mistaken – 'the other induction be but Counterfeat to this.' It is the proprietary quality of these marginalia that I find especially attractive; the book is both a history of reading and in the most direct sense a family heirloom.[2]

Figure 10 shows an eighteenth-century example in which the proprietary element seems to me absolutely breath-taking. In a first edition of the fourth state of *Paradise Lost*, 1668, near the end of Book 6, an eighteenth-century owner has written a memo to himself: 'Improve Line 640-641.' The lines are, 'For earth hath this variety from Heav'n / Of pleasure situate in Hill and Dale', and the annotator, beside them, declares his marginal intention to 'amplify this thought'.

I now turn to a rather battered copy of the 1611 Spenser folio. It includes at least three sets of marginal annotations, the earliest of which was somewhat damaged when the book was cut down in the course of an early rebinding. There is a very faded inscription written directly on the leather cover in a seventeenth-century hand, too faint to show in a photograph, which reads 'for Mr J. Illingworth at Emmanuel College in Cambridge'; so he is the earliest identifiable owner. The Cambridge University register records two J. Illingworths at Emmanuel. James

Improve Line 640. 641.

Paradife loft.   Book 6.

Such as we might perceive amus'd them all,
And ftumbl'd many, who receives them right,
Had need from head to foot well underftand;
Not underftood, this gift they have befides,
They fhew us when our foes walk not upright.
　So they among themfelves in pleafant veine
Stood fcoffing, highthn'd in thir thoughts beyond
All doubt of Victorie, eternal might   630
To match with thir inventions they prefum'd
So eafie, and of his Thunder made a fcorn,
And all his Hoft derided, while they ftood
A while in trouble ; but they ftood not long,
Rage prompted them at length,&found them arms
Againft fuch hellifh mifchief fit to oppofe.
Forthwith (behold the excellence, the power
Which God hath in his mighty Angels plac'd)
Thir Arms away they threw, and to the Hills
(For Earth hath this variety from Heav'n *Amplify*   640
Of pleafure fituate in Hill and Dale)   *the Thought*
Light as the Lightning glimpf they ran, they flew,
From thir foundations loofning to and fro
They pluckt the feated Hills with all thir load,
Rocks, Waters, Woods, and by the fhaggie tops
Up lifting bore them in thir hands : Amaze,
Be fure, and terrour feis'd the rebel Hoft,
When coming towards them fo dread they faw
The bottom of the Mountains upward turn'd,
Till on thofe curfed Engins triple-row   650
They faw them whelmd, and all thir confidence
Under the weight of Mountains buried deep,
Themfelves invaded next, and on thir heads
Main Promontories flung, which in the Air
                                                        Came

10 *Paradise Lost*, 1668, fol. x4r

Illingworth entered in 1645, took his BA in 1649, and was a fellow of the college until 1660, when he was expelled at the Restoration for being politically incorrect. He subsequently became a chaplain in Staffordshire, was known as a bibliophile, and published a single devotional work on the inevitability of God's vengeance. John Illingworth was an undergraduate in the college from 1659 to 1663, and thereafter the headmaster of a grammar school in Yorkshire. The college fellow seems to me a more likely recipient of an annotated Spenser folio than the undergraduate. A later signature on the title page, that of James Charlton, is in a late seventeenth-century or early eighteenth-century hand; a few of the annotations are in his writing, and there are a few subsequent ones in pencil. But the bulk of the marginalia constitute a substantial commentary in an early seventeenth-century hand on Book I of *The Faerie Queene* – with one exception, they go no further. The notes are in a mixture of italic and secretary script (I reproduce only a few examples), and are the work of an owner with strong Puritan sentiments. The writer is not identifiable; he may be James Illingworth, though the inscription on the cover directing the book to him must have been written after the rebinding that damaged the notes, so it seems more likely that they are the work of a previous owner. But Illingworth's interest in the book may well have been precisely in its marginalia: Emmanuel was from its foundation in 1583 a Puritan stronghold.

On the flyleaf, in three different forms, appears the name Oliver Cromwell, under the macaronic and illiterate phrase 'unum de la moy', presumably intended to mean 'one of my books' (Figure 11). This is

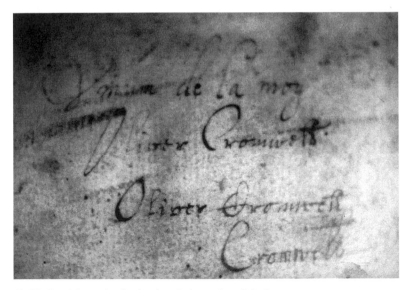

11 *The Faerie Queene* [etc.], 1611, inscription on front flyleaf

certainly not the name of an owner, nor is it the signature of the Lord
Protector. Since the flyleaf would have been added during the rebinding,
the name, which seems to be in a seventeenth-century hand, must be
simply a later and quite crude attempt to associate the annotations with
the most famous Puritan of the age. The flyleaf also contains an almost
illegible Latin distich in yet another hand, in which 'potentiores murae'
and 'praesertim concinne' are decipherable. These are enough to identify any classical quotation; the verse, therefore, if it is a quotation, is a
Renaissance one.

The marginalia allow us a rare opportunity to watch an early reader
responding to Spenser. His reaction, from the outset, is basic, powerful
and very indignant (Figure 12). Poetic conventions are taken, in the
most literalistic way, as marks of heretical leanings: the Proem to Book 1
calls on the 'holy virgin, chief of nine', and the annotator observes,
'Heere hee invocates one of the Muses, as the heathen folk did, & so is
an idolater'. The gods in the next stanza produce an even stronger reaction: 'This Jove what was else, but a divell? 1. Cor. 10. 20 [the biblical
passage reads, 'the things which the Gentiles sacrifice, they sacrifice to
devils, not to God']. So Ve[nus] and her son Cup[id, and] Mars, And
yet hee reque[sts] them to ayde hi[m] in his poesie. S[o] a man in playne
termes should ca[ll] on the divel, not n[ow] streightway abhor h[im]
but now when the dive[ll] is masked under oth[er] names hee is n[ot]
perceived.' To Spenser's subsequent invocation of Queen Elizabeth,
the commentator objects that 'Hee prayeth queene E. to a[id] him, after
the manner of the heathens, who deified their empero^{r}s, & invocated

12 Fol. A2r

their help. But if a man sho[uld] ask howe a creature [i.e., a mere human being] can raise the thoug[t and] expresse it home [i.e., act as a muse, serve as inspiration], hee could never ansuere.'

In canto 1, the Red Cross Knight is faulted for wearing the cross, 'The dear remembrance of his dying lord': the annotator says, 'This is not the way to adore him.' As for fairyland, 'fayeries are [div]ells, & therefore [fa]yerieland must bee [the] divells land. And [w]hat a glorie is this [to] any, to [ca]ll her queene [of] such a place?' Throughout Book 1, the designation of fairies as devils every time they are mentioned forms a tedious marginal refrain. By stanza 20 of canto 1, the poem itself has been consigned to the mass of heretical tracts vomited forth by the dragon Error: the margin proclaims that 'A part of this book was there.' Most readers experiencing this sort of difficulty with the most basic premises of a work would simply stop reading, but this reader is unusually tenacious, and the invective soon becomes more specific and more interesting.

When the Red Cross Knight and Una encounter a hermit saying his rosary, the figure elicits an immediate marginal objection: 'Is this a signe of holynesse, to pray on beades? A papist would lyk this well.' Spenser's account of the hermitage is similarly criticised: 'This commendation of an heremeticall lyfe, is naught: for god hath not commanded us to forsake the society of men, but to doe good to all.' By the time the hermit is found talking of saints and popes and singing Ave Marys, one would have thought that Spenser's attitude toward him was clear enough; the annotator, however, remains indignant: 'Yet hee callcth him a godly fathcr.' And hcrc, of coursc, though thc indignation is misplaced, the reader is on to something, and his reading is perfectly correct: the hermit is Hypocrisy, the disguised Archimago, who proceeds to trouble the sleeping knight with lustful dreams, to present him, on awaking, with the lascivious Duessa, and to separate him successfully from Una.

But even when the hermit is revealed as a villain, and the Roman Catholic paraphernalia is revealed as a sign not of his virtue but of his iniquity, the annotator remains contemptuous of both Hypocrisy's power and Spenser's narrative: 'This is an idle [f]iction, for I sup[p]ose, that never [w]as any good man, [or] woman so delud[ed], as these were. [I]f Sathan could [th]us doe, wee [w]ere in a mise[r]able case.' The contempt, no doubt, is a function of the annotator's realisation that he has in fact mistaken Spenser's allegiances; but this early reader's moral discomfort is surely not entirely misplaced, and it is worth considering just how mistaken he has actually been. Much later, in canto 10, Una leads the Red Cross Knight to the House of Holiness, where they meet the devout Celia, who is described, this time without irony, as 'busy at her beads'. The reader duly comments, 'Why beades, & not prayer? [If] any say, it is poe[tic]all. I say, poesie [mu]st not grace [in]iquitie.' A little further on the hermit Contemplation is encountered, 'That day and night said his devotion, / Ne other worldly business did apply.' The commentator remarks, 'The comendation of hermites is naught' – this time surely not unreasonably. Vices and virtues, villains and heroes often do look the same in the poem, and this is certainly part of its moral structure; but our Puritan reader also provides a good index to the degree to which Roman Catholicism remained an indispensable and genuinely troubling element in Protestant poetics, as in the Elizabethan religious imagination generally. The problem is tartly epitomised in the gloss on Contemplation's promise that the Knight of Holiness will become 'Saint George of merry England': 'A popish saint devised by idle Monks.'

Most of the marginalia constitute carping of this sort, simpleminded though not therefore inconsequential; but there are a few that show a more subtle mind at work. The writer has, to begin with, a classical education. When in canto 2 the Red Cross Knight unexpectedly draws blood from a tree, which turns out to be the transformed Fradubio, the annotator disapprovingly notes the Virgilian parallel: 'a fond fable lyk that of po[li]dorus. a wo[n]der it is that Christian[s] should delyte in suc[h] fopperies.' However, when the Red Cross Knight defeats and kills the Saracen Sansfoy, the reader comments, 'The good knight should have saved him, & not killed. you will say heere is a mysticall meaning. I think so, but all know not that, & therefore it is not safe to teach murther under such pretenses.' This is the first place where the fact that the poem is an allegory and requires a certain sophistication of the reader is acknowledged. In canto 7, when the forging of the knight's arms by Merlin is described, the comment reads, 'Thus the red crosse knight must bee releeved by Magick. as you may after see Canto 8 [– he is now reading ahead before he annotates, so as not to get caught out again]. What simple reader will not comend Merlin & his magick if hee listen to this.' In canto 3, when Una's beauty is credited with taming the savage lion – 'O how can beauty master the most strong' – the reaction is entirely predictable: 'Heere beauty (n[ot] gods) stayes the [li]ons fury'; but the comment on Una's musings in the next stanza is quite shrewd (Figure 13). Here is the stanza:

13 Fol. Bir

The Lyon Lord of euery beast in field,
Quoth she, his princely puissance doth abate,
And mighty proud to humble weake does yield,
Forgetfull of the hungry rage, which late
Him prickt, in pitty of my sad estate:
But he, my Lyon, and my noble Lord,
How does he find in cruell heart to hate
Her that him lov'd, and euer most ador'd,
As the God of my life? why hath he me abhord?

This is the marginalium: 'Heere is no thank[s] to god for her de[li]verance. Is it shame for a po[et] to pray? Not so for heathen virgi[ls] & Homers have m[ade] prayers to their g[ods].' And below this, on Una's characterisation of her knight as 'the god of my life', he remarks that 'Shee hade need of some earthly god, for I do not [see] that shee prayes to the god of heaven'.

Two things strike me here: first, the acknowledgement of a genuine religious sensibility in pagan poetry, and the insistence on its validity as a poetic model (even for this reader, there are clearly two ways of looking at the invocation of muses and the praise of Olympian deities); second, the perception that here Una has somehow lost her mystical status and turned into a perfectly conventional romance heroine abandoned by her

perfectly conventional knight. The reading is acute and accurate.
Milton was unquestionably a more sympathetic reader of Spenser – he
told Dryden, after all, that 'Spenser was his original' – but his problems
with *The Faerie Queene* were not unlike those of our critic: he firmly
rejected the Arthurian subject matter, and made his case for Spenser by
reading him not against romance but against Scotus and Aquinas.

Two final marginalia may serve as summaries of the conflicting attitudes of Spenser's early readers. The only mark made by the original
annotator outside Book 1 of *The Faerie Queene* silently calls attention to
this passage in *Mother Hubberds Tale* (Figure 14):

> But ah! for shame,
> Let not sweet Poets praise, whose onely pride
> Is vertue to advaunce, and vice deride,
> Be with the worke of losels wit defamed,
> Ne let such verses Poetry be named:
> Yet he the name on him would rashly take

Spenser is made to condemn himself. But in canto 4 of *The Faerie
Queene*, history, or more precisely provenance, takes its revenge. Beside
this passage:

14 *The Faerie Queene* [etc.], 1611, 'Mother Hubberds Tale,' lines 810-15

> And eke the verse of famous Poets wit
> He does backbite, and spightfull poison spues
> From leprous mouth on all, that euer writ:
> Such one vile *Enuie* was, that first in rowe did sit,

a later annotator – not, judging from the hand, James Charlton – has inscribed, 'The picture of him that made the former notes' (Figure 15). If this is the Reverend Mr Illingworth's comment, it gives us a nice index to the breadth of Puritan critical opinion about Protestant canonical texts.

At what point did marginalia, the legible incorporation of the work of reading into the text of the book, become a way of defacing it rather than of increasing its value? At what point did the legible evidence of ownership become a detriment? I suggest that the desire for pristine books, unmediated by use or even by prior possession, relates to the increasing centrality of the author in the way we construe the idea of the book – postmodern theory has not reached the world of bibliophile practice. That centrality is, nevertheless, largely fictitious, as any writer who has dealt with the constraints of modern publishers' budgets, house styles and editorial intransigence will be well aware.

Notes

1 Item 50 in Catalogue 1243 (1997).
2 Since completing this chapter, I have done additional work on the Lady Anne Clifford material and have arrived at some further conclusions regarding the marginalia in her text. My revised interpretation of the volume will appear under the title 'Marginal Maternity: Reading Lady Anne Clifford's *Mirror for Magistrates*'. In particular, the 'childish italic' reproduced in figure 8 is in fact Clifford's own hand.

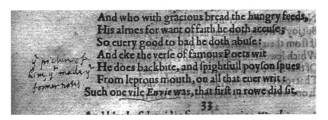

15 *The Faerie Queene* 1.4.32

Naming, renaming and unnaming in the Shakespearean quartos and folio

Peter Stallybrass

It comes as something of a surprise to find the extent to which the personal name does not figure in the early Shakespearean texts.[1] The desire to establish personal names is the desire of most editors, from Alexander Pope to the present. R. B. McKerrow influentially argued that 'The use of the personal name, besides probably coming closer to the author's original intention, has the advantage that it fixes the name in the reader's memory and prevents him from being puzzled as to the identity of the persons referred to in the text, as might otherwise be'.[2] Why does McKerrow believe that the 'personal name' comes closest to Shakespeare's 'original intentions', when he argues at the same time that Shakespeare's hypothetical manuscripts were systematically irregular in their naming of characters?[3]

Although there is no single principle of naming in Shakespeare's plays, I believe that Shakespeare usually moves away from personal names as he writes. Furthermore, the act of being given a personal name, at least for those of high status, is often an act of *unnaming*. To the extent that Shakespeare is interested in unnaming, he is indeed interested in personal names. Nowhere is our own regime of the individual more entrenched than in the belief that the personal name gives access to the person in a way that 'mere' generic labels do not. But in Shakespeare's theatrical scripts, as in the great majority of Renaissance theatrical scripts, the generic name is the generative one, the personal 'merely' personal. That 'merely' can, of course, be of interest to dramatists, particularly when they are exploring deprivation. I believe that in the Renaissance the personal name is often the name of deprivation, the name of a person when stripped of social function. The 'private' person is he or she who has been deprived of public status.

Anne Barton has done much to refute McKerrow's working principle. She writes of Shakespeare's 'characteristic reluctance either to start from names, or to regard them, once given, as necessarily fixed'.[4]

Even so striking a name as 'Perdita' in *The Winter's Tale* is, she points out, only a temporary designation: 'In exchanging "Perdita" for "Princess," the recovered royal child loses nothing. She merely crosses over to join the ranks of those characters, many of them important, for whom Shakespeare in these late plays preferred generic over individual designations' (151). Or again, she comments perceptively on the naming of characters in *The Comedy of Errors*. While the personal name 'Egeon' is significant in relation to the reunion of husband and wife ('if thou be'st the same Egeon, speak'), the speech prefixes tell the generic narrative of a 'merchant', who, as a result both of his profession and his search for his sons, has put his life in jeopardy. And the work of the play is to rename the 'merchant' as 'father' and 'husband' and to rename the Antipholuses and the Dromios as brothers. From this latter perspective, the play is less about the discovery of the proper name than about the restoration of relational identity: husband and wife; father and son; brother and brother (161). Similarly, in *The Winter's Tale*, the process of discovery is that 'Perdita' is really the 'Princess'.

But Shakespeare, like most professional dramatists, took a particular interest in two forms of personal naming: when a personal name is applied to more than one person (as in the case of the twins in *The Comedy of Errors*) and when one person has more than one personal name. Or, to put it another way, he is most interested in the personal name when it is least personal. His interest develops, I believe, from two crucial aspects of Renaissance staging: mimesis and doubling. Renaissance theatrical mimesis, I would argue, begins not less with a person than with a costume.[5] All the records of the early professional theatres show the extraordinary expenses involved in establishing a wardrobe before a play could be undertaken. When an actor puts on a costume (or, we might say, when a costume takes an actor over), one body is absorbed into another, one status into another status. If two actors step into identical costumes, they have usually within the conventions of the Renaissance theatre stepped into the 'same' body. Antipholus and Antipholus, to the bemusement of their fellow characters, share a single body. But what that means in theatrical terms is that they share a single (doubled) costume. Similarly, to the embarrassment of a realist aesthetic, Viola and Sebastian and Cesario share a single body: a single (doubled) suit. This is because Viola deliberately imitates her brother's clothes. Yet once that logic is established, it has consequences. Viola does not know that her brother is alive, but the other characters see that she *is* her brother, just as her brother *is* her, even though, at the same time, the audience recognises the splitting of the suit between the body of an adult player and the body of a boy apprentice.

In the theatre, names are attached less to bodies than to what were called then as now 'properties': the name 'man' can be attached to a boy's body by the attachment of the property of a beard; the name 'lady' can be attached to a boy's body by the putting on of a dress.[6] We consequently might want to reverse our usual way of thinking about bodies and prostheses. For here, the name is attached to the garment or property, and the actor's body is itself supplementary, the ghost that activates a name that is already there, stored in the wardrobe as much as in the actor's parts or a theatrical script.[7] Indeed, even theatrical scripts are at times supplementary to the costumes, and this because of the simple economics of the theatre. As Jean MacIntyre has finely argued, if a company invested in a particular set of costumes (for a play about Robin Hood, or a play set in Asia), it often could not recoup the money it had spent from the performance of a single play. So suites of plays might be commissioned to fit the costumes.[8]

The simplest, and most theatrical, way of thinking about how many characters there are in any one play is to ask how many costumes the play requires. This is because of the centrality of doubling in the Renaissance professional theatres. Thus, *Mucedorus* tells us that ten actors can easily play all the parts, which means that ten actors will have time to put on as many costumes as the parts require.[9] We know from the plot of 2 *The Seven Deadly Sins*, probably revived in the 1590s, that Burbage was to perform two parts, Cowley eight, Duke six, Pallant six and Holland five (Bentley, 230). We also know from the 1631 promptbook of Massinger's *Believe as You List* that single parts could be divided up between two or three players (Bentley, 231).[10] To put it another way, Renaissance theatrical conventions might require not only that one body wear many different costumes but also that many bodies fit into a single costume. Now what most theatrical historians argue, quite rightly, is that the more prominent the part the less likely the player was to double (Bentley, 230). But I would put this a different way: the prominent parts were usually *already* doubled. That is, if doubling is above all about the timing required to get an actor off stage and into another costume before he could return, then Lear and Cordelia and Edgar are doubled parts. For the prominent actor is usually divided up amongst a set of costumes, just like any other doubling actor. And the change of costume always, I would argue, marks a transformation of identity. The King, divested of his crown and of his

train, is merely Lear; Edgar, divested of the clothes of an aristocratic
son and heir, will say '*Edgar* I nothing am' and be transformed by his
nakedness and the blanket round his loins into Tom of Bedlam;
Cordelia, invested in new robes, becomes Queen of France; Kent,
divested of his aristocratic robes, will lose his name, and (belatedly)
take on the name of Caius.[11]

But if a change of costume is, within the conventions of the
Renaissance professional theatre, necessarily a change of identity, it is
not necessarily a change of name. There is a relative autonomy
between clothing and naming. At its simplest, a dramatist,
bookholder, compositor or later editor has a choice between naming
the player's existing costume or naming a prior costume (often the
first costume that the actor wears). At the beginning of both *The
Taming of the Shrew* and *The Taming of a Shrew*, a boy puts on the costume of a lady. In *The Shrew*, the boy (named Bartholomew) can 'wel
vsurpe the grace, / Voice, gate, and action of a Gentlewoman' (Norton
facsimile, TLN 143-4 [Ind.1.132]). When Bartholomew enters, the
stage direction reads '*Enter Lady*' and the subsequent speech prefixes
are all to '*Lady*.' and '*La*.' (TLN 252-98 [In.2.99–143]). Bartholomew,
in other words, a boy being played by a boy, is absorbed into the costume he puts on, which renames him 'Lady.' But in *A Shrew*, the more
common procedure is followed by which the first costume gives the
character his or her name, a name that will persist, often with many
vagaries, throughout the play.[12] So there, the boy apprentice puts on
the costume that names him 'Boy', and even when he dresses as a
woman and is addressed as a woman, the stage directions and speech
prefixes assert the continuity of the imprint of the first costume. In *A
Shrew*, the boy actor remains within the naming practices of the script
'Boy' despite his women's clothes. We are looking, then, at two different systems of naming. The conflict between these two systems has
radical implications. Moreover, and this is perhaps the most striking
point, dramatists can play between the two systems and play one off
against the other.

Twelfth Night presents perhaps the most radical playing off of the
one system against the other and as a result, as Stephen Orgel has
shown, it is one of Shakespeare's least-known plays.[13] That is, although
the play is frequently read, taught and performed, one element of the
conclusion of the plot remains unknown, even (as I have discovered
through malicious tests) by the most distinguished Shakespearean
scholars. On the one hand, *Twelfth Night* clearly follows the convention

of *A Shrew* in that the name of the character follows the imprint of the
costume in which we first see the actor appear. The boy actor appears
first as 'Ladie' and 'Madam' and the speech prefixes and stage directions follow the gendering of the first costume throughout the play.[14]
When the 'Ladie' is re-dressed as a 'Eunuch', it is the previous costume
that still marks the character's gender: '*Enter ... Viola in mans attire*'
(Norton facsimile, TLN 250 [1.4]). The costume gives the gender, but
it does not give the name itself as far as speech prefixes and stage directions are concerned. Yet, as Anne Barton notes, the character is never
actually called Viola within the performed text prior to the final scene.
Before that, she is 'Ladie', 'Madam', or 'Cesario'. Naming is, Barton
argues, deliberately withheld, so that, in the final discovery scene, the
restoration of name can return 'the anonymous "lady," the pretended
"Cesario," to her family, her social identity, and estate' (Barton, 138).

   In an important sense, though, the name is actually not given even in
the final scene. Sebastian says that he *would* name Cesario as Viola
'Were you a woman' (TLN 2405 [5.1.239]). Cesario repeats the name
'Viola' and yet still withholds it from him/her self:

> VIO. If nothing lets to make vs happie both,
> But this my masculine vsurp'd attyre:
> *Do not embrace me*, till each circumstance,
> Of place, time, fortune, do co-here and iumpe
> That I am *Viola*, which to confirme,
> Ile bring you to a Captaine in this Towne,
> Where lye my maiden weeds.
>
>   (TLN 2415-21 [5. 1. 249-55])

The embrace that will restore sister to brother, brother to sister, is elab-
orately held back by the eruption, at the last gasp of the play, of a whole
new narrative, the narrative of Viola's maiden weeds. It is this narrative
that shapes the ending of the play.

   Cesario will become Viola when, and only when, her maiden weeds
have been restored to her. And so the Captain, who is scarcely a significant character in the play if character is what you're looking for, suddenly becomes crucial since he has the clothes that will rename Cesario
as Viola. But where is he? In prison, we discover, at the suit of Malvolio:

> DU. Giue me thy hand,
> And let me see thee in thy womans weedes.
> VIO. The Captaine that did bring me first on shore
> Hath my Maides garments; he vpon some Action

Is now in durance, at *Maluoio's* suite,
A Gentleman, and follower of my Ladies.
OL. He shall inlarge him: fetch *Maluolio* hither ...

TLN 2439-45 [5.1.272-8])

Malvolio, in other words, is only brought back on the stage so that he can release the Captain so that the Captain can give Cesario his 'Maides garments' so that Cesario can become Viola. In fact, Malvolio returns only to depart again in anger. It is solely so as to secure Viola's clothes, which are still as captive as the Captain who has them, that the Duke seeks a reconciliation with Malvolio after he has walked out: 'DU. Pursue him, and entreate him to a peace: / He hath not told vs of the Captaine yet' (TLN 2550-51 [5.1.380-1]). With the Captain still in prison, Cesario is without the clothes that will translate him into Viola. And it is with this failure of Cesario to become Viola that the play concludes:

> DU.   *Cesario* come
> (For so you shall be while you are a man:)
> But when in other habites you are seene,
> *Orsino's* Mistris, and his fancies Queene.   *Exeunt*
>
> (TLN 2555-8 [5.1.385-8])

In *Twelfth Night*, then, there is an absolute conflict between two naming systems. The textual apparatus of the Folio allows only for the existence of Viola, as the character is named in stage directions and speech prefixes alike. But the performed play refuses to allow Viola to emerge at all. This conflict derives from the extent to which both the published text and the performed play are invested in the imprint of clothes. The text follows the imprint of the clothes that the anonymous 'Ladie' is wearing; the play follows the imprint of the clothes that translate the 'Ladie' into 'Cesario'.

In the radically different context of *Richard II*, we find similar conflicts and overlappings between name and clothes. In Q4 and F1, Richard quite literally divests himself of monarchy; that is, he takes off the clothes that name him king and transfers them to Bolingbroke. The question of naming is of particular significance at this moment. Is Richard still king, by which we might mean, in the language of the theatre, have the robes of monarchy imprinted him as king to the extent that, even without them, he retains the name that he had acquired through them? Or is Bolingbroke now king, by which we might mean that, in investing himself in Richard's robes, he is invested as monarch?

We cannot give a single answer to this question, because, as Randy McLeod has brilliantly noted, *The Tragedie of King Richard the second* (Q1) and *The Life & death of Richard the second* (F1) give antithetical answers.[15] In Q1, Bolingbroke, having acquired the crown, enters as '*the King with his nobles*' (sig. Iv); in F1, he enters as '*Bullingbrooke*' with '*other lords*' (TLN 2496 [5.3]). 'King' versus 'Bullingbrooke'; 'his' versus 'other'. The name 'King' is inflated by the whole of his train, which is no less than the kingdom. Everything is his; he is in the possession of no one. But 'Bullingbrooke' is just one lord among others, or even less, since the name, unlike Hereford or Lancaster, conjures up no property, no train to support it.

There is no simple opposition, though, between Q1 and F1 since, as McLeod has shown, the two texts are totally divided within themselves. Indeed, one of the dangers of the two-text theory that now presides over much of Shakespeare scholarship is that it tends to reify each of the two texts, erasing both their own multiplicities and their mutual interweavings.[16] The texts are both less and more than two. So in Q1 (*The Tragedie*), while Bolingbroke is consistently named in the speech prefixes from 5.3 to the end of the play as '*King.*' or '*King H.*', in his final stage entrance he is named '*Bullingbrooke*' (sigs Iv-K2). Equally curiously, in F1 (*The Life & death*), where Bolingbroke is *never* named as 'king' in stage directions or speech prefixes, Richard is named as '*King*' in stage directions only through Act 2, and he is only named '*King*' and (once) '*King Richard*' in the speech prefixes in the very first scene, after which he is merely '*Ri.*', '*Ric.*' or '*Rich.*' This is in contrast to Q1, which gives the speech prefix '*King*' to Richard as late as the last act. Two kings, one king, no king: both texts waver, although in strikingly different ways, between the naming and the unnaming of monarchs. The name of king and the robes of monarchy merge and reinforce each other; or the robes and the name change hands; or the robes remain but the name goes; or the name remains but the robes go.

Names, though, are constantly inter-related with things, as Margreta de Grazia has shown.[17] In the social life of Renaissance England the most powerful names are those associated most directly with land; on the professional Renaissance stage, names are directly associated with what the theatre called its properties. The name then, whether of an actual aristocrat or of a player's persona, is in a very specific sense extrinsic to the person. At the end of Renaissance plays, a ring or a mantle or a chain or some other object again and again restores both proper name and relational identity.

I want to explore now the articulations and the disarticulations between aristocratic and theatrical modes of naming. Both forms of naming are, I believe, profoundly opposed to interiority. Interiority is indeed often literalised in both forms, but in terms of unnaming. If a later regime of individuality will try to trace its most fundamental traits through an interior subjectivity, the interiority of aristocratic monuments and tragic drama alike is displayed in the fully material skull beneath the skin.[18] What characterises that skull is anonymity. The body, given over to death, could be anyone's: the skull may be Alexander's or Yorick's or whomever's. Without a memorial or a gravestone or a gravedigger to tell you whose the skull was, you don't know. But while the depths of the body display only the workings of anonymous death, the surfaces of the body trace the insignia of identity.

If property named person, though, the only landed property of the professional companies was the theatres themselves (if and when they owned them).[19] And the stage was not a suitable medium, nor had it ever been, for the presentation of landed wealth. The properties displayed on the stage were, like women's inheritances more generally, moveables. It is, of course, true that land could be alienated, but with nothing like the ease of moveables, which could pass in a moment from hand to hand, body to body.[20] In other words, stage properties conjured up precisely what aristocratic properties were imagined as overcoming: rapid transformability, the sliding of name into name. None the less, theatre companies used stage properties as material gestures towards an imagined permanence that could never be attributed to the players themselves. On the one hand, the permanence of theatrical properties (and a very temporary one it usually was) was the financial capital of the company itself. The capital consisted of the costumes, props and scripts in which the company had invested. They were their bank which they could sell or pawn in times of hardship. On the other hand, within the theatrical fictions that they performed, the properties could be used to invoke an imagined permanence: the suit of armour or the bracelet or the ring or the mantle that would secure identity, that would lock thing to name, name to person. The name need in no sense be personal. When Perdita is discovered by her father, the witnesses to that discovery do not mention her name, but rather ask that whether the king has 'found his Heire' (TLN 3039 [5.2.29]). And if Perdita's resemblance to her mother and her natural majesty are adduced as proofs of her identity, her identity is secured by the discovery of her mother's mantle and her mother's jewel about her neck, as well as by

the letters of Antigonus (TLN 3042-5 [5.2.32-5]). Her name as
princess and heir is inscribed in material properties, even if these are
properties that the audience never gets to see. Similarly, Thaisa recognises her lost husband Pericles by his voice and his form, but his identity is secured by the ring that 'the king my father gaue you'.[21]

Moveable properties in the theatre were in fact put to radically con-
tradictory ends. On the one hand, they conjured up the instability of
identity as servant assumed the properties of master, woman the properties of man, king the properties of beggar, Roman general the properties of mean exile. On the other hand, they asserted the continuity of
identity over time and distance. It is the process of unnaming and forgetting that Hamlet, the son, attempts to prevent as he mourns his dead
father. He wants to find some further means to memorialise the dead
father and monarch than the mourning clothes which are 'but the trap-
pings and the suites of woe'.[22] His claim, though, in both Q2 and F1
although not in Q1, is that it is not '*alone*' his inky cloak that names him
as mourner (TLN 28 [1.2.77]). That is, even if his clothes alone are
inadequate for the work of mourning, they are still a constitutive part of
it, even if a part that anyone could play. But just what the work of
mourning clothes is differs in Q2 and F1. In F1, not clothes, not the
facial expressions of grief, not 'all Formes, Moods, shews of Griefe'
(TLN 264 [1.2.82]) can '*denote*' him truly. In Q2, the 'chapes of griefe'
cannot '*deuote*' him truly. The difference between the two versions is a
difference of no more than an inverted letter: 'n' or 'u' (modern 'v').
F1's 'denote' is familiar to us: clothes are signifiers, symbolic systems
directed at the observer, detachable from both the body and the inner
state of their wearer. Q2's 'deuote' is not familiar. It suggests the power
of clothes to shape and in-habit (note the contrast between Q2's
'chapes' and F1's 'shews' of grief). Mourning clothes devote the wearer
to what he or she mourns; more than mere fashions, they fashion both
who the wearer is and what the wearer will remember.

Retaining his mourning clothes, and thus refusing to celebrate the
remarriage of his mother, Hamlet attempts to perpetuate his father's
name and memory. And for all his claims to have 'that within which
passes showe' (Q2, TLN 266 [1.2.85]), he berates his mother for not
wearing mourning, claiming that, between the funeral and the marriage, it has been 'A little month or ere those shooes were old / With
which she followed my poore fathers bodie' (Q2, TLN 331–2
[1.2.147–8]). Taking off her mourning shoes, Gertrude takes her feet
out of the past. She unnames herself as old Hamlet's widow. Similarly,

in asking Hamlet to 'cast [his] nighted colour off' (Q2, TLN 248 [1.2.68]), Gertrude asks him to cease staging himself as his dead father's son. For mourning clothes enact the materiality of memory, daily reminding both wearer and observer of the dead.

Twelfth Night, probably written within the same year as *Hamlet*, enacts a curious inversion of Gertrude's brief mourning.[23] Hamlet attacks his mother for the 'little month' of her mourning; Orsino attacks Olivia for her refusal to give up her mourning clothes, even though her brother died seven years before. It seems likely, indeed, that when John Manningham saw the play in 1602, the actor who played Olivia was dressed in mourning clothes throughout, since Manningham remembered her, mistakenly, as a widow.[24] The emphasis in both plays is less upon the proper than upon the relational name. What should a widow, a sister, a brother, a friend, a son, a father, an uncle, a mother, a wife, a lover be? How should they act?

I have immediately to qualify this, since the name 'Hamlet' is obsessively repeated in all three of the early *Hamlet* texts. Yet this personal name partially functions, I believe, as a form of *un*naming. It is striking, for instance, that the dead king and father is only named as 'Hamlet' four times in both Q2 and F1: three times in connection with his battle with Fortinbras, thus emphasising single combat as against national war; once by his son. And his son's act of naming is itself uncannily close to an act of unnaming. The father is already unnamed in the return of his suit of armour. The armour is Hamlet's, but what activates the armour in the present is repeatedly called an '*it*'. And the stage directions and speech prefixes of Q1, Q2 and F1 alike unname the dead Hamlet as simply 'Ghost'. For the Ghost to become a revenant of the dead Hamlet thus depends upon an act of naming, an act of naming that the living Hamlet performs: 'Ile *call* thee *Hamlet*, / King, Father, royall Dane' (Q2, TLN 629-30 [1.4.44-5], my emphasis). There are two things I want to note about this act of naming. The first is that it is 'preposterous' in the rhetorical sense that Pat Parker and Jonathan Goldberg have taught us to recognise.[25] The 'preposterous' puts the posterior prior to its genealogical or social pre-cedent, the son before the father, the wife before the husband, the servant before the master, the bottom before the head. In a patriarchal culture, it is fathers who have the power to name their children. But in *Hamlet*, it is the son who is put in the position of naming the father.

The second point I want to note is that the name of 'Hamlet', although prior, is in this particular rhetorical phrasing the unmarked term. 'Hamlet' is absorbed into 'King', 'King' into 'father', 'father' into 'royall Dane'. The personal name is the least significant, the generic the most. And even the name 'Hamlet' is not unique in the way that, say, 'Coriolanus' is. That is, 'Hamlet', like so many of the names that fascinated Shakespeare, is divided between more than one character. As Anne Barton notes, 'Hal' is a name unique to Henry IV's son, yet *1 Henry IV* is organised around the displacement of 'Hal' by 'Harry' a 'personal' name split between three different persons (Harry Bolingbroke, Harry Hotspur and Harry, Prince of Wales) (Barton, 110–12). 'Harry' is also potentially a common noun, referring to any 'Tom, Dick or Harry', although the play swerves away from that doubling of the name of the monarch by changing the expression to '*Tom, Dicke*, and *Francis*' (Norton facsimile, TLN 972-3 [2.4.8]). In *Hamlet*, the name 'Hamlet' is split between a dead warrior-king and his antic and bedlamite son. And the trajectory of the play will be towards the undoing of the connection between Hamlet and monarchy and the dispersal of the name along with the dispersal of the aristocratic clothes of the antic son.

If the name 'Hamlet' is split, so also is the title 'royall Dane', attributed to the dead Hamlet but now shared by the king and his 'imperiall ioyntresse' who occupy 'the royall bed of Denmarke' (Q2, TLN 767 [1.5.82]). Similarly the names 'King' and 'father' have been appropriated by Claudius. But, as many scholars have reminded us, it isn't quite right to say that Claudius takes on the name of King. In any staging of the play, the name 'Claudius' is never mentioned, and it appears nowhere in the text of Q1. In Q2 the name appears in the stage direction for his first entrance and as his first speech prefix and never again. In F1 it appears only in the first stage direction. The person we call Claudius is in all three texts called 'King'. While we think of a personal name as an *addition* to the identity of the King of Denmark, from the perspective of aristocratic naming it makes as much sense to think of it as a *diminution*.

But in *Hamlet*, even the single name 'King' is troubled by the spectre of doubling. The Ghost haunts the name 'King' both with an idealised past and with a present in which the spectral dead threaten to vampirise the living. At the same time, the play is haunted by alternative forms of rule: the rule of an invading Norway; popular rule (Laertes and the people) in place of elective monarchy. Moreover, the name 'King' is itself doubled in Q2 and F1 through the selfconscious staging of kingship in the play within the play. It is worth noting that such doubling is carefully avoided in Q1. There, the 'Player' enters in 'The Mousetrap' as '*Duke*'; and the boy actor ('My yong lady and mistris', who has in fact nearly grown out of female roles) takes the part of '*Duchesse*' (Q1, TLN 2023 [3.2.154 s.d.]). But in Q2 and F1, at least in the stage directions which start the play within the play, the 'Player' performs as '*King*', the boy as '*Queene*' (Q2 and F1, TLN 2023 [3.2.154 s.d.]). Both Player and Boy are absorbed into their parts, as is Bartholomew into the part of 'Lady' in *The Taming of the Shrew*. That is, the speech prefixes in Q2 and F1 *Hamlet* are not '*Player*' and '*Boy*' but in Q2 '*King*' and '*Quee.*' and in F1 '*King*' and '*Bap.*' (for 'Baptista') or '*Qu.*'. In other words, the Player and (intermittently in F1) the Boy textually double the names that a modern editor names 'Claudius' and 'Gertrude' but that F1 and Q2 consistently name 'King' and (intermittently in the case of Q2) 'Queen'. There is, though, a curious twist here. While the Boy who plays 'Queen' mimics the role of Gertrude, the Player who plays 'King' mimics the part of old Hamlet, a part now played by a Ghost. In the play within the play, the role of Claudius, the present king, is mimicked not by the brother of the fiction's monarch but by the nephew, one Lucianus. The king who watches the play thus watches himself unnamed as king, unnamed even as uncle. This transposition has not escaped the notice of Freudians. Within the plot of the play within the play, the usurper is the nephew, thus corresponding in the audience to the King's nephew, that is, Hamlet; within the audience, the usurper is the regicide, Claudius, who corresponds to the regicide, Lucianus, in the play within the play. The speech prefixes, in fact, direct us to the latter reading, since the texts of Q2 and F1 require that we split 'King' (Gonzago) from 'King' (Claudius), 'Queen' (Baptista) from 'Queen' (Gertrude). Such a splitting of names is accomplished on the stage through casting; but in the text the names are conflated.

Despite the doubling of the name 'King', the fact that remains more surprising and more resistant to our own expectations is that *this* king, whom we call Claudius, is unnamed *except* as 'King'. Similarly, in *Measure for Measure*, the Duke's function is asserted by the withholding of any personal name, whether in the play itself or in the stage directions and speech prefixes. The name 'Vincentio', by which the Duke is known in most modern editions, only appears amongst 'The names of all the Actors' at the end of the F1 text. Within the play, he is simply 'the Duke', just as Claudius is simply 'the King'. The power of the name in both cases is put in tension with the actions of the persons who fulfil those ruling functions. In *Measure for Measure*, the Duke has invested the ironically named Angelo with rulership, together with the 'figure of vs' and 'our selfe' (TLN 19, 49); in *Hamlet*, the king will be accused of regicide, fratricide and incest. But, having no personal names, the Duke and the King are to a surprising extent immune to the interrogation of their ruling functions; 'Richard', on the other hand, through the very act of naming him as such, can be divorced from the name of King, as can his successor Bolingbroke and Bolingbroke's successor Harry. Hal's strategies, indeed, can be seen as his attempt to obscure his own dubious genealogy as claimant to the throne by turning to advantage the disadvantage of his doubled name, absorbing Harry Percy's deeds into Harry Monmouth's.[26]

In general, to have a personal name (Richard or Bolingbroke or Harry) is a limitation on the unqualified name of King. The character modern editors have reduced to 'Claudius' has absorbed the power and authority of the previous king, who is himself reduced to a Ghost. And in the course of the play, at least according to the stage direction of Q1, the Ghost is further reduced from the spectre of a warrior in his memorialising armour to the spectre of a private citizen 'in his night gowne' (Q1, TLN 2482 [3.4.101]). In contrast to the doubled figure of the Ghost, the King (Claudius), for all the splittings of his conscience, increasingly asserts the 'diuinitie' (Q2, TLN 2868 [4.5.124]) that hedges him around within even more 'strength and armour' than that which binds a 'singuler and peculier life' (Q2, TLN 2283–9 [3.3.11–16]). The body of this king is both multiple, absorbing the 'generall' (Q2, TLN 2296 [3.3.23]) into itself, and monolithic, as the Ghost at first appears to be but in fact is not. The person of the 'Queen', on the other hand, is more complex, particularly in Q2, where she is radically split between the naming of her function and her personal name, 'Gertrard'. This very split lends itself all too easily to our own understanding and thus erases the difficulty that confronts us. Recall McKerrow's assertion: the editor should emend speech prefixes and stage directions to '[t]he use of the personal name' since personal names 'probably com[e] closer to the author's original intention'. Q2, then, would on those grounds already be the text closest 'to the author's original intention', as it is there that the personal name emerges most closely from behind what McKerrow would think of as the obscuring generic name. For in Q2, and in Q2 alone, the 'Queen' is renamed as '*Gertrard*' or '*Ger.*', a single time in the speech prefixes up to 3.2, throughout 3.4 (with a single exception of '*Quee.*' at TLN 2435

[3.4.52]), throughout 4.1, and in the opening stage direction to 3.4. But
this emergence of the name 'Gertrard' is, I would argue, only a temporary undoing of both the name and power of the Queen, a kind of textual complicity with the violence of the son against his mother.

'Gertrard' is actually named as such thirteen times within the performance text of Q2, and she is named that exclusively by the King, signifying the intimacy between them. In contrast, 'Gertrard' emerges in
speech prefixes and stage directions exclusively in relation to her son,
Hamlet. To put it a different way, the naming of 'Gertrard' within the
performed play and the naming of 'Gertrard' within the apparatus of
the text are culturally and ideologically distinct. Within the performed
play, the name asserts the closeness of husband and wife, although a
closeness that remains hierarchical. The Queen can be 'Gertrard' to
her husband; the King remains 'my Lord' (Q2, TLN 3761 [5.2.291]) to
his wife. But as speech prefix and stage direction, the name 'Gertrard'
unnames her as queen and wife. The first time that 'Gertrard' occurs
within the textual apparatus of Q2 is, I think, doubly motivated so as to
detach her from her husband and so as to situate her in relation to
Hamlet both as her son and as her potential lover:

> GER. Come hether my deere *Hamlet*, sit by me.
> HAM. No good mother, heere's mettle more attractiue.
>
>   (Q2, TLN 1963–4 [3.2.108–10])

It is as if Hamlet's response has the retrospective power to rename his
mother in her preceding request, no longer as queen, or even as mother,
but as a woman whose sexual attractions (whose magnetic 'mettle') can
be compared to the sexual attractions of Hamlet's former lover,
Ophelia. If Claudius names his lover as 'Gertrard' within the staged
play, the textual apparatus names 'Gertrard' as potential lover in relation to Hamlet. Such a renaming is resisted (or simply not imagined) in
either Q1 or F1. The Q2 naming of the Queen as 'Gertrard' this single
time within the textual apparatus of 3.2 prepares the way for the
repeated naming of her as 'Gertrard' in Q2's closet scene. There,
Gertrard/the Queen will say, 'thou hast cleft my hart in twaine' (TLN
2539 [3.4.156]), even as Q2 cleaves her name in two. 'Cleaving', of
course, carries the antithetical meanings of separation and union.
Within the marriage service, it is required that the daughter be cleft
(divided) from her father and cleave (be united) to her husband.
Hamlet wants to cleave the Queen/wife from her King/husband so
that she will cleave to Hamlet (both the dead King/husband and his

proxy, the son/prince). And he will attempt to unname his mother as Queen by detaching her from the properties that name her Queen, the properties which prop and substantiate her name.

I am, of course, fully aware that in the *staging* of a play textual markers such as speech prefixes disappear, absorbed into the action and the roles. I even believe that speech prefixes are quite commonly absorbed even in the act of reading, coming to our notice only when something 'goes wrong' in our making sense of a passage. But in Renaissance reading practices, I would suggest, the absorption of speech prefixes was not, in the first instance, into 'character', but rather into a system of difference without positive term, the system of difference that, at its simplest, marks dialogue as a differentiation of two positions, without any need to solidify either of those positions immediately into a specific person. That, I think, is the implication of Renaissance scripts where positional difference in a dialogue can and is frequently redistributed from one character to another in different versions of a play (as I argue below in relation to the frequent redistribution of lines between characters in Q1 and F1 *Lear*). These redistributions and the anxiety they now cause remain extraordinarily revealing of the gap between the assumptions of the modern editor or critic and those of the Renaissance dramatist or bookholder or compositor. The gap marks a rupture in cultural assumptions. At its extreme, I would say that a character cannot have much interest within bourgeois ideology unless it is an individual, whereas the 'individual' cannot have interest within aristocratic ideology unless it explicitly partakes of a generic or social field. Names within Shakespearean dramatic practice are of most interest not when they define an individual but when they most tensely and contradictorily act as the markers of the convergence and splitting of identities.

The splitting and undressing of 'Hamlet' that will transform Hamlet (the armoured but dead father) into the pale shadow of Hamlet (the 'naked' but living son) is reworked in *Lear*, where the King is split and transformed into a pale shadow of the King. At the same time, the King in *Lear* is split like the Queen in Q2's *Hamlet* between the name of his status and his personal name. But the splitting that hovers round the textual margins of Q2's 'Gertrard' becomes theatrically central in *Lear*. The name 'Lear', like the prefix 'Gertrard', works, I want to argue, as a form of unnaming. In fact, the name 'Lear' occurs surprisingly rarely in the performance speeches of any of the three early texts. The name appears, of course, on the title page of Q1 and as a running header both there and in F1. And it is also the exclusive speech prefix and dominant stage direction in Q1 and F1 (the name 'King' appears a single time but in a different location in the stage directions of both Q1 and F1). Within the performance script, though, the name 'Lear' occurs only sixteen times in the composite text of the Riverside edition, compared to the thirty-one namings of 'Edmund' (the most frequently repeated personal name) and the twenty-one namings of both 'Cordelia' and 'Tom'. The infrequency of the naming of Lear is in striking contrast to the frequency of the naming of Shakespeare's Roman heroes: according to the concordance to the Riverside edition, the two Caesars are named 376 times in *Julius Caesar* and *Antony and Cleopatra*; Antony is named 211 times in the two plays; Brutus is named 145 times in *Julius Caesar*.[27] But these Roman names had already become *generic*, and thus had at least partially shifted from proper to common nouns. One could be 'a Caesar', 'an Antony', 'a Brutus'. Indeed, names seem to interest Shakespeare to the very extent to which they are becoming generic, when the 'General' (Caesar, Antony, Coriolanus) has become 'general' (a commonplace).[28] It is not surprising, then, that the name that recurs most frequently in *Lear* is 'Fool' (more than fifty times), simultaneously the designation of a particular role and a name that will be attached to Lear, Kent, Albany and Cordelia.

The name 'Lear' mediates between the generic power of the name 'King' (the power of the particular to absorb the general) and the generic powerlessness of 'Fool' or 'madman' (the power of the general to absorb the particular). Not having generic force, the name 'Lear' can act as a diminution of the title 'King'. Indeed, 'Lear' is first used in the play by Kent as a way of opening up the space of detachment and rebuke:

> Royall *Lear*,
> Whom I haue euer honor'd as my King,
> Loued as my Father, as my maister followed,
> As my great patron thought on in my prayers[29]

'*Royall*' Lear. Yet Kent's emphasis is upon the conditional rather than the absolute quality of the monarch. Kent has honoured Lear *as* his king, father, master, patron, but that 'as' opens up the possibility of detachment. (Lear is 'like' a king as Madonna is 'like' a virgin.) The naming of 'Lear' as such is a significant step in his uncrowning. As 'Lear', he is a, not the, king. In fact, Kent immediately goes on to repeat

the name 'Lear' with a subversive lack of any honorific 'royall': 'Be *Kent*
vnmannerly when *Lear* is man [F1: 'mad']' (Q1, TLN 137 [1.1.145]).
All modern editors follow F1's 'mad', but it is worth noting that 'man'
is invariant in the existing copies of Q1. 'Man' is, in fact, a perfectly
plausible reading, picking up punningly on the transformation of Kent
from man to 'vnmannerly' and of Lear from king to 'man', while at the
same time giving a literal and symbolic priority of 'Kent' (the name of
an earldom) to 'Lear' (the name of a mere man [in the Folio, of a
madman], even if one who still claims the title of monarch). In both
texts, at any rate, the name 'Lear' is a diminishment of the plenitude
and potency of 'king'. The naming of 'Lear' is the beginning of the
unnaming of the 'King'. If this is right, it is the less surprising that the
phrase 'King Lear' occurs only a single time in both the *Historie* (Q1)
and the *Tragedie* (F1) of Lear: 'King *Lear* hath lost, he and his daughter
taine' (Q1, TLN 2651 [5.2.6]). He is named King Lear, then, only at
the very moment when he has absolutely lost the throne, and when he is
the prisoner of the Bastard. 'Lear', like 'fool' or 'madman', inscribes
dispossession. The names of possession – 'King' and 'father' (sixty-
seven and seventy-nine times respectively in the Riverside edition) –
recur with much greater frequency in the *Historie* and *Tragedie* of Lear.
But they, like any generic title, are open to doubling: the doubling of the
title King with the King of France; the doubling of the title of father
with Gloucester.

Let me give a very crude summary of the naming practices within
the actual speeches of the *Lear* texts so as to try and bring out the relation between personal names and generic or status names. The names
most commonly repeated are the proper names that also function as
generic names (King, Fool). After such names, the most commonly
repeated name is a personal name: it is the name of Edmund, despite
the fact that in the speech prefixes (always in Q1; usually in F1) and the
stage directions (more commonly than not in Q1; less commonly than
not in F1) he is named generically as 'Bastard'. The third most
common name is 'Gloucester', a name that defines a status and that can
refer to three people in the play (Gloucester, the father; Edmund;
Edgar), although it is in fact only used to refer to two (Edmund and
Gloucester). The fourth most common name is about equally Cordelia
(a personal name) and Tom (both a personal and a generic name). The
name 'Lear' is less common than any of these names; the name 'Edgar'
is less common again. This, despite the title page of Q1, which gives
particular prominence to the names of Lear and Edgar.

What is immediately striking in this crude summary is the unusual significance given to one particular personal name: the name of Edmund. It is striking both because it undoes the declared priorities of the Q1 title page and because it works against a textual apparatus that most commonly names Edmund 'Bastard'. It is true that the 'Bastard' first appears as 'Edmund' in stage direction and speech prefixes in the *Tragedie* (F1). But the name 'Edmund' is soon displaced by the name 'Bastard' in F1's speech prefixes, probably because F1 is following Q2 in regard to its textual apparatus. Q2 in turn usually follows Q1, and Q1 had to print 'Edmund' as 'Bastard' (or at least, not as Edmund) for mechanical reasons, even if the name in the copy behind it was 'Edmund'. Peter Blayney has given the evidence for this in his magisterial work on the printing of the first quarto of *Lear*.[30]

Blayney notes that the play-quarto of *Lear* which Nicholas Okes's shop printed in 1607-8 was the first play-quarto that the shop had ever printed. Now play-quartos, as Blayney shows, make peculiar demands upon the upper-case italic *E* for the stage directions '*Enter*' and '*Exit*' and '*Exeunt*' (Blayney, 129). The fact that upper-case italic *E* had not been in much demand previously is suggested by the fact that several of the letters in Okes's shop 'had been deliberately defaced for use as *F*' (Blayney, 129). But the text of *Lear* put quite extraordinary demands upon upper-case italic *E* because, in addition to the usual demands in a play of entrances and exits it also required *E*s for every speech prefix for '*Edgar*' and would also have required *E*s for every speech prefix for '*Edmund*' if he was called that in the copy. But, as it turned out, there were not even enough *E*s to cover the entrances, exits and Edgar, let alone Edmund, with the visible result that the *E* of *Edgar* had to be composed from a mixture of the correct italics, swash *E*s, roman E*s and *E*s that had been defaced to make *F*s, and with the invisible result that formes that had already been set up had to be cannibalised for *E*s, thus delaying the whole printing process. So if the F1 *Tragedie* suggests that the name 'Edmund' may have been at least sometimes in the textual apparatus of the copy that lay behind it, the Q1 *Historie* suggests that literal shortages of 'characters' unnamed Edmund.

If the shortage of upper-case italic *E*s in Q1 may have led to the unnaming of Edmund, it certainly led to the defacing of Edgar. That is, in one of those extraordinary coincidences that are impelled by the determinations of materiality, the defacing of Edgar within Q1, as he is transformed from aristocratic son and heir to beggar and madman, is mimicked by the defacement of the material characters out of which Q1 is composed. My interest in these parallel defacements is the greater because they cannot be reconciled within a single field of intentionality or causality. The theatrical defacement depends upon a deliberate reworking of a widely known *topos*; the textual defacement depends upon the specific limitations of a specific printshop. If Nicholas Okes had printed more play-quartos before, he would probably have acquired a larger stock of upper-case italics, and the problem would not have occurred. But he didn't, and it did.

It is to the defacement of Edgar that I now want to turn, emphasising to begin with the printed text rather that the theatrical script. If the theatrical script necessitated cutting up the roles of Edmund and Edgar into two distinct players' parts, the printed text threatens to merge the two names. In the Q1 *Historie*, the compositor or the copy text twice confuses the two names. In Q1, Goneril, addressing the man defined in the stage direction as '*Bastard*', says 'backe *Edgar* to my brother [Cornwall], / Hasten his musters, and conduct his powers' (Q1, TLN 2013-14 [4.2.15]), which in F1 correctly becomes 'Backe *Edmond*'. Again, when Gloucester enters in Q1, supposedly climbing up towards the cliffs of Dover, he is led by '*Edmund*', whereas F1's Gloucester is correctly led by '*Edgar*' (Q1, TLN 2221 [4.6 s.d.]). In fact, the printed texts pull the reader in antithetical directions: on the one hand, towards Q1's absolute distinction between the speech prefixes '*Ed.*', '*Edg.*', '*Edgar.*' and '*Fdg.*' and the speech prefixes '*Ba.*' and '*Bast.*'; on the other hand, to the overlap and merging of the alliterative 'Edgar' and 'Edmund'.

But this overlapping and merging of names is much less conspicuous in the performed script. There, Edgar is absorbed by Edmund, as Edmund appropriates Edgar's potential title, Gloucester. Edmund, in fact, is addressed as Gloucester eight times in the Q1 *Historie*, and not only by Goneril and Oswald but also by Albany and Edgar. Edgar, in contrast, is never addressed as Gloucester. As Edmund moves towards assuming the name of Gloucester, Edgar is defaced both literally ('my face ile grime with filth' [Q1, TLN 1071 (2.3.9)]) and through his unnaming as 'Tom of Bedlam'. As Margreta de Grazia has finely observed, the name 'Tom of Bedlam' is a perverse version of the aristocratic form 'Edmund of Gloucester'.[31] The 'of' in the latter case ties the personal name to the property that will entitle it. But the 'of' of 'Tom of Bedlam' ties the common noun 'Tom' (the Tom of any Tom, Dick or Harry) to the hospital that not only unnames a person's reason but also disentitles him from the getting or leaving of property. '*Edgar* I nothing am' (Q1, TLN 1083 [2.3.21]); 'my name is lost' (Q1, TLN 2780 [5.3.121]). What *Lear* sets forth, as de Grazia argues, is the mutual implication of name and property (de Grazia, 21–7). Without property, Edgar is Tom, the King is Lear, Lear is Lear's shadow. It is the 'lendings' which both Lear and Edgar dispose of that name them as king and heir respectively, that name them even as person as opposed to thing. Without such accommodations one is 'the thing it selfe': not some uncovered essence but a thing that is less than a beast because a 'bare ... Animall', without even the property of wool or hide (F1, TLN 1886-8 [3.4.107–8]).

But the connection between name and 'lendings' draws attention not only to the possibility of divestment – i.e., that losing one's clothes one loses one's name – but also to the ways in which a name is composed through the absorption of the bodies and possessions of others. Lear's train, as de Grazia argues, is the men who attend him, but men conceived as if Lear had absorbed them into his own body as his clothing (cf. the bride's 'train') (de Grazia, 22). The clothed person owes his protective covering to the animals from which he has taken that covering; the aristocratic name owes its protective power to the liveried servants who are absorbed into that power. The naming of clothes by Lear as 'lendings' thus points to the construction of identity through the dispossession of another. The word 'robe' is in fact derived from the Old French *robe*, meaning spoil or booty – that which has been robbed. This derivation is exploited in the Admiral's Men's play *Patient Grissil*, where the Marquess claims: 'I rob'd my wardrop of all precious robes / That she [Grissil] might shine in beautie like the Sunne.' [32] If the Marquess here claims that he has robbed himself, the more usual implication is that the rich have robbed to attain such robes. As the Tuscan Renaissance proverb had it, 'chi ha roba, ruba' ('he who has property/robes is a thief').

The play upon 'robe' and 'rob' is part of a larger Renaissance discourse on the relation between clothes and theft. Thus, Scipione Mercurio, rewriting Laurent Joubert's book on popular errors, notes that humans, although the most noble of animals, are born without 'vestimenti'. To clothe themselves, they plunder the rest of the animal world: ' ... atae che per procacciarsene, e proedersi di quanto avaramente gli fu' dalla Natura negato, a' guisa di publico ladrone, toglie a' questo animale la pelle, a' quell'altro la lana, in somma ne spoglia molti per vestir se stesso'. [33] Lear articulates this sense of clothes as stolen when, using Tom o' Bedlam as his model, he strips himself on the heath: 'Is man no more then this? Consider him well. Thou ow'st the Worme no Silke; the Beast, no Hide; the Sheepe, no Wooll; the cat, no perfume ... Off, off you Lendings' (F1, TLN 1882-8 [3.4.103-8]). Rejecting 'lendings', which have been taken from the backs of others, Lear goes on to attack the 'robbed [i.e. robed] man of Iustice' (Q1, TLN 1742 [3.6.36]), the robber whose thefts are concealed by the 'robes & furd-gownes' of 'the great image of authoritie' (Q1, TLN 2371-2, 2366 [4.6.165, 158]).

But in *Lear* 'the great image of authoritie' is quite literally disrobed through the disrobing both of present authority (the King) and of authority to come (Edgar, entitled through primogeniture as 'son and heir'). In place of the rules of inheritance that bind land to name, name to the succession of the eldest son, *Lear* imagines every possible inheritance system *except* primogeniture. The king himself begins this process: in the absence of male issue, women will inherit. But they will inherit through the divisions of gavelkind, a system of partibility that is itself shadowed in the play by the alternative of ultimogeniture (inheritance by the youngest), an alternative only hinted at in the case of Cordelia, but achieved in the case of Edmund.[34] And in the succession of Gloucester to Gloucester, three possibilities are imagined or encompassed: the disposing of the patriarch so that his sons may reign jointly in his stead; the inheritance of the older son; the rights of the illegitimate over the legitimate child. Finally, *Lear* imagines male heirs as dependent upon the wives they have married or might marry (Albany upon Goneril, Cornwall upon Regan, Edmund upon Goneril or Regan) and native kings as dependent upon their invading daughters (Lear upon Cordelia).

The two most subversive images of this undoing of entitlement are, I think, in the relation of Edgar to Edmund and of Albany to Goneril. As Edgar is unnamed, so Edmund acquires a name. Note first that, despite the shortage of upper-case italic *E*, the stage directions of both Q1 and F1 move in the final act from naming him as '*Bastard*' to naming him consistently as '*Edmund*'. Even more striking is the ordering of the names in the stage directions of the last act: '*Enter Edmund, Regan, and their powers*' in Q1, as if Regan had already declared, as she later will:

> Generall,
> Take thou my souldiers, prisoners, patrimonie,
> Witnes the world that I create thee here
> My Lord and maister.

(Q1, TLN 2734-7 [5.3.74-7])

Even more striking is the first stage direction of the final scene of the *Tragedie* (F1): '*Enter in conquest with Drums and Colours, Edmund, Lear, and Cordelia, as prisoners, Souldiers, Captaine*' (F1, TLN 2938–9 [5.3]). The illegitimate younger son as virtual monarch, with a king and a queen as his prisoners. Edmund's ascent to unchallenged supremacy has already been envisaged through the fantasised killing of Albany and Goneril by Regan or of Regan by Goneril. The restoration of an undivided kingdom is imagined, then, but under the rule of a bastard, of a younger son, of a child who has disinherited his father. It is as if the play encourages its audience to imagine and encompass treason. In the place of 'Edgar, son and heir to Gloucester', 'the Bastard' will rule.

But the Bastard is, of course, defeated; Edgar is restored to his rights. More than that, there are, I think, some curious suggestions that Edgar, like the demonised Edmund, is imagined as future king. Nahum Tate was not simply making up the centrality of Edgar to any supposedly 'happy ending': he was picking up significant cues in the play.[35] Edgar is, as Regan tells us, the King's godson and it was Lear who named him Edgar (Q1, TLN 862-3 [2.1.91–2]). Similarly, Cymbeline, prefiguring the incorporation of his foster child into his own family, had given him his name, Posthumus. Moreover, the concepts of 'majesty' and the 'royal' disappear from the play after their repeated use in the first scene, to reappear again only towards the end of the play in relation to Lear ('this old maiesty' [Q1. TLN 2962 (5.3.300)]). But the last use of the term 'royal' is not in reference to Lear but in reference to Edgar. After Edgar has declared his name, Albany responds: 'Me thought thy very gate did prophecie, / A royall noblenesse' (Q1, TLN 2835-6 [3.175-6]). His 'royall noblenesse' suggests that he may become heir to more than an earldom.

The impossibility of any such inheritance is contained in the extraordinary limitations of Edgar's reassertions of his name, when he tells Edmund, in the F1 *Tragedie*:

> My name is *Edgar* and thy fathers Sonne,
> The Gods are iust, and of our pleasant vices [Q1: 'vertues']
> Make instruments to plague vs:
> The darke and vitious place where thee he got,
> Cost him his eyes.
>
>   (F1, TLN 3130–4 [5.3.170–4])

His claim is to the limited personal name alone. His genealogy is, through a strange rhetorical twist, distanced and even disowned. He is

the son of *Edmund*'s father, his name thus established through his relation to the illegitimate son. And his father is unnamed, or named only
indirectly and generically through his relation to the unnamed mother
of Edmund, herself imagined as the very source of namelessness: a
'darke and vitious place'. In Shakespeare's *Lucrece*, what issues from
that place is imagined as 'blur'd with namelesse bastardie'.[36] In *The
Tragedie* (F1) the blinded father is imagined as having unnamed himself through the act of lechery; producing 'nameless bastardy', he has
produced himself as nameless. The violent imagination of that 'darke
and vitious place', though, rebounds against Edgar himself, unnaming
him by cancelling out the imagined place of legitimacy. It is as if, even
here, the name of Edmund has swallowed up the name of Edgar, swallowed up the name of Gloucester, leaving no name to which Albany's
promised 'rights / With boote' (F1, TLN 3272–3 [5.3.301–2]) could
accrue. It is also as if the naming of the sexual scene undoes the possibility of any renaming and of any inheritance within the play. The
absorbative power of the aristocratic name is here reversed by the
absorbative power of a principle of unnaming.

Yet in F1, that principle of unnaming is so general that there is no particular shock to the ascription of the final speech in the play to '*Edg.*'. A
'royall noblenesse' has been discerned in him, even if he is not the man of
highest rank. But the ascription of the last speech to Edgar would have
been far more surprising in the text of Q1. This is, I think, largely because
of the significance of the 'non-theatrical' speech prefixes. In F1, the
speaking characters at the end of the play are Edgar, Kent and Albany.
Despite the fact that Kent and Albany name estates, whereas Edgar is a
personal name, the aristocratic names are not foregrounded. But that is
not true of Q1, where the three concluding speakers are named in the
speech prefixes as Edgar, Kent and '*Duke*'. In other words, Q1 distinguishes Albany from Edgar and Kent by specifically naming his status. In
fact, this is an act of renaming during the course of the final scene. For
although he enters 5.3 as '*Duke*' in Q1 (in F1, he is '*Albany*' and '*Alb.*'
throughout the final scene), in the speech prefixes he is at first '*Alb.*'.
'*Duke.*', indeed, is a speech prefix which, in Q1, refers to two dukes:
Albany and Cornwall. In 1.4 '*Duke.*' refers to Albany; in 2.1, 2.2 and 2.4 it
refers to Cornwall (although once in 2.1 his speech prefix is '*Corn.*').
After 2.4 and prior to the last scene, '*Duke.*' disappears as a speech prefix.
Instead of the doubled 'Duke', we have Cornwall and Albany.

Unnaming is written into the practices of making scripts for the
professional theatre in the Renaissance. This is not, I think, a 'deep'

question, as most character analyses would make it. Recent character analyses tend to trace the differing consistencies of Albany and Edgar as if they were discrete individuals in Q1 and F1. But that is not, I think, how character emerges in Shakespearean drama. At its simplest, and judging from the Hand D pages of *Sir Thomas More* which most scholars presume to be the hand of Shakespeare, we can suggest the following principle: the assignment of character is belated, a question of how one divides up what is, at its most basic, monologue or dialogue, between one, two, or more actors.[37] Hand D seems first to have written the speeches, and then, only afterwards, assigned speech prefixes. And they are, particularly to begin with, of the most minimal kind. The speeches are simply divided between 'Lincoln', taken over from the existing play, and 'other'. But 'other' has been divided by Hand C into no less than three different parts: George Betts; his brother, a clown; Williamson, a carpenter.

We can see the same principle at work (whether by Hand D or Hand X I have no idea) in *Lear*. '*Three Gentlemen*' in Q1 becomes '*a Gentleman*' in F1 (Q1, TLN 2384; F1, TLN 2630); a Doctor and a Gentleman in Q1 are condensed into the single figure of a Gentleman in F1. Between Q1 and F1, lines are transferred from Kent to Lear, from Lear to Kent, from Lear to the Fool, from Regan to Cornwall, from Edmund to Regan, from Edmund to the Herald, from Goneril to Lear, from Goneril to Edmund, from Goneril to Albany, from Goneril to Regan and from Regan to Goneril, from Cornwall to Goneril, from Albany to Edgar. It is, I believe, within the very nature of Renaissance theatrical writing that speeches preceded character and could be reassigned. They could be reassigned by a scribe, as in the case of the part made for Edward Alleyn for *Orlando* by a scribe. They could be reassigned by another dramatist, or by the acting company, or by a particular actor so as to facilitate a performance by a bigger or a smaller company or so as to pad out the part of a particularly good actor and diminish the part of a weaker one. They could be reassigned by a compositor who could not read the handwriting of the manuscript he was following or was trying to regularise the speech prefixes or was short of a specific letter or was trying to disambiguate 'Duke' from 'Duke' (e.g. Albany from Cornwall) or 'Cor.' from 'Cor' (e.g. Cornwall from Cordelia). They could be reassigned by the dramatist who wrote the play. Once a part had been assigned, it was attached to a range of things: a player or (as in the case of *Believe as You List*) two or three players; a costume or costumes (which might then be transferred to another part, like the speech prefixes themselves); specific props. But, like Edgar, every part could be unnamed, could be reassigned. If the fictions that the theatre presented were often haunted by the fantasy of a name that was embedded in a property or a person, the conditions of theatrical representation always worked towards the splitting and doubling of the part, the splitting and doubling of the name, the unnaming and renaming which underpinned theatrical mimesis itself.

Notes

1 This essay owes its existence to an invitation from John Kerrigan and Anne Barton, and I am deeply grateful to them and for criticisms of an early draft made by Juliet Fleming, David Kastan, Andrew Murphy and Phyllis Rackin. It is in more ways than I can acknowledge a footnote to the work of, and conversations with, Margreta de Grazia, Randy McLeod, Jeffrey Masten and Stephen Orgel. I am also indebted to the work of Jonathan Goldberg and Paul Werstine. See in particular Goldberg's *Voice Terminal Echo: Postmodernism and English Renaissance Texts* (New York, Methuen, 1986), pp. 68–100, 'Textual properties', *Shakespeare Quarterly*, 37:2 (1986), pp. 213–17 and *Writing Matter: From the Hand of the English Renaissance* (Stanford, Stanford University Press, 1990); and Werstine's 'McKerrow's "suggestion" and twentieth-century Shakespeare textual criticism', *Renaissance Drama*, n.s. 19 (1988), pp. 149–73 and 'Narratives about printed Shakespeare texts: "foul papers" and "bad" quartos', *Shakespeare Quarterly*, 41:1 (1990), pp. 65–86.

2 Ronald B. McKerrow, *Prolegomena for the Oxford Shakespeare: A Study in Editorial Method* (Oxford, Clarendon Press, 1939), p. 58. See also W. W. Greg, *The Editorial Problem in Shakespeare: A Survey of the Foundations of the Text* (Oxford, Clarendon Press, 3rd edn, 1954), pp. 102–5, and Werstine's critique, 'McKerrow's "suggestion"'.

3 McKerrow, *Prolegomena*, p. 57, where he argues that 'in the heat of composition, [the characters'] qualities or the part which they played in the action were often more strongly present to [Shakespeare's] imagination than their personal names'.

4 Anne Barton, *The Names of Comedy* (Oxford, Clarendon Press, 1990), p. 89.

5 On the relation between costumes and identity on the Renaissance stage, see Richard Southern, *The Staging of Plays before Shakespeare* (London, Faber & Faber, 1973), particularly pp. 132–42; G. K. Hunter, 'Flatcaps and bluecoats: visual signals on the Elizabethan stage', *Essays and Studies* (1980), pp. 39–40; David M. Bevington, '"Blake and wyght, fowll and fayer": stage picture in *Wisdom*', in Milla Cozart Riggio (ed.), *The 'Wisdom' Symposium, Papers from the Trinity College Medieval Festival* (New York, AMS Press, 1986), pp. 18–38; Scott McMillin, *The Elizabethan Theatre and 'The Book of Sir Thomas More'* (Ithaca, NY, Cornell University Press, 1987), pp. 53–4; Stephen J. Greenblatt, *Learning to Curse: Essays in Early Modern Culture* (London, Routledge, 1990), pp. 161–2; Jean MacIntyre, *Costumes and Scripts in the Elizabethan Theatres* (Edmonton, University of Alberta Press, 1992); Laura Levine, *Men in Women's Clothing: Anti-Theatricality and Effeminization, 1579–1642* (Cambridge, Cambridge University Press, 1994); Peter Stallybrass, 'Worn worlds: clothes and identity on the Renaissance stage', in Margreta de Grazia, Maureen Quilligan and Peter Stallybrass (eds.), *Subject and Object in Renaissance Culture* (Cambridge, Cambridge University Press, 1996), pp. 289–320; Stephen Orgel, *Impersonations: The Performance of Gender in Shakespeare's England* (Cambridge, Cambridge University Press, 1996), pp. 83–105.

6 I am deeply indebted to Will Fisher's unpublished work on beards on the Renaissance stage.

7 See, for instance, R. W. Ingram (ed.), *Coventry, Records of Early English Drama* (Toronto, University of Toronto Press, 1981), pp. 226, 224; MacIntyre, *Costumes*, p. 80.

8 MacIntyre, *Costumes*, p. 104. For the significance of costumes in the economic calculus of the Restoration stage, see John Downes, *Roscius Anglicanus*, ed. Judith Milhous and Robert D. Hume (London, Society for Theatre Research, 1987), pp. 53, 101, 94 and 89.

9 See G. E. Bentley, *The Profession of Player in Shakespeare's Time, 1590–1642* (Princeton, Princeton University Press, 1984), p. 229.

10 See also David Bradley, *From Text to Performance in the Elizabethan Theatre: Preparing the Play for the Stage* (Cambridge, Cambridge University Press, 1992), pp. 86–7.

11 William Shakespeare, *The Tragedie of King Lear*, in *The Norton Facsimile: The First Folio of Shakespeare*, ed. Charlton Hinman (New York, Norton, 1968), TLN 1272 (2.3.21) and 3249 (5.3.284). Except where otherwise stated, all further references to F1 texts will be from this edition and will be incorporated parenthetically into the text.

12 Anon., *A Pleasant Conceited Historie called The taming of a Shrew* (1594), in Geoffrey Bullough (ed.), *Narrative and Dramatic Sources of Shakespeare* (London, Routledge & Kegan Paul, 1966), scene 2, ll. 34, 39, 54, 56. The stage direction at line 34 reads: '*Enter the boy in Womans attire*'.

13 Orgel, *Impersonations*, pp. 50, 104. For an important earlier analysis of the significance of Viola's clothes at the end of the play, see Phyllis Rackin, 'Androgyny, mimesis and the marriage of the boy heroine on the English Renaissance stage', *PMLA*, 102:1 (1987), pp. 29–41.

14 Yet as Jonathan Goldberg notes, '[w]hat becomes [Viola] she may become'. See his 'Shakespearean characters: the generation of Silvia', *Voice Terminal Echo*, pp. 68–100, p. 86.

15 My comments on *Richard II* are directly indebted to unpublished work by Randy McLeod/Random Cloud. Quotations from Q1 are from the facsimile of *The Tragedie of King Richard the second* in Michael B. Allen and Kenneth Muir, *Shakespeare's Plays in Quarto* (Berkeley, University of California Press, 1981). Quotations from F1 are from *The Life & death of Richard the second* in the Norton facsimile.

16 For a good account of these multiplicities, see Paul Werstine, 'The textual mystery of *Hamlet*', *Shakespeare Quarterly*, 39:1 (1988), pp. 1–26; see also Margreta de Grazia and Peter Stallybrass, 'The materiality of the Shakespearean text', *Shakespeare Quarterly*, 44:3 (1993), pp. 255–83.

17 Margreta de Grazia, 'The ideology of superfluous things: *King Lear* as period piece', in Margreta de Grazia, Maureen Quilligan and Peter Stallybrass (eds.), *Subject and Object in Renaissance Culture* (Cambridge, Cambridge University Press, 1996), pp. 17–42.

18 For a critique of the concept of the individual as an anachronism in Renaissance England, see my 'Shakespeare, the individual, and the text', in Lawrence Grossberg, Cary Nelson and Paula Treichler (eds.), *Cultural Studies* (London, Routledge, 1992), pp. 593–610.

19 The theatres themselves could be notoriously moveable. On 28 December 1598, the Burbages and others pulled down the Theatre and carried 'all the wood and timber therof unto the Banckside in the parishe of St. Marye Overyes, and there erected a new playehowse [the Globe] with the sayd timber and woode'. See E. K. Chambers, *The Elizabethan Stage*, vol. 2 (Oxford, Clarendon Press, 1923), p. 415.

20 On the gendering of moveables and immoveables in wills and testaments, see Amy Louise Erickson, *Women and Property in Early Modern England* (London, Routledge, 1993).

21 *The Play of Pericles Prince of Tyre* in Michael B. Allen and Kenneth Muir, *Shakespeare's Plays in Quarto* (Berkeley, University of California Press, 1981), sig. I2v (5.3.39).

22 All quotations from *Hamlet* are from Paul Bertram and Bernice W. Kliman, *The Three-Text Hamlet: Parallel Texts of the First and Second Quartos and the First Folio* (New York, AMS Press, 1991). Q2, TLN 267 (1.2.86).

23 See MacIntyre, *Costumes*, p. 187.

24 John Manningham, *Diary*, excerpted in G. Blakemore Evans (ed.), *The Riverside Shakespeare* (Boston, Houghton Mifflin, 1997), p. 1966.

25 Patricia Parker, 'Preposterous events', *Shakespeare Quarterly*, 43:2 (1992), pp. 186–213 and 'Preposterous reversals', *Modern Language Quarterly*, 54:4 (1993), pp. 435–82; Jonathan Goldberg, *Sodometries: Renaissance Texts, Modern Sexualities* (Stanford, Stanford University Press, 1992), pp. 4, 179–92.

26 On the absorption of the deeds of '*Harrie Percy*' by '*Harry Monmouth*', see *The First Part of King Henry the Fourth* in the Norton facsimile, TLN 3021–15 (5.4.59–73).

27 Marvin Spevack, *The Harvard Concordance to Shakespeare* (Cambridge, MA, Harvard University Press, 1973).

28 I draw here upon Patricia Parker's fine analysis of 'general' in *Literary Fat Ladies: Rhetoric, Gender, Property* (London, Methuen, 1997), pp. 85–9.

29 All quotations from Q1 (*The Historie of King Lear*) and F1 (*The Tragedie of King Lear*) are from William Shakespeare, *The Parallel King Lear 1608–1623*, ed. Michael Warren (Berkeley, University of California Press, 1989), Q1, TLN 130 (1.1.139–42).

30 Peter W. M. Blayney, *The Texts of King Lear and their Origins*, vol. 1, 'Nicholas Okes and the First Quarto' (Cambridge, Cambridge University Press, 1982).

31 De Grazia, 'The ideology of superfluous things', p. 27. My whole analysis of *Lear* is profoundly indebted to Margreta de Grazia.

32 Thomas Dekker, *Patient Grissil*, in *The Dramatic Works of Thomas Dekker*, ed. Fredson Bowers, vol. 1 (Cambridge, Cambridge University Press, 1953), 3.1.81–2.

33 *De gli errori popolari d'Italia. Libri sette* (Padova, Francesco Bolzetta, 1645), p. 182. I am grateful to Mary Galucci for this reference and for her analysis of *spogliare*.

34 For a fine analysis of inheritance systems and *King Lear*, to which I am indebted, see Richard Wilson, *Will Power: Essays on Shakespearean Authority* (Hemel Hempstead, Harvester Wheatsheaf, 1993), pp. 215–30.

35 Nahum Tate, *The History of King Lear*, in Christopher Spencer (ed.), *Five Restoration Adaptations of Shakespeare* (Urbana, University of Illinois Press, 1965), 5.6, pp. 269–73.

36 'Lucrece' in William Shakespeare, *The Poems*, edited by Hyder Edward Rollins, New Variorum (Philadelphia, Lippincott, 1938), p. 163, l. 522.

37 For useful commentaries on Hand D in *Sir Thomas More*, see McMillin, *The Elizabethan Theatre*, 'Hand D', pp. 135–59; Barton, *The Names of Comedy*, p. 89.

Composition/decomposition: singular Shakespeare and the death of the author

Laurie E. Maguire

'Editing is a ritual we perform over the corpus of an author who has passed away.' (Gary Taylor)[1]

Introduction: *in memoriam*

My subject is memory and memorial, the abstract and the concrete: editions as receptacles to house an author's remains and perpetuate his memory. This chapter is thus about the death of the author in its most literal form. I begin, appropriately, at the end, with a contemporary account of Renaissance death.

In 1600 Francis Tate (1560–1616) described 'the Antiquity, Variety, and Ceremonies of Funerals in England' (30 April 1600).[2] Eschewing description of aristocratic funerals (which were regulated by the College of Heralds), and avoiding eschatological matters (pre-Reformation rituals had not been entirely displaced by their Protestant descendants), Tate provides a prosaic and pragmatic account of thanatological procedures. 'When life beginneth to forsake the bodie, they which are present close the eies and shut the mouth ... Then is the body laid forth ... upon a floore in some chamber covered with a sheete, and candels set burning over yt on a table day and night, and the body continually attended or watched' (216).[3] There is no 'sett and determinate time how longe the corps should be kept', Tate says, although we know from other sources[4] that two to three days was usual, prompt interment being necessary to avoid the olfactory effects of decomposition; however some wills request periods of fifteen to forty days before burial, presumably to assuage the testator's fear of being buried alive (Gittings, *Death*, 30). Where state funerals, requiring elaborate preparations, were planned, the corpse was embalmed (an expensive process), and interment safely delayed for some months. Tate touches on both these matters (217).

Tate continues: 'The appointed day for the funeral being neere, the body is wrapt up with flowers and herbes in a faire sheet, and and [sic] this we call Winding a Corpse. ... After this, the body is put into a coffin of wood or stone, or wrapped in lead, and sometime there is put up with it somethinge which he principally esteemed' (217). 'On the day of the interment the body is brought forth of the chamber, where before it lay, into the hall or great chamber, and there placed till the mourners be reddy and marshalled' (218). Covered in a sheet, over which is draped a black cloth or velvet covering, the coffin is carried to the grave by servants or specially selected poor people. The poor and/or the rest of the servants (dressed in black) precede the corpse, with family and friends following behind in black mourning cloaks and hoods. Tate says that it is customary for the route to the grave to follow the most direct and least public ways possible (219). And so the deceased is buried.

Probate accounts and private papers expand Tate's bare summary. In preparation for burial, the dead body was washed, shaved (where necessary), dressed in a smock or shirt, and (in the seventeenth century, if not before) given a cap, gloves and cravat.[5] The shroud came from the household linen supply unless the deceased were unusually tall, in which case it was specially made. The body was displayed, strewn with flowers and herbs, face uncovered. Neighbours paid their last respects, after which the shroud was tied at top and bottom (loosely so as not to 'impede the wearer on the day of resurrection' – Gittings, 112).

Sir Thomas Overbury describes a milkmaid concerned to die in the spring so she could have 'store of flowers stucke upon her winding sheet'.[6] The most common sweetening herb was rosemary: in Q1 *Romeo and Juliet* the Friar invites the mourners to 'sticke your Rosemary in this dead coarse', and the stage direction which concludes the scene instructs everyone but the Nurse to '*goe foorth, casting Rosemary on her*' (T2v). Rosemary was often additionally carried by mourners in the funeral procession. Perfumed water was also used to sweeten the corpse (in Q2 *Romeo and Juliet* Paris vows to dew Juliet's tomb nightly with sweet water, which is provided for, along with flowers, in the stage direction in Q1 [I4v]). Decomposition was further disguised by burning perfume during the wake.

Mourning clothes for grieving relatives were provided by the family of the deceased. This was 'an expensive business and so it was in general confined to wealthier people' (Gittings, 119); poor people wore their everyday clothes. Black palls (white for a bachelor, maid or a woman deceased in childbirth) were hired from the parish. The many yards of black cloth which swathed the church at funerals of wealthier people were hired from several cloth merchants (one merchant being insufficient to supply the amount needed). The deceased's family also distributed gifts to the assembled mourners: gloves, ribbons, points and thread, for example, to friends, and 'dole' (bread, cheese, wheat, malt, 1d.) to the poor.

Funerals were costly affairs, with the expenses usually anticipated in advance and provided by the deceased; however, descendants often spent far more on the obsequies than was specified in the deceased's will. Food and drink regularly account for half and sometimes three quarters of the funeral expenses. If a substantial meal were required, it took place later, at the deceased's house, after the 'drinking', which took place in the churchyard immediately following the interment (Gittings, 97).

Although many Renaissance funeral customs derive from the Middle Ages (for example, burning candles, walking with the corpse),[7] new trends reflect the increasing sense of individualisation which characterises the early modern. Funeral sermons gave biographical details of the deceased and were printed in pamphlet form (a forerunner of the obituary); and funeral monuments marked the deceased individual, providing permanent commemoration in an age in which tombstones were not yet widely used. Funeral monuments in England had long existed for the royal and aristocratic, a demonstration of the continuation of the Body Politic despite the demise of the Body Natural;[8] from the early fourteenth century, memorials to non-royal deceased began to increase in number, and, whereas earlier monuments had often been anonymous, the name of the deceased was now an important feature. A simplified version of this commemorative custom, in the form of tombstones, would later extend to ordinary people. (Until the last years of the seventeenth century, churchyards were full of unmarked graves; bones disturbed when digging a new grave were put in the charnel house (Gittings, 143–4).)

Francis Tate's near contemporary, John Weever (1576–1632) supplements Tate's brief description of death with the comprehensive Folio volume entitled *Ancient Funerall Monuments* (1631). However, Weever does not restrict the definition of monument to architectural tomb:

A Monument is a thing erected, made, or written, for a memoriall of some remarkable action, fit to bee transferred to future posterities. ... Now aboue all remembrances (by which men haue endeuoured, euen in despight of death to giue vnto their Fames eternitie) for worthinesse and continuance, bookes, or writings, haue euer had the preheminence ...

The Muses workes stone-monuments out last;
Tis wit keepes life, all else death will downe cast (B1r).[9]

A few pages later Weever refines his definition. Returning from the literary to the literal, he offers an architectural model: 'Now to speake properly of a Monument, as it is here in this my ensuing Treatise vnderstood, it is a receptacle or sepulchre, purposely made, erected, or built, to receiue a dead corps, and to preserue the same from violation' (B3r).

I want to unite Weever's two models, the literary and the literal, by considering what happens when an author's writing – a self-reflexive monument – is housed in a purpose-built receptacle, erected by others – an edition, a collected works – 'to preserue the same from violation'. The result is increased liminality, the nexus of life and death, failure to be and continuing to be, a Derridean metaphysics of presence.[10] Walter J. Ong has considered this paradox in relation to *Pippa Passes*, in which Browning refers to the practice of pressing flowers in books. In Ong's analysis

The dead flower, once alive, is the psychic equivalent of the verbal text. The paradox lies in the fact that the deadness of the text, its removal from the living human lifeworld, its rigid visual fixity, assures its endurance and its potential for being resurrected into limitless living contexts by a potentially infinite number of living readers.[11]

Simply put: the author is dead; long live the author.

In this chapter I pursue the connection between physical death and literary memorial in the general context of editing. In the first section I adopt Weever's monumental image to reconsider the First Folio (a memorial monument erected by Heminge and Condell to Shakespeare), and link it to grief theory to contextualise editorial attitudes: the tidying of the deceased's *corpus*, which burial practices have long demanded, and the idealisation of the deceased are two of the early stages of mourning. In the second section I use these linked issues (tidying, commemorating, idealising) to revisit the concept of memorial reconstruction and the twentieth-century construction of texts as 'good' or 'bad', focusing on the work of Peter Alexander on the *Henry VI* plays. As we shall see, the concept of memorial reconstruction both stems from and supports the editorial need to fix a playtext in a singular permanent form, to privilege one text over another, and is powerfully related to the tidying and idealising stages of grief and recovery.[12] My concluding section considers the current state of editing in a society that is in denial about death.

The First Folio

John Heminge and Henry Condell: actors in the Chamberlain's (subsequently King's) Men, sharers in the Globe, fellows of Shakespeare and editors of the First Folio. Shakespeare remembered these men as his friends in his will of 1616, leaving them (along with Burbage) 26*s.* 1*d.* each to buy a commemorative ring. We remember Heminge and Condell because they remembered Shakespeare, collecting thirty-six of his plays in the First Folio of 1623 '*onely to keepe the memory of so worthy a Friend, & Fellow aliue, as was our* SHAKESPEARE' (A2v). The volume is thus both a relic of the deceased and a memorial to him.

As Heminge and Condell explain in their dedicatory epistle to the Earls of Pembroke and Montgomery, the plays have outlived the author and '[*w*]*e haue but collected them, and done an office to the dead, to procure his Orphanes, Guardians*'. However, as the prefatory material proceeds, it becomes clear that rumours of Shakespeare's death have been greatly exaggerated. Although 'sad mortality' has denied him the opportunity to become an editor, he survives as an author. With the eulogising paradoxes familiar to us from sonneteering tradition, Ben Jonson writes '*My Shakespeare ... / Thou ... art aliue still, while thy Booke doth liue, / And we haue wits to read*' (A4r), and Hugh Holland concludes '*For though his line of life went soone about, / The life yet of his lines shall neuer out*' (A5r). 'I.M.' (James Mabbe?) recasts the paradox in a theatrical form:

> *WEE wondred* (Shake-speare) *that thou went'st so soone*
> *From the World = Stage, to the Graues-Tyring-roome.*
> *Wee thought thee dead, but this thy printed worth,*
> *Tels thy Spectators, that thou went'st but forth*
> *To enter with applause. An Actors Art*
> *Can dye, and liue, to acte a second part*
> *That's but an* Exit *of Mortalitie;*
> *This, a Re-entrance to a Plaudite.* (A7r)

The rest is not silence, and the spirit of the First Folio is thus one of cel-ebration: the contributors to, and editors of, the volume come to praise Shakespeare, not to bury him. The volume is a memorial, and, like all memorials, it celebrates life in the midst of death. Although the plays in the First Folio span a period of more than two decades and represent different phases of composition (the unrevised and possibly incomplete draft of *Timon of Athens*; the revised texts of *The Taming of the Shrew*, *Romeo and Juliet* and *Love's Labour's Lost*, still bearing the internal evi-dence of revision;[13] Ralph Crane's scribal transcripts of *Measure for Measure* and *The Two Gentlemen of Verona*), they combine, as Graham Holderness and his colleagues note in their contribution to this volume, to give a coherent overview of Shakespeare, the man and his work. The plays may contain internal contradictions or changes of thought, but no alternative versions of the plays are allowed admission to the First Folio to compete with and complicate our unified memorial vision. As literary executors, Heminge and Condell perform the tidying-up operations which death requires, preparing the corpus, the inevitably single corpus, of Shakespeare for public view. As Tate describes, the foul copy of the deceased body must be 'wrapt ... in a faire sheet', turned into the fair copy of the edited Folio.

Shakespeare's corpus is presented to us rhetorically, through an invitation to read and understand not the plays but the person, William Shakespeare himself, who is preserved in the First Folio: 'Reade him, therefore; and againe, and againe: And if then you do not like him, surely you are in some manifest danger not to vnderstand him'. The invitation applies to multiple readings of a single text, and that text is the Author.

The equation of people with books is an appropriate Shakespearean conceit, familiar to us from Lady Macbeth's description of her hus-band – 'Your Face, my Thane, is as a Booke, where men / May reade strange matters' (TLN 417–18) – and from Lady Capulet's instruc-tions to Juliet before the ball (TLN 427–32).[14] In reading Paris's linea-ments, Juliet is invited to 'share all that he doth possesse, / By hauing him, making your selfe no lesse' (TLN 439–40). In the same manner, familiarity with the First Folio will lead to personal possession: for Heminge and Condell, and for Leonard Digges, the poet is 'our Shakespeare'; for Ben Jonson he is 'my Shakespeare' and 'my beloued'; for the prospective purchaser he is, in a sense, 'yours that read him'.

The duality which characterises the First Folio's discussion of the author (his life/death, presence/absence) extends to the reader, who is characterised in both commercial and literary fashion. For the reader, spiritual possession of Shakespeare must be prefaced by commercial; Shakespeare has to be owned fiscally before he can be owned mentally or emotionally. This duality links the reader with the editors and publishers, for (as *The Merchant of Venice* makes clear), emotional and commercial possession are connected through the notion of risk. The first paragraph of Heminge and Condell's address to 'The Great Variety of Readers' has a desperate jocularity which can be loosely summarised as 'Hey, do we ever need you to buy this volume'. But, despite the desperate injunctions to purchase, this, we are told emphatically, is, as far as the editors are concerned, a memorial tribute rather than a commercial venture. Heminge and Condell have collected Shakespeare's plays '*without ambition either of selfe-profit, or fame*' (A2v) and Leonard Digges commends the editors' piety in giving the world this collection.[15]

The First Folio has indeed become something of a symbol for selfless generosity, as represented in texts as diverse as Ethel Wilson's autobiographical essay (1961) which contemplates the editors' allegiance to a dead friend, and the set of the Royal Shakespeare Company's production of Richard Nelson's play, *Some Americans Abroad* (London, 1989), where the sentiments represented by the backdrop (the First Folio address 'To the great Variety of Readers') contrasted sharply with the competitive and back-stabbing petty-mindedness of the academic *dramatis personae* squabbling in the various Shakespearean venues in which they were leading student seminars.[16] Charles Connell's short biography of Heminge and Condell, *They Gave Us Shakespeare*, takes Ethel Wilson's essay one step further, producing a hyperbolic paean of praise to the under-fêted editors for their generous literary undertaking: 'without their devotion, assiduity and indefatigable efforts, the world would have been poorer'.[17]

In fact, Connell's book presents an even more effusive homage. His tribute to the dead editors was prompted, he explains, by F. E. Cleary, a British civil servant who became intrigued by the roles of Heminge and Condell in the First Folio when he was given responsibility for the garden in which they are buried. Connell's book turns Cleary's tribute to the first editors into Connell's tribute to Cleary, who, significantly, shares the book's first photographic plate with Heminge and Condell's memorial plaque. The same transference of tribute can be seen architecturally. After the Second World War, Heminge and Condell's bomb-damaged parish church was dismantled and shipped to Missouri to be rebuilt as the Winston Churchill Memorial and Library.

The title of Connell's book, *They Gave Us Shakespeare*, comes from Leonard Digges's exordium in the First Folio: 'Shake-speare, *at length, thy pious fellowes giue / The world thy Workes*' (A7r). It is worth collating these sentiments with the inscription on the memorial plaque to Heminge and Condell in the garden of St Mary the Virgin Aldermanbury, dedicated in 1896, which rewrites Digges's sentiments in a proleptically postmodern way: 'To the Memory of John Heminge and Henry Condell ... To their disinterested affection the world owes *all that it calls Shakespeare*' (my emphasis). Heminge and Condell did not give us Shakespeare; they gave us all that we call Shakespeare.

Heminge and Condell's epistle 'To the great Variety of Readers' is (like most advertising ploys) explicit in its claim to completeness: whereas before the reader was exposed to inferior copies, now the reader has those copies 'cur'd, and perfect of their limbes; and all the rest' (A3r). Heminge and Condell give us the complete dramatic works. They not only remember Shakespeare; they literally re-member him. In what must constitute the most confident, the most cryptic – and the briefest – statement of editorial policy in the history of editing, Heminge and Condell explain the foundation of their text:

> where (before) you were abus'd with diuerse stolne, and surreptitious copies, maimed, and deformed by the frauds and stealthes of iniurious impostors, that expos'd them: euen those, are now offer'd to your view cur'd, and perfect of their limbes; and all the rest, absolute in their numbers, as he conceiued the[m].

This is the language of embalmment, and the anthropomorphising vocabulary both of this epistle (where plays are conceived, maimed, deformed, cured and furnished with limbs) and of the dedicatory epistle which precedes it (where plays are orphaned) is taken further in the reifying/deifying word-made-flesh metaphor examined above ('Read *him*'; my emphasis) which accords with Leonard Digges's sentiments: the editors give us not an editorial construct, but the real thing – Shakespeare. However, the phrasing on the Heminge and Condell memorial plaque is equally correct: the editors give us all that we call Shakespeare. The First Folio, like editing in general, is a construct: a time-dependent product of informed and arbitrary choices in varying combinations. 'What we call Shakespeare' varied between 1621 and 1623 (and indeed has done so continually since).[18]

As Margreta de Grazia points out, 'what we call Shakespeare' might have been very different had two stationers, Jaggard and Pavier, succeeded in their attempt to publish a Shakespeare collection in 1619.[19] In that year the printer William Jaggard and the publisher Thomas Pavier entered into partnership, not for the first time. They aimed to produce a collection of ten Shakespeare plays in quarto and their motive in collecting and editing the plays, unlike the proclaimed motive of Heminge and Condell a few years later, was obviously commercial.

In preparing the Folio, Heminge and Condell rejected eight of the Pavier playtexts, a rejection that makes sense in the context of death; death may offer an occasion to celebrate the deceased, but it also provides an opportunity for spurious claims to patrilineal succession and inheritance. Bastardy compromises reputation as well as finances, and it is no accident that in the Renaissance the term 'bastard' applied to illegitimate coins as well as to illegitimate persons, while, in the printing house, bastard fonts were used for legal documents.[20] Shakespeare's bastard offspring (e.g. Q1 *Pericles* – a collaborative work? a memorial reconstruction? a rough draft?) as well as those claimants who falsely advertise themselves as Shakespeare's legitimate offspring (e.g. *1 Contention*, *A Yorkshire Tragedy*) must be excluded.

As executors, Heminge and Condell try to distinguish Shakespeare from what Jaggard and Pavier merely call Shakespeare, the Author from the Other, the true child from the false copy. Their conventional paternal tropes remind us that children, like monuments, are ways to remember the dead, to find continuity in annihilation, to give a voice to silence. Their vocabulary of legitimate and illegitimate textual offspring is also conventional in prefatory epistles, but in its legalistic concern to distinguish true from false it invokes, quite naturally, the language of death and inheritance.

Memorial reconstruction

For consideration of these issues – truth, falsehood, death, succession, memory – I now turn to the work of Peter Alexander (1894-1969). Alexander first achieved fame for applying Greg's theory of memorial reconstruction to *1 Contention* and *The True Tragedy of Richard, Duke of York*. As I shall show, Alexander's textual work, like Heminge and Condell's editorial work, illustrates the connection between the editorial creation of a single, unified ('good') text and the death of the author.

The field of enquiry into suspect texts, as Alexander found it, dealt with texts (Q1 *The Merry Wives of Windsor*, Q *Orlando Furioso*) whose problems are discernible on even a cursory reading,[21] and whose language and action vary considerably from that represented in the parallel Folio or manuscript text, respectively.[22] The focal texts in Alexander's investigation, *1 Contention* (Q 1594) and its sequel *Richard Duke of York* (O 1595), have no such obvious problems. Considered in isolation, they are sound textually and sophisticated dramatically. Considered alongside F *2 Henry VI* and F *3 Henry VI*, they show few verbal or situational differences. At *c.* 2300 lines Q *1 Contention* and O *Richard Duke of York* are not unduly short, at least not in relation to most other plays of the 1590s (the 3000-plus lines of plays by Jonson and Shakespeare are exceptional), and are not shorter than their F counterparts to an extent that might cause critical alarm or raise accusations of truncation in Q/O. Metre and phrasing give no undue or sustained cause for alarm, and what differences there are in dialogue and stage directions between Q/O and F suggest that the F texts represent Shakespeare's revision of earlier plays by himself or another, rather than that Q/O represent failing and inaccurate memory.

Alexander's concern was not relative excellence, but manifest error, such as the confused genealogy of the Yorks in *1 Contention*, which is 'not merely ... incorrect; the argument ... as a whole has no point whatever'.[23] Errors of this kind were deemed incompatible with authorial composition, and so Alexander concluded that Greg's theory of memorial reconstruction for *The Merry Wives of Windsor* and *Orlando Furioso* held good for (parts of) the early texts of *Henry VI*: *1 Contention* and *Richard Duke of York* are 'pirated versions of *2* and *3 Henry VI*, put together by two of the leading players in Pembroke's Company, after the failure of the tour in 1593' (116). Whether Alexander's conclusions are right or wrong is neither important nor relevant to the concerns of this chapter. What interests me are the conditions under which Alexander researched his topic, for his conclusions are prompted by the death of an author.

Alexander's argument begins with the death of the author Robert Greene, who died in penury in 1592. In an autobiographical pamphlet apparently composed on his deathbed, Greene warns his fellow dramatists to have nothing to do with actors, and he levels a particular accusation against Shakespeare:

> trust them not: for there is an vpstart Crow, beautified with our feathers,
> that with his *Tygers hart wrapt in a Players hyde*, supposes he is as well
> able to bombast out a blanke verse as the best of you: and beeing an
> absolute *Iohannes fac totum*, is in his owne conceit the onely Shake-scene

in a countrey … let those Apes imitate your past excellence, and neuer more acquaint them with your admired inuentions.[24]

Malone's *Dissertation on Henry VI* (1787) inaugurated the view that this passage, with its parodic line from *3 Henry VI*, meant that Shakespeare began his career by rewriting the plays of other men, Greene among them; hence Greene's envy of Shakespeare's artistic and financial success, since Greene, one of the unacknowledged sources of this success, was dying prematurely and penniless.

This interpretation had made inevitable the view that suspect texts, such as the quarto of *1 Contention*, were first sketches by a playwright, later revised by Shakespeare in the text of the First Folio. Alexander agreed with Malone that Greene ridiculed Shakespeare's dramatic ability, and that the line from *3 Henry VI* was cited contemptuously as an example of the bombast which the parvenu author was producing. Alexander argued, however, that Greene's bitterness was not caused by the actor-turned-author's plagiarism. Greene was bitter because Shakespeare, having spoken others' lines as an actor, had the temerity to presume that he could turn dramatist. In other words Greene taught Shakespeare all he knows and, having been eclipsed by the newcomer, is abandoned. He goes to his death without physical, financial or emotional support from the players and player-playwright whose careers he enabled. Such an interpretation removes the need for Shakespeare to serve a dramatic apprenticeship as reviser of earlier plays by others. It therefore removes the need to view *1 Contention* and *Richard Duke of York* as examples of those earlier plays. (That *1 Contention* and *Richard Duke of York* could still represent early versions of plays written entirely by Shakespeare was an alternative not mentioned).

I mentioned above that Alexander's work begins with the death of Robert Greene. Indeed, Greene's deathbed accusation is the subject of Alexander's first chapter. His work, however, as he explains in the preface, stems from the death of another author, John Semple Smart. Smart held the Queen Margaret College Lectureship at the University of Glasgow from 1907 until his death in 1925. At the time of his death Smart was working on a volume which was to be part biography, part textual study. Combining archival research, historical context and textual analysis, Smart intended to scrutinise the accepted facts and legends about Shakespeare's life in order to analyse the textual problems which cloud understanding of the early Shakespeare. The textual element was to focus on Greene's vituperative remarks in *Greene's Groatsworth of Wit*, the relationship between *3 Henry VI* and *Richard*

Duke of York, the relationship between *The Taming of the Shrew* and *The Taming of a Shrew*, and the date of *The Comedy of Errors*.

When Smart died, six chapters of biographical material had been brought to a state of near-completion. Three chapters of textual material remained in jotted fragments. The book was published posthumously in 1928 as *Shakespeare. Truth and Tradition*. In 'A Memoir of the Author' W. Macneile Dixon tells us that it is to Peter Alexander that 'we owe the transcription of the pencilled chapters and notes, a labour of love, which made it possible to send this book to the press'.[25] In imposing order on Smart's papers (written we are told 'often on stray sheets, within and without the ordinary limits of the page, [and] sometimes difficult to decipher'),[26] Alexander, like Heminge and Condell before him, was concerned 'onely to keep the memory of so worthy a friend'.

While editing Smart's book, Alexander was also writing one of his own, and in 1929 he published *Shakespeare's Henry VI and Richard III*, a version of the textual study which his mentor did not live to complete. This work of Alexander also arises directly from Smart, as Alexander acknowledges in the preface: 'it was at the suggestion of the late Dr Smart that I first examined the text of *Henry VI*' (v). In the introduction which he contributed to the volume, A. W. Pollard presents the debt in a more dramatic fashion: 'Mr Alexander, who succeeded Dr Smart in his lectureship at Glasgow, has not only helped to preserve his teacher's work, he has been continuing it, *as Dr Smart on his death-bed bade him*' (1, my emphasis). In other words: 'Remember me'. Alexander's editorial work on Smart's text, like Heminge and Condell's on Shakespeare's, is a memorial tribute, a homage to the dead author. We see this most obviously in the epigraph from Dante which Smart intended to apply to Shakespeare but which Alexander reapplies to Smart:

> Onorate l'altissimo poeta:
> l'ombra sua torna, ch'era dipartita.
> (Honour the most lofty poet:
> His shade, which had departed, returns [to us]).

Just as Heminge and Condell's tribute to Shakespeare becomes Connell's tribute to Heminge and Condell, so Smart's tribute to Shakespeare becomes Alexander's tribute to Smart.

As a work which has its origin in death (Greene and Smart), Alexander's book is a scholarly undertaking in the most literal sense, and it presents, coincidentally or not, a tidy narrative which aims to validate the reputation of the dead author Shakespeare, to keep the memory of so worthy a poet. The contradictions and multiplicities of the early Shakespearean chronology are resolved into a coherent whole, a single text, through the convenient construct of memorial reconstruction. Memorial reconstruction, like Heminge and Condell's editing, simplifies the author and his text, turning diversity into singularity. This is not the place to consider the pros and cons of memorial reconstruction (Paul Werstine shows how oversimplified the concept is, and how conveniently it served the purposes and biases of the New Bibliographical editors who invented it[27]). What interests me here is the way memorial reconstruction parallels grief theory: it resolves inconsistencies by positing a single, idealised, re-membered text; it imposes a dichotomous value system which overvalues the 'good' and ignores the 'bad'; and it sanitises the messy complexity of the textual *corpus* into a wholesome wholeness.

After death/afterlife

Life and death were closely linked in the early modern period. This link manifests itself in many ways: the traditional herbs and flowers of nuptials were the same herbs and flowers of funerals; ritual sexual games were played around the corpse during the wake; children, representatives of the continuation of life, were a prominent presence at funerals; death, like birth, took place in the home; and churchyards were not restricted to burials but used for domestic and artistic purposes such as grazing cattle, hanging washing, emptying chamber pots, disposing of dung and performing drama; funeral drinking took place in the churchyard, sometimes in the church, and in *Hamlet* 5.2, in the grave itself.[28] The funeral ceremony proclaims this liminality in a poignant fashion. As Richard Leppert explains, the coffin 'protects something precious at the same time its protection confirms loss'; it alludes to 'vitality, to sound, to breath, though only by announcing death and silence'.[29] To use Derrida's formulation, the funeral, like the text, is the ultimate in 'presence' as 'generalised absence'.

Renaissance humanism was a project of bringing the dead back to life: recovering the Romans, remembering the Greeks. Translating the classics literally carried the dead across cultures (*trans-latio*). And, as Francis Tate's account, with which I began, demonstrates, the Renaissance was not afraid to interact with the dead. What they did to a corpse – washing, cleaning, perfuming, preparing it for public display – they did equally to the literary corpus. Thomas Drant prefaces his translation of Horace, *A Medicinable Morall, that is, the two Bookes of Horace his Satyres* (1566) as follows:

> I haue interfarced (to remoue his obscuritie and sometymes to better his matter) much of myne owne deuysinge. I haue peeced his reason, eekede, and mended his similitudes, mollyfied his hardnes, prolonged his cortall kynd of speeche, changed, & much altered his wordes, but not his sentence: or at leaste (I dare say) not his purpose. (A3v)

Robert S. Miola shows how Chapman's translation of Homer, like Drant's of Horace, is 'an intertextual field'. Chapman's *Iliad* has 'three not two principal coordinates – Scripture, Homer, Chapman'.[30] Like Drant and Horace, Christian and pagan, Chapman and Homer, the living and the dead, comfortably co-exist.

Twentieth-century editing is also a project of recovering the dead. The difference lies in our attitude to death. No longer comfortable with death as a facet of life, we compartmentalise the dead and the dying: the geriatric home, the palliative care hospice, the funeral parlour, the mortician, the undertaker. Death, like birth, now takes place whenever possible in a clinically professional, rather than domestically familiar, atmosphere: the hospital. Robert Nisbet points out that many of us have never seen a dead body.[31] In contrast to the Renaissance, we actively discourage children from attending funerals, and we are ourselves protected from images of death by press regulatory bodies which disallow media representation of the dead unless they are shrouded by body bags. Such attitudes were confronted audaciously by Joe Orton in his satiric comedy on death, *Loot* (1965), where the corpse is repeatedly mishandled, and is the source of irreverent one-liners:

> TRUSCOT: Whose mummy is this?
> HAL: Mine.
> TRUSCOT: Whose was it before?
> HAL: I'm an only child.[32]

The play provoked a torrent of angry and offended letters in the daily newspapers. Orton had violated one of the remaining twentieth-century taboos: death.

Medieval and Renaissance iconographic tradition gave us the dance of death – skulls and skeletons visiting the living and leading them to the grave, a visual equivalent of the *ars moriendi* as a means to the *ars vivendi*. Death was the ultimate sense of an ending. Instead of the *dance* of death, the late twentieth-century model is the *denial* of death. Woody Allen sums it up: 'I'm not afraid of dying; I just don't want to be there when it happens.' From cosmetic surgery to funeral parlours, we seek to protect ourselves from bodies – our own and others' – decomposition. Death is viewed as an unnatural terminus; it, and the stages marking our progress towards it, are to be postponed by whatever means possible. Death was, until recently, a subject deemed unsuitable for conversation, and even now we address it only indirectly, in euphemism: 'passed on', 'passed away', 'crossed over'. This denial leads, not unexpectedly, to untidying, unediting the body of the text. Variant texts are but various stages in the ongoing, hopefully unending, life of, say, *King Lear*; Q/F variants are part of a continuum that embraces *King Leir*, Nahum Tate, Olivier, Shattuck promptbooks and RSC archives. Texts, like bodies, can have corporeal reconstruction, improvement, repair, augmentation, reduction, transplant, bypass, correction, to prolong their life, improve its quality, satisfy the prevailing aesthetic, defer oblivion.

But the issue is more complicated than this straightforward summary suggests, for death is a *terminus ad quem* with a curiously shifting definition of 'terminus'. To the early modern theocentric mind, the Last Judgement was a more significant indicator of finality than burial – thus corpses could be exhumed for 'posthumous honours or (as in the case of Cromwell) punishments' – and burial was more final than physical expiry (the fact that corpses could be arrested for debt en route to the grave shows that death and annihilation were not the same).[33] In our own era, definitions of what constitutes the end of life have also shifted. Life-support machines mean that cardiac arrest or pulmonary failure no longer signify 'death'; instead, 'brain death' now provides the new definition of the end. Thus the early modern and the postmodern overlap in their flexible attitude to death, a flexibility mirrored in their similarly tolerant attitudes to textual variation and plurality. It is the New Bibliographical period that is the anomaly in textual/editorial attitudes – the period, not coincidentally, of Freud and the death drive, where the death drive's impulse to return to life's 'primeval, inorganic state'[34] parallels the New Bibliographers' desire to strip the veil of print from Renaissance texts and return to one originary text.

Conclusion

If editing is about grief, it is so because scholarship in general is about loss. This is obvious in certain localised and easily locatable moments: the Short Title Catalogue was in part, as Gary Taylor has shown, a response to the death of Pollard's two sons, his boss and his wife during the Great War.[35] The rare-book trade developed, as Joseph Loewenstein has demonstrated, in the same period: in the face of overwhelming loss, one starts to catalogue what one has, to search for origins, to remember and value antecedents.[36] But the view that scholarship is about loss is true in a larger cultural sense too. In *Cultural Selection* Gary Taylor argues that culture is 'always the gift of the survivor. It is always bereaved, always retrospective'.[37] He is not alone in observing the elegiac nature of literature. Jonathan Bate observes that 'the epitaph, the monumental inscription, is the earliest form of written poetry, perhaps one of the earliest forms of any kind of writing'.[38] For Geoffrey Hartman, 'inscribing, naming, and writing are types of a commemorative and inherently elegiac act',[39] just as they are, more nostalgically and wistfully, for Derrida. Literature – the written – is essentially (according to Bate and Taylor) and inevitably (according to Derrida and Hartman) about loss.

The author is always inevitably absent, as postmodern critics have observed. Andrew Murphy provides the most sustained examination of what this absence means to editors, concluding that 'every vision of textual presence ... is doomed to failure'.[40] Grief is the process of coming to terms with absence, and this process has several stages. In its earliest stages it involves denial and idealisation: the mourner urges the dead not to be dead; the mourner invents rather than recalls, the mourner creates the person mourned, the mourner remembers. Recovery is signalled by paradox: grieving and celebrating, looking back while planning forward, remembering and forgetting. The task in recovery is not to reduce these oppositions to singularity as did Heminge and Condell, Peter Alexander and the New Bibliographers, but to enable them to co-exist. Editing is, it seems, a matter of life and death.[41]

Notes

1 Gary Taylor, 'The rhetoric of textual criticism', *TEXT*, 4 (1988), p. 5.

2 Printed in Thomas Hearne, *A Collection of Curious Discourses*, 2 vols (London, W. & J. Richardson, 1771). vol. l, pp. 215–21. Further references to this work are included parenthetically in my text. The *DNB* (vol. 55, pp. 376–7) gives Tate's dates as 1560–11 November 1616.

3 Tate characterises the custom of candle-burning as 'now growen into disuse, being thought superstitious' (p. 16).

4 See the probate accounts, theological works, diaries, letters and records of overseers of the poor cited by Clare Gittings in *Death, Burial and the Individual in Early Modern England* (London, Croom Helm, 1984). I quote mostly from Gittings' convenient overview (further

references are included parenthetically in my text); however, the following works have also provided helpful information about funeral procedures, grief and attitudes to death: Lawrence Stone, *The Family, Sex, and Marriage in England 1500-1800* (London, Weidenfeld & Nicolson, 1977), pp. 66-82 and *The Past and the Present Revisited* (London, Routledge & Kegan Paul, 1987); Philippe Ariès, *Western Attitudes Toward Death* (Baltimore, MD, Johns Hopkins University Press, 1974); Phillis Cunnington and Catherine Lucas, *Costumes for Births, Marriages and Deaths* (London, Adam & Charles Black, 1972), pp. 123-293; G. W. Pigman, *Grief and English Renaissance Elegy* (Cambridge, Cambridge University Press, 1985); Nigel Llewellyn, 'The royal body: monuments to the dead, for the living', in Lucy Gent and Nigel Llewellyn (eds), *Renaissance Bodies: The Human Figure in English Culture c. 1540-1660* (London, Reaktion Books, 1990), pp. 218-40; Nigel Llewellyn, *The Art of Death: Visual Culture in the English Death Ritual c. 1500-1800* (London, V&A Museum and Reaktion Books, 1991); Robert N. Watson, *The Rest is Silence: Death as Annihilation in the English Renaissance* (Berkeley, University of California Press, 1994); and ch. 1 of Tricia Lootens, *Lost Saints: Silence, Gender, and Victorian Literary Canonization* (Charlottesville, University Press of Virginia, 1996). The description of the practicalities of dealing with the dead in David Cressy's comprehensive study, *Birth, Marriage, and Death* (Oxford, Oxford University Press, 1997), like my own account, is based on Tate's description.

5 Gittings, *Death*, pp. 112-13, quoting M. Misson, *Memoirs and Observations of His Travels over England*, trans. J. Ozell (London, 1719).

6 Sir Thomas Overbury, 'A faire and happy Milk-mayd', in *Miscellaneous Works in Prose and Verse*, ed. by Edward F. Rimbault (London, Reeves & Turner, 1890), pp. 118-19 (p. 119).

7 For a good account of medieval practices, see Christopher Daniell, *Death and Burial in Medieval England 1066-1550* (London, Routledge, 1997).

8 None the less, the erection of royal funeral monuments does not constitute an unbroken trend. Tracing such monuments from the reigns of Henry VII through James I, Nigel Llewellyn argues that the need for monuments 'was manifestly greater at the establishment of the dynasty, but that once the lineage was safely established, monuments became less important, could be left unfinished, or even dispensed with' ('The royal body', p. 225).

9 Weever is not the first to view literature as a memorial edifice: Horace, whom he quotes, refers to his three books of *Odes* as a 'Monument then brasse more lasting' (Weever, B 1r; Horace, *Odes*, 3.30. 1), and similar sentiments are voiced by Martial and Ovid. In the Renaissance Herrick's *Hesperides* (1648), influenced by Martial, selfconsciously presents itself as a funeral monument, and Milton's *Areopagitica* (1644) describes a good book as 'the precious life-blood of a master spirit, imbalm'd and treasur'd up on purpose to a life beyond life' (Don M. Wolfe, ed., *The Complete Prose Works* of John Milton, 8 vols (New Haven, CT, Yale University Press, 1953-82) II, 493). For an interesting analysis of literary lament and celebration in the Caroline period see Warren Chernaik, 'Books as memorials the politics of consolation', *Yearbook of English Studies*, 21 (1991), pp. 207-17.

10 For an excellent analysis of this phenomenon, see Andrew Murphy, '"Came errour here by mysse of man": editing and the metaphysics of presence', *Yearbook of English Studies*, 29 (1999), pp. 118-37.

11 Walter J. Ong, *Orality and Literacy* (London, Methuen, 1982), p. 81.

12 For information about grief theory see Jane Littlewood, *Aspects of Grief* (London, Routledge, 1992); Colin Murray Parkes, *Bereavement* (Harmondsworth, Penguin, 1991); Margaret S. Stroebe, Wolfgang Stroebe and Robert O. Hanson (eds), *Handbook of Bereavement: Theory, Research, and Intervention* (Cambridge, Cambridge University Press, 1993); Elisabeth Kübler-Ross, *On Death and Dying* (London, Macmillan, 1969). G. W. Pigman's *Grief and English Renaissance Elegy* provides a particularly helpful discussion

of changing Renaissance attitudes to grief and mourning. Robert Burton's *Anatomy of Melancholy*, ed. by Thomas C. Faulkner, Nicolas K. Kiessling and Rhonda L. Blair (Oxford, Clarendon Press, 1989), part I, section 2, subsection 7, deals briefly with loss. Mourning is surprisingly underrepresented in Renaissance documents. Cressy's researches give him three pages on mourning, in comparison to eighty-seven pages on death. In part this may be because the Reformation, with its erasure of Catholic burial rites, took away the outlet for grief, leaving Protestants 'alone with their memories'. See Michael Neill, *Issues of Death: Mortality and Identity in English Renaissance Tragedy* (Oxford, Clarendon, 1997), pp. 244–6.

13 See Stanley Wells and Gary Taylor, 'No shrew, a shrew, and the shrew: internal revision in *The Taming of the Shrew*', in Bernhard Fabian and Kurt Tetzeli von Rosador (eds), *Shakespeare: Text, Language, Criticism* (Hildesheim, Olms-Weidmann, 1987), pp. 351–70, and Grace Ioppolo, *Revising Shakespeare* (Cambridge, MA, Harvard University Press, 1991), pp. 89–103.

14 All references to Shakespeare's plays come from the First Folio; Through Line Numbering is taken from the facsimile edition prepared by Charlton Hinman (New York, W. W. Norton, 1968).

15 The fiscal and the thanatological are two separate 'genres' (or ritualised behaviours) in Bakhtin's sense (see 'The problem of speech genres', in Mikhail Bakhtin, *Speech Genres and Other Late Essays*, trans. V. W. McGee, ed. C. Emerson and M. Holquist (Austin, University of Texas Press, 1986), pp. 60–102); that is, they are domains with separate languages and symbolic practices. Obviously, death often involves finance (inheritance, taxes, bills), but in Western culture the interaction of the genres is not acknowledged: it is the clash of these genres that made Joe Orton's *Loot* such a daring piece of drama in 1965.

16 Ethel Wilson, 'To keep the memory of so worthy a friend', in *Mrs Golightly and Other Stories* (New Canadian Library. Toronto, McClelland & Stewart, 1990), pp. 94–101; Richard Nelson, *Some Americans Abroad* (London, Faber & Faber, 1989).

17 Charles Connell, *They Gave Us Shakespeare: John Heminge and Henry Condell* (London, Oriel Press (Routledge & Kegan Paul), 1982), p. 2.

18 1621–23 represents the two-year period in which Heminge and Condell were preparing the First Folio and encountering enforced fluctuations in their choice of plays. For subsequent versions of 'what we call Shakespeare' see the second issue of the third edition of the Folio (1664), Alexander Pope's edition of Shakespeare (1725), Charles Knight's *Pictorial Shakespeare* (1841), Wells and Taylor's Oxford *Shakespeare* (1986), the Norton Shakespeare ed. Stephen Greenblatt et al (1997), and the second edition of the Riverside Shakespeare ed. G. Blakemore Evans (1997).

19 Margreta de Grazia, *Shakespeare Verbatim* (Oxford, Clarendon Press, 1991), p. 30.

20 For an excellent analysis of the nexus of fiscal and personal bastardy in *The Revenger's Tragedy*, see Michael Neill, 'Bastardy, counterfeiting, and misogyny in *The Revenger's Tragedy*', *Studies in English Literature*, 36 (1996), pp. 397–416.

21 In fact, as I have argued elsewhere (*Shakespearean Suspect Texts* (Cambridge, Cambridge University Press, 1996)) the 'problems' in *Orlando Furioso* are slight and were exaggerated by Greg. However, at the time Alexander was researching, Greg was publicising his opinions about the 'bad' nature of *Orlando Furioso*, opinions which quickly won acceptance. See W. W. Greg, ' "Bad quartos" outside Shakespeare - "Alcazar" and "Orlando" ', *Library*, 3rd series, 10 (1919), pp. 193–222, and *Two Elizabethan Stage Abridgements* (Oxford, Frederick Hall, 1922).

22 The Alleyn manuscript (so-called because it was prepared for, and marked by, Edward Alleyn) contains Orlando's part and its cues.

23 Alexander, *Shakespeare's 'Henry VI' and 'Richard III'* (Cambridge, Cambridge University Press, 1929), p. 62. Further references are incorporated into the text.

24 Robert Greene, *Greene's Groatsworth of Wit, Bought with a Million of Repentance* (London, 1592), sig. Flr. For a defence of Greene's authorship of this pamphlet see Harold Jenkins, 'On the authenticity of *Greene's Groatsworth of Wit* and *The Repentance of Robert Greene*', *Review of English Studies*, 11 (1935), pp. 28–41. John Jowett has recently provided convincing evidence for Chettle's authorship; see 'Johannes Factotum: Henry Chettle and *Greene's Groatsworth of Wit*', *Proceedings of the Bibliographical Society of America*, 87 (1993), pp. 453-86. Chettle's authorship does not affect my analysis of Alexander's argument.

25 J. S. Smart, *Shakespeare: Truth and Tradition* (1928, repr. Oxford, Oxford University Press, 1966), p. xxiii.

26 Smart, *Truth and Tradition*, p. xxiii.

27 Paul Werstine, 'Narratives about printed Shakespeare texts: "foul papers" and "bad quartos"', *Shakespeare Quarterly*, 41 (1990), pp. 65–86.

28 See Gittings, *Death*, and Cressy, *Birth, Marriage, and Death*.

29 Richard Leppert, *The Sight of Sound: Music, Representation, and the History of the Body* (Berkeley, University of California Press, 1993), p. xxiv.

30 Robert S. Miola, 'On death and dying in Chapman's *Iliad*: translation as forgery', *Journal of the Classical Tradition*, 3 (1996), p. 17.

31 Robert Nisbet, *Prejudices. A Philosophic Dictionary* (Cambridge, MA, Harvard University Press, 1982), p.120.

32 Joe Orton, *Loot*, in *Joe Orton: The Complete Plays*, introd. by John Lahr (New York, Grove Press, 1976), p. 231.

33 Watson, *Death as Annihilation*, p. 4. Watson further argues that since the conditions of death - 'silence, coldness, containment, and passivity' - were also the living conditions of the Renaissance wife, the early modern male must have been reassured about the tolerability of post mortem conditions (p. 31).

34 Jonathan Dollimore, *Death, Desire and Loss in Western Culture* (London, Routledge, 1998), p. 186.

35 Taylor, 'Rhetoric', p. 50.

36 Joseph Loewenstein, 'Authentic reproductions: the material origins of the New Bibliography', in Laurie E. Maguire and Thomas L. Berger (eds), *Textual Formations and Reformations* (Newark, DE, University of Delaware Press, 1998), pp. 23–44.

37 Gary Taylor, *Cultural Selection* (New York, Basic Books, 1996), p. 5.

38 Jonathan Bate, *Romantic Ecology* (London, Routledge, 1991), p. 87.

39 Geoffrey Hartman, *Beyond Formalism* (New Haven, Yale University Press, 1970), p. 223.

40 Murphy, '"Came Errour Here"', p. 136.

41 I am grateful to Douglas Brooks, Stephen Greenblatt, Robert S. Miola and Peter Stallybrass for helpful comments on, and discussion about, earlier incarnations of this chapter.

Biblebable[1]

Graham Holderness, Stanley E. Porter and Carol Banks

'Renove that bible'
(Joyce, *Finnegans Wake*, 3rd edn, London, Faber & Faber, 1964, p. 579:10)

When castaways appearing on the classic BBC radio programme *Desert Island Discs* are offered, as a staple resource to sustain their imaginary marooned condition, two books – the Bible and the *Complete Works of Shakespeare* – there is no particular specification as to text or edition. It is reasonable to assume, however, that the Bible would be best represented for these purposes by the 1611 *Authorised Version* (*AV* – or as it tends to be known in biblical studies, the *King James Version* or *KJV*), or something very much like it; and the *Complete Works of Shakespeare* can only be, in terms of its basic contents, one of the many different versions of the 1623 First Folio, with the addition of the sonnets and the narrative poems.[2] From the breadth of choice available across over a millennium of writing in English, therefore, the castaway gets to take, in terms of literary provisions, two books that were printed within a decade of each other, in the generally undistinguished and culturally decadent (at least in the estimation of many historians) reign of King James I.

It is natural to assume that this apparently to some degree fortuitous, perhaps even arbitrary, contingency owes more to subsequent appropriations of Shakespeare for quasi-religious ideologies, than to any substantive cultural and historical connection. Theatre and reformed church were of course to some degree enemies in this period: stage-plays were vigorously denounced from pulpit and pamphlet, and the theatres were eventually closed during the Commonwealth. The Puritans who initiated the new translation were certainly hostile to the theatre: the Dr John Reynolds, President of Corpus Christi College Oxford, who put the proposal for the *AV* to the King – 'moued his Maiestie, that there might bee a newe *translation* of the *Bible*, because, those which were allowed in the raignes of *Henrie* the eight, and *Edward* the sixt were corrupt and not aunswerable to the truth of the Originall'[3] – was the same Dr Reynolds who had delivered in 1599, in the form of a published controversy with Dr William Gager, a particularly aggressive denunciation of the theatre (together with other sports and leisure pursuits), *Th'overthrow of Stage-Playes*.[4]

It has been argued that the strategy of linking the Bible and *The Complete Works of Shakespeare* together, as master-documents of English culture, has much to do with efforts to confer on Shakespeare's work a quasi-divine status comparable to that of the Bible. 'The telling juxtaposition of the Bible with the *Complete Works of Shakespeare*', argues John Drakakis, constitutes 'a tacit acknowledgement of Shakespeare as universal, transcendent, and eternal': '*Desert Island Discs* attributes to Shakespearean influence … a divine status. Shakespeare, thus removed from human history, becomes for us the "Absolute Subject" whose all-embracing "Word" takes its place alongside the Bible as our guarantee of civilisation and humanity.'[5]

But the two books display other affinities beside their traditional linking in the castaway's two-volume set of the greatest stories ever told. Both were published under the aegis of royal patronage: the new translation of the Bible was a project explicitly sponsored by James at the Hampton Court Conference in 1604;[6] the First Folio was an edition, compiled by two actors of the King's Men, of works by the royal company's foremost playwright. Both carry dedications to royal or aristocratic patrons: the *KJV* is dedicated to 'The Most High and Mightie Prince, Iames' (Pollard facsimile, 'The Epistle Dedicatorie') and the Folio 'To the Most Noble and Incomparable Paire of Brethren, William Earle of Pembroke, &c. Lord Chamberlaine to the *Kings most Excellent Maiesty*; and Philip Earle of Montgomery, &c. Gentleman of his Maiesties Bed-Chamber. Both Knights of the most Noble Order of the Garter, and our singular good Lords' (Norton facsimile, p. 5). Both represent canonical compilations of works initially written and published as individual texts that bore quite different relations (or even no relation at all) to one another. (There is also, it should be noted, at this point a substantive difference, in that the First Folio is the initial point of Shakespearean canon-formation, whereas the canon of the biblical books had been substantially agreed and approved by the fourth century AD.[7])

Both books were produced in the same publishing format, a bound folio text, printed in roman type with double columns, and both were aimed to some degree at a new publishing market. The contents of both the Bible and the First Folio of Shakespeare's plays had been, and remained, freely available in oral performative media. Both volumes therefore collected and circulated writings already accessible to lettered and unlettered alike, through the ear, from every church pulpit and from the stages of the metropolitan theatre. The 'godly-learned', claimed the editors of the *KJV*, 'prouided Translations into the vulgar for their Countreymen, insomuch that most nations vnder heauen did shortly after their conuersion, heare Christ speaking vnto them in their mother tongue' (Pollard facsimile, 'The Translators To the Reader'); 'these Playes', say Heminge and Condell, drawing for a parallel on the oral procedures of the law-courts, 'haue had their triall alreadie, and stood out all Appeales' ('To the great Variety of Readers', Norton facsimile, p. 7). The writings in each case were converted by editing and publication into a form that could possibly have been used as a text for performance, but was more likely to be used for private reading. Although these are big books by modern standards, it was still to private readers, rather than to their natural performative contexts, that they seem to have appealed. The First Folio could have been used as a promptbook, but not as a source for actors' parts; and though the Folio *KJV* was intended to replace the 'ordinary Bible read in the Church, commonly called the *Bishops' Bible*',[8] it is clear that it did not automatically replace the existing bibles that were held in churches and used by the clergy for liturgical and devotional purposes. As evidence that other and earlier editions continued to be used after the publication of the *KJV*, we can find them quoted not only in sermons by such clerics as John Donne, but even in those of Lancelot Andrewes, one of the *KJV*'s leading translators, and in those of Miles Smith, a translator and a co-author of the *KJV*'s prefatory essay 'The Translators To the Reader'.[9]

The two volumes were aimed therefore primarily at new 'market segments', divergent sections of the small but print-hungry literate reading public (they were not of course aimed at the same readers, and possibly even at two different and to some degree mutually exclusive categories of reader). Heminge and Condell in their brief preface address 'the great Variety of Readers', many of whom, as both the preface and some of the commendatory poems indicate, would have been expected to know the plays from performance, but are now assumed to have the inclination to 'buy', 'read' and if necessary 'censure' the scripts of those performances, collected and presented in an approved and authoritative literary text (Norton facsimile, p. 7).

*

Translation of the Bible into English began, as all other vernacular translations began, from the requirements of a local or national appropriation of scriptures previously retained by the authority of the Roman church in the form of St Jerome's Latin 'Vulgate' text ('how shall men meditate in that, which they cannot vnderstand?' asked the translators of the *KJV*, and 'How shall they vnderstand that which is kept close in an vnknowen tongue?' [Pollard facsimile, 'The Translators To the Reader']). Erasmus wanted every farmer to be able to sing parts of the scripture at his plough.[10] This did not necessarily in the first instance of course imply access to individual and private readings of the scriptures. Attempts were made by the church authorities to restrict the circulation of vernacular translations such as those of Wycliff.[11] William Tyndale, whose translation of the New Testament provided, it is calculated, some 90 per cent of the *KJV*'s, was burned at the stake for unauthorised translation and publication of an English Bible.[12] But the *KJV*, like the Puritan Geneva Bible,[13] was certainly connected with the general strategy of the reforming movement within the English church to widen direct access to the scriptures. The need for published texts that would enable such access went hand in hand with the cultural and technological changes – the growth of literacy and the development of printing – that provided the means to further that aim.

There is one final respect in which these two books closely resemble one another in terms of cultural efficacy and function. Both were apparently published in order to supersede earlier variant versions of the same text or texts. Although, as indicated above, the First Folio was opening and defining a canon, whereas the *KJV* was re-presenting a canon closed some twelve centuries earlier, both publications were, in the modern jargon of marketing, seeking a larger market share by eliminating competition. It is clear that the editors and translators presented their products to the public in the expectation that they would supplant those existing and still competitive versions (see below for detailed references). At the same time they were claiming for their new products substantial cultural power and authority: whether in presenting the words of Shakespeare or the Word of God, they claimed to be doing so in a form authorised and approved by higher secular and ecclesiastical authorities. Both sets of editors assume that the cultural and literary value of the material they were reproducing was not in dispute, having already been well established and authenticated; but both claimed that this particular publication had a unique importance in defining and establishing the authority and value of the works in question.

Some nineteen of the plays modern scholars attribute to Shakespeare appeared in cheap quarto format during his lifetime, often with their theatrical provenance clearly signalled by an emphasis on the companies who owned and produced the plays, rather than on the author. In the case of the Shakespeare Folio, the texts to be supplanted were identified by the editors as some of these 'stolne, and surreptitious copies':

> It had bene a thing, we confesse, worthie to haue bene wished, that the Author himselfe had liu'd to haue set forth, and ouerseen his owne writings; But since it hath bin ordain'd otherwise, and he by death departed from that right, we pray you do not envie his Friends, the office of their care, and paine, to haue collected & publish'd them; and so to haue published them, as where (before) you were abus'd with diuerse stolne, and surreptitious copies, maimed, and deformed by the frauds and stealthes of iniurious impostors, that expos'd them: euen those, are now offer'd to your view cur'd, and perfect of their limbes; and all the rest, absolute in their numbers, as he conceiued the[m]. Who, as he was a happie imitator of Nature, was a most gentle expresser of it. His mind and hand went together: And what he thought, he vttered with that easinesse, that wee haue scarse receiued from him a blot in his papers. But it is not our prouince, who onely gather his works, and giue them you, to praise him. It is yours that reade him. (Norton facsimile, p. 7)

The figurative language deployed here however goes much further than an assertion that some texts previously published had been pirated and printed without authorisation. The copies previously printed were not only 'stolne, and surreptitious', but 'maimed, and deformed', like diseased parts of a body cut off and 'expos'd' to public view by 'iniurious impostors'. The writer's *oeuvre*, the complete body of his dramatic work, as represented by the Folio, has been carefully reassembled by a process of miraculous healing ('cur'd') and restoration.

The link between the 'body' of the text and the now absent body of the writer himself is then pursued further. The textual body that remains now stands for the mortal body that has departed. This idea naturally runs as a common theme through the Folio's prefatory poems: 'For though his line of life went soone about, / The life yet of his lines shall neuer out' (Hugh Holland, 'Vpon the Lines and Life of the Famous Scenicke Poet, Master William Shakespeare', Norton facsimile, p. 11); 'death may destroy, / They say, his body, but his verse shall live.'[14] Since Shakespeare himself, as author, exhibited a perfect unity of body and spirit, a perfect correspondence of intellect and physical action – 'His mind and hand went together' – the editors assume an identity between the textual body and the resurrected 'spiritual body' that exists and awaits ultimate occupation by Shakespeare's departed soul.

The claims made for the unique cultural value of the Folio go far beyond affirming that the texts have now been accurately corrected and responsibly compiled. As they 'gather' Shakespeare's works together, the editors are also reassembling the 'Author', represented here by the figure of the risen body that is identical with the body of the text. In theological terms, the imagery leans on Christian ideas but also hints at something like the Egyptian myth of Isis and Osiris, in which the scattered fragments of the god are patiently found and reassembled into a new whole. The Folio editors reinstate, through their construction of the 'author', the Shakespearean body that is 'by death departed'.

Finally, as the preface and the Folio's commendatory poems strongly emphasise, the Shakespearean 'work' pre-existed both the Folio redaction and the earliest printed versions, in the form of the theatrical productions upon which the texts were based, and from which, in some senses, at least some of them, or some elements of them, derive.[15] Heminge and Condell point out that 'these Playes haue had their triall alreadie, and stood out all Appeales': they have been tried and tested in the demanding laboratory of the public playhouse; though they may have been censured by dissatisfied customers, audiences have continually come back for more. In this sense the *Collected Works* gathers and enfolds within itself the physical life of these plays in the theatre, as well as their previously inauthentic, now authorised, existence as literary texts. In 'I. M.'s' (James Mabbe's) epitaph 'To the memorie of M. W. Shake-speare', the works, together with the actor-dramatist, have briefly retired from the stage, as their author has briefly withdrawn from the world, only to reappear, in this published volume, to tumultuous applause: 'Wee thought thee dead, but this thy printed worth, / Tels thy Spectators, that thou went'st but forth / To enter with applause' (Norton facsimile, p. 15).

*

The *KJV* had its origin in the Millenary Petition presented to King James on his accession to the English throne in 1603. So styled because it was said to contain 1000 signatures (or one-tenth of the English clergy), it put forward the views and expounded the grievances of the Puritans in the English church. Having little sympathy with these representations, James grudgingly agreed to have them presented and debated at a conference in 1604, which would focus, in his words, on 'things pretended to be amiss' in the church. James responded more positively to the proposal for a new translation of the Bible than to most of the other complaints:

> he [Dr Reynolds] moued his Maiestie, that there might bee a newe *translation* of the *Bible* ... Whereupon his Highnesse wished that some especiall paines should be taken in that behalfe for one vniforme translation (professing that hee could neuer yet see a Bible well translated in English; but the worst of all, his Maiestie thought the *Geneua* to bee) and this to bee done by the best learned in both the Vniuersities, after them to be reuiewed by the Bishops, and the chiefe learned of the Church; from them to bee presented to the *Priuie-Councell*; and lastly to be ratified by his *Royall authoritie*; and so this whole Church to be bound vnto it, and none other.[16]

However, the views recorded in the translators' preface to the *KJV*, 'The Translators To the Reader', are rather those of the dominant church authorities than those of the signatories to the Millenary Petition:

> the very Historicall trueth is, that vpon the importunate petitions of the Puritanes, at his Maiesties comming to this Crowne, the Conference at Hampton Court hauing bene appointed for hearing their complaints: when by force of reason they were put from all other grounds, they had recourse at the last, to this shift, that they could not with good conscience subscribe to the Communion booke, since it maintained the Bible as it was there translated, which was as they said, a most corrupted translation. And although this was iudged to be but a very poore and emptie shift; yet euen hereupon did his Maiestie beginne to bethinke him-selfe of the good that might ensue by a new translation, and presently after gaue order for this Translation which is now presented vnto thee. Thus much to satisfie our scrupulous Brethren. (Pollard facsimile, 'Translators To the Reader')

The bishops, who clearly dominated the operation, were not however in a position to present their project simply as a supersession of previous defective works, since they were confident that 'the very meanest translation of the Bible in English, set foorth by men of our profession ... containeth the word of God, nay, is the word of God' (Pollard facsimile, 'Translators To the Reader'). They therefore presented their work as traditional rather than revolutionary, as a synthesis rather than a supplanting of previous efforts: 'Truly (good Christian Reader) wee neuer thought from the beginning, that we should neede to make a new Translation, nor yet to make of a bad one a good one, ... but to make a good one better, or out of many good ones, one principall good one, not iustly to be excepted against' (ibid.). Their ultimate objective, a universalisation and standardising of the scriptures through the English church and nation, was defined as follows: 'we desire that the Scripture may speake like it selfe, as in the language of *Canaan*, that it may bee vnderstood euen of the very vulgar' (ibid.). The language of Canaan was Hebrew, believed at the time to have been the oldest of all languages, and used here to indicate the possibility of a universal language shared by all members of a society. Thus where, previous to vernacular translations, the educated and the clerisy had possessed the Latin, Greek and Hebrew that were the keys to the unlocking of Holy Scripture, now the Bible in English translation could be a common property of all who could read.

The translators naturally saw themselves as mediating the Word of God: God was the ultimate 'author' of the *Authorised Version*. Translation is defined, in a series of metaphors, as a process of opening, unlocking, releasing the light and energy of the scriptures to a new audience and readership:

> Translation it is that openeth the window, to let in the light; that breaketh the shell, that we may eat the kernel; that putteth aside the curtaine, that we may looke into the most Holy place; that remooueth the couer of the well, that wee may come by the water, euen as *Iacob* rolled away the stone from the mouth of the well, by which meanes the flockes of *Laban* were watered. (Pollard facsimile, 'Translators To the Reader')

But the translators were also well aware that the Word of God, though manifestly communicated by direct inspiration to the original biblical 'authors', from Moses to St John the Divine, is written and recorded only by human hands. Even accounts of divine autograph such as that found on the Commandments – 'And the Tables were the worke of God; and the writing was the writing of God, grauen vpon the Tables' (*Exodus*, 32.16) – had to be mediated through the Hebrew texts then believed to have been written by Moses himself, and were now translated into English. However important the responsibility of the translator, then, he stands at several removes from the 'original'. The 'Authorship' of the *KJV* is attributed directly and primarily to God; at a secondary level to the original biblical authors (Moses, the Prophets, the Apostles, etc.); but then at the most immediate and contemporary historical level, to a man who so far as we know had no hand at all in the enterprise, King James himself:

now at last, by the Mercy of God, and the continuance of our Labours, it
being brought vnto such a conclusion, as that we haue great hope that
the Church of *England* shall reape good fruit thereby; we hold it our
duety to offer it to your Maiestie, not onely as to our King and
Soueraigne, but as to the principall moouer and Author of the Worke.
(Pollard facsimile, 'To The Most High And Mightie Prince, Iames,
Epistle Dedicatorie')[17]

At the most literal level, the *KJV* has become not, as it in reality was, a
Puritan proposal, but the king's own personal suggestion and pet project. But much more is entailed in that language of 'motion' and
'authorship'. James is here literally understood to be God's 'Deputie
elected by the Lord' (*The life and death of King Richard the Second*,
TLN 1412, Norton facsimile), a worldly substitute for the divinity
itself.[18] James was the Prime Mover of the *KJV* as God was the Prime
Mover of the universe; he is the 'Author', the enabler and facilitator, of
the new translation, in the same sense that he is (elsewhere in the same
dedication) the 'immediate Author' of his people's 'true happiness'.
James is the Author of the *KJV* in the sense that he 'authorises' it,
licenses and lends it his authority; and by creating the cultural space for
it in the first place. He is the Author of his own Authorised Version, in
the same way that the dedicatee of Shakespeare's *Sonnets* is credited as
their 'only begetter' and only he brought them into being.[19]

*

In order briefly to trace the processes by means of which the respective
contents of the Bible and the *Complete Works of Shakespeare* found their
way into these two seventeenth-century volumes, it is necessary to
adopt two very different timescales: the one measured in decades, the
other in millennia. The processes are none the less in some ways surprisingly similar.

    The 1611 Bible contained three sections: the Old Testament, the
Apocrypha and the New Testament. The process of Old Testament
canonisation took place over many centuries. Virtually all scholars
agree that the 'Pentateuch' (the first five books of the Old Testament,
supposedly written by Moses, and also known in Judaic culture as 'The
Law') was the first part of the Old Testament to find a relatively stable
form, and to be widely accepted in Judaism, followed by the Prophets
(the prophetic and historical books) and probably the Psalms. These
were very likely the basic constituents of a recognised body of documents that existed and were used by Jews around 1000 BC. In the third

century BC the Hebrew writings were translated into Greek in Alexandria, producing the *Septuagint*, so called from the seventy-two scribes who completed it in seventy-two days.[20] A less colourful historical explanation would be simply that Greek translations were needed because Egyptian Jews could no longer understand Hebrew. Nor is the *Septuagint* one cohesive translation of a single Jewish document, but rather a number of differing versions produced over time and from different Hebrew texts (e.g. the Greek *Jeremiah* is shorter than, and differently structured from, the Hebrew). The *Septuagint* was copied and used in Jewish communities throughout the Graeco-Roman diaspora, and evidently even in Palestine (parts of the *Septuagint* were actually found among the Dead Sea Scrolls).

In the second century AD, translations of the *Septuagint* into Latin began to appear, now to meet the needs of those Jews who could understand neither Greek nor Hebrew. Only fragmentary relics of the Old Latin versions remain, since it was superseded after the fourth century by St Jerome's *Vulgate*. This, the first monoglot Bible, established an authoritative and regularised text for the Latin or Western church. Jerome rejected the *Septuagint*, and made his translation of the Old Testament directly from the Hebrew. The Jews also rejected the *Septuagint* when during the first and second centuries AD it became established in use among Christians.[21] After the Jewish Revolt of 66–70 the major group to maintain Jewish traditions, a successor to the Pharisees, established what became known as 'Rabbinic Judaism'. A particular group of scribes, the Masoretes, took special responsibility for the preservation of the Hebrew Bible, which thus developed and was formalised in the first few centuries of the Christian era. Until the discovery in 1947 of the Dead Sea Scrolls, virtually all of the Hebrew texts considered reliable were Masoretic texts, which are embodied in documents such as the Leningrad (*c.* 1008 AD) and Aleppo (c. 930 AD) Codices. Yet most of these did not date to earlier than the ninth century AD.

The discovery among the Qumran documents of the Isaiah Scroll (*1Q Isaiah*) provided detailed comparison between the Masoretic tradition and a much older text, and showed clearly that there must have been several, if not many, Hebrew Bible traditions in existence when the Dead Sea Scrolls were in use.[22] Thus a period of around a millennium separates the writing of the original documents from the earliest complete texts of the Hebrew Bible.

Scholars are not agreed on when the canon of the New Testament as we know it was established. Whereas the individual documents

of the Hebrew Bible had been collected into unity by the scroll, the
compilation of the Gospels and Epistles into the New Testament was
facilitated by the newer technology of the codex. Codices dating from
the fourth century, such as Codex Sinaiticus and Codex Vaticanus, contain most of the Old Testament in Greek, all (or much) of what we
know as the New Testament, plus additional books later eliminated
from the canon.[23] Evidently even in the fourth and fifth centuries it was
still common for individual writings to circulate without being gathered into a single 'book'. Copies of individual books survive from as
early as 200 AD (e.g. P. Bodmer II [=P[66]], with St John's Gospel, and the
Chester Beatty Papyrus, with many of Paul's letters).

   The biblical sources available to scholars such as Erasmus and
Tyndale were relatively limited by comparison with those available
today. Thousands of papyri, discovered in the sands of Egypt in the
nineteenth and twentieth centuries, have provided MS sources additional to, and different from, manuscripts extant in the Renaissance.
Biblical scholars classify these fragments into the Alexandrian, dating
from the second century; the Western, which influenced the Latin
texts; and the Byzantine, the latest of the three major text-types, not
appearing before 350 AD.[24] Erasmus built his Greek text of the New
Testament on a limited number of Byzantine minuscule texts (though
it should be noted that the majority of the extant documents are
Byzantine, hence the term 'majority text'), since the most important
codices, together with the papyri, had not as yet been discovered.[25] For
part of the *Book of Revelation* Erasmus had no manuscript to follow,
and so translated the Latin Vulgate back into Greek himself. Erasmus's
Textus Receptus, in its second edition of 1633, became the standard
Greek text until the mid-nineteenth century. Approximately 5000
manuscripts of various-sized portions of the New Testament are now
available to scholars. Erasmus used five, relatively late manuscripts, all
dating from later than 1100 AD, most from the fourteenth century. The
modern biblical scholar can get almost 1000 years nearer to the time of
the original writings than could the translators of the *KJV*.

   By the time the *KJV* was constructed, the Christian scriptures had in
English Protestant culture long since ceased to be the *biblia* ('books') in
the form of which its various writings had been originated, and had not as
yet encountered the 'disintegrationist' tendencies of a modern biblical
criticism faced with a much greater diversity and plurality of texts.[26] It
was, very definitely, *the* Bible. Yet the brief history provided above of its
formation prior to the seventeenth-century can be seen to characterise a

scripture with a vast multiplicity of origins, and with a far more iterable canon than seventeenth-century scholars could have been aware of. As Robert Carroll and Stephen Prickett observe: 'if the Bible is essentially a book in exile from its original context, we should note that this has *always* been true of it. As we understand more of its cultural context we are also coming more and more to see how eclectic and diverse are its origins.'[27] The question of language is as important as these issues of canon and origin. Early Christians shared with Jews a scripture, that became both the Judaic Bible and the Old Testament, written in a language that neither Jew nor Christian spoke (Jesus, from the evidence of the Gospels, spoke primarily Aramaic), and that had already been translated, presumably for the use of Jews, into Greek.[28] The maintenance of the Hebrew scripture was no uninterrupted survival of the language of Canaan, but a specific initiative to preserve Hebrew tradition in conditions of national defeat and cultural collapse. 'For Europe the Bible', according to Carroll and Prickett, 'has always been a translated book'; by contrast with the *Qur'an*, indissolubly embedded in its native Arabic:

> Three-quarters of the Christian Bible ... is acknowledged, even by its most fundamentalist adherents, to be originally the scriptures of another religion and written in a language never spoken by any Christian community ... it is not an aberration but actually a recurring characteristic of the Bible that it is written in a language at some remove from that actually spoken by its readers.[29]

The *KJV*, in its textual and linguistic conservatism, is no exception to this general observation:

> in a period when the English language was changing more rapidly than ever before or since, the Bible was set in words that were designed to stress the essential continuity of the Anglican settlement with the past by recalling the phraseology not merely of the familiar Geneva Bible, but of Coverdale and Tyndale – and beyond that even of the Vulgate itself ... the language of the new translation was often deliberately archaic and Latinized. Similarly, the variety of styles in the Old Testament writings was flattened and archaised into the form that we have now come to think of instinctively as 'biblical'.
>
> As a result, the language of the Authorised Version forms a curiously and even uniquely self-referential whole – in many ways, indeed, much more so than the original writings of which it is composed.[30]

*

There is no record of the transactions which precipitated the publication of the First Folio of Shakespeare's collected works: no surviving

letters between the editors (John Heminge and Henrie Condell), and
the publishers and printers (William and Isaac Jaggard and Edward
Blount), nor any accounts of the meetings which must have taken place
to discuss the production of this costly venture.[31] This was not a project
on the national scale of the Authorised *King James Version*, debated in
full conference of church and state at Hampton Court. Consideration
of the process of compiling the Shakespeare canon is therefore
restricted to evidence supplied by the book itself, the surviving earlier
editions of some of the individual plays contained therein and general
intelligence relating to sixteenth- and seventeenth-century theatrical
and publishing practices.

When the editors and publishers of the First Folio took it upon
themselves to produce a collected volume of Shakespeare's work, the
author may have departed this life but his words, like those of the Bible,
were still very much alive, freely scattered abroad as the plays continued to enjoy popular success in performance and print. His non-
dramatic works *Venus and Adonis* and *The Rape of Lucrece* (both
dedicated to the wealthy aristocratic patron, the Earl of Southampton)
and the collection of his sonnets were likewise in public circulation, the
former enjoying repeated reprinting.[32] Records from the years 1616–23
show the continued popularity of plays such as *Twelfth Night* and *The
Winter's Tale*, performed at court in 1618, 1619–20 and 1623,[33] and
some of the older plays continued to be reprinted (six editions of
Richard III were published in quarto between 1597 and 1622, whereas
a more recent play, *Othello*, had in 1622 only just been released, the year
before publication of the First Folio). However, prior to 1623 these free
and fragmentary products were yet to achieve canonical status: they
were, like masterless men, unleashed to the 'great Variety' of readers
and playgoers. Yet, unlike the long history of scriptural formation, the
Shakespeare canon took little more than thirty years to come into
being; the oldest play, probably *The Two Gentlemen of Verona*, dates
only from the early 1590s. Nevertheless, notwithstanding its relatively
rapid formation, there are numerous parallels with the Bible.

In compiling the first collected edition of Shakespeare's plays a
variety of sources were available to the editors. Of the thirty-six plays
included in the volume, eighteen already existed in print as single
quarto playtexts. A nineteenth also in print in 1623, *Pericles*, was not
included, although it has been reclaimed by subsequent editors, along
with the non-dramatic poems which were also excluded, and *The Two
Noble Kinsmen* (acknowledged as co-authored), in the same way as

rediscovered and reconsidered texts were, over a period of time, added to the Bible. Some of these earlier Shakespearean quartos existed, like the early scriptures, in plural and contested forms. For example the 1604/5 quarto edition of *Hamlet* is almost double the length of the 1603 text and renames many of the leading characters, a situation not dissimilar to the Greek and Hebrew versions of *Jeremiah*. Several of these quarto editions differ significantly from their counterparts in the Folio, and were therefore condemned, first by Heminge and Condell as those 'maimed, and deformed' texts they endeavoured to replace, and by the early twentieth-century editors who branded them as simply 'bad quartos', a condemnation some recent critics and editors have sought to revise.[34]

To the eighteen plays which had previously appeared in print, the Folio editors added a further eighteen which had never been printed before, although two of them (*The life and death of King John* and *The Taming of the Shrew*) existed in very similar dramatisations, which are still regarded by some critics as further 'bad quartos'. However, it is important to observe that all the plays existed at some point in the form of hand-written scripts: the playwright's own drafts (known as 'foul papers' because these were presumably covered in changes and crossings-out, or 'blottings'), the actors' individual scripted parts (the Elizabethan actor only received a copy of his own lines with cues) and at least one complete 'fair copy' to be used as a promptbook and to obtain the approval of the censor.[35] These manuscripts were a component part of the plays as theatrical performance, as the property of the theatrical companies which owned them, and they were officially printed only when the theatres were temporarily closed, or when the company needed extra money, or if a particular play had ceased to draw the crowds profitably in performance. We might therefore reasonably assume that at least some of the unpublished plays in 1623 were either those of more recent origin or those which continued to draw the crowds, plays such as *The Winter's Tale* and *Twelfth Night* – new testaments, we might say, that were added to the old.

It is generally assumed that the First Folio editors worked from such manuscripts for all the plays in their collected edition, not least since the title page carries the assurance that they are 'Published according to the True Originall Copies', copies which in the preface are praised for being more 'fair' than 'foul', since 'wee have scarse receiued from him a blot in his papers' (Norton facsimile, p. 7). But the close correlation between many of the plays in the folio and some of the previously published quartos suggests that the editors must also have made use of the printed versions. In other words they worked with a variety of sources, 'fair' and 'foul', 'good' and 'bad' – some already in public circulation, others still privately owned – discriminating as they saw fit, just as did the men who compiled the *KJV*. Both volumes therefore involved a process of selection and refinement, in which texts regarded as suspect, fragmentary or deformed would either be 'improved' or discarded.

The traditional editorial process endeavours to regularise spelling, lineation and punctuation, to 'correct' foreign or mistaken words, and remove words and passages which the censor might regard as profane or libellous. As Charlton Hinman (the first editor of *The Norton Facsimile*) explains, the editors of the First Folio 'made it their task not merely to "gather his works" but to furnish the printer with carefully corrected texts of them' (Charlton Hinman, 'Introduction', Norton facsimile, p. x). Some of these corrections can be identified by comparing the quarto plays with the Folio, but we have no way of knowing the full extent of this editorial intervention for, although many of the quartos have survived, all of the manuscripts have been lost in the dark backward and abysm of time. Lost, that is, for the present. The example of the Dead Sea Scrolls, miraculously rediscovered in 1947, gives hope to the perennial scholarly dream of finding the resurrected document that would correct or redefine the Shakespeare canon. Indeed, the attribution to Shakespeare's hand of a section in the manuscript of *Sir Thomas More* justified the inclusion of that multiply authored play in some *Collected Works* of Shakespeare, such as that of Jaspar Sisson.[36]

Once the process of selection was complete, the fragmentary body of the author's work could be reassembled into a new whole. As in the *KJV*, the 1623 volume comprised of three sections: 'Comedies', 'Histories' and 'Tragedies'. Most of the plays, which in the quartos had no divisions, were themselves likewise tidily arranged, some into acts, others into acts and scenes, like chapter and verse of the Bible. But the generic grouping of the plays meant that the order in which the plays had first been written and produced could now be changed. If the First Folio was to be perceived as the work of an author whose 'mind and hand went together', it was not designed to present them in the order in which 'he conceiued them' (Norton facsimile, p. 7), to trace the growth of the poet's mind, as in Wordsworth's *The Prelude*, but rather to map the distribution of it in its various stages of development, a dissemination of his greater achievements across the entire collection, in the way that the Word of God is distributed and redistributed across the scriptures, mediated through the prophets, disciples and apostles. Thus, one of the last to be written, *The Winter's Tale*, the product of the mature playwright, was included in the first group – the 'Comedies' – whilst one of the first, *Titus Andronicus*, produced when Shakespeare was relatively new to the profession, is placed in the last group – the 'Tragedies'. The three groups within the First Folio also served another function. These fixed groups did not readily accommodate plays of mixed generic content, hence plays once capable of dual interpretation, signalled by designating them 'comicall histories' or 'tragicall histories', were streamlined into a single genre and redefined as comic, tragic or historic. But perhaps the most significant changes effected by the tripartite division relate to the plays centrally placed within the canon – those classed as 'Histories'.

The 'Histories' included only the English history plays set within the period 1200 to 1533, ten plays in total, eight of which (if we include the 'bad quarto' *The Troublesome reign of King John*), already existed in single, disaggregated editions. All the Roman plays and the other histories which focused on the more distant past were subsequently categorised as 'Tragedies', hence a play once entitled *M. William Shak-speare: His True Chronicle Historie of the life and death of King Lear and his three Daughters* (a Q text dated 1608), was renamed in its revision *The Tragedie of King Lear*, to suit its new generic status within the 'Tragedies'. Many of the plays in the 'Histories' group were themselves renamed, binding the events to the life of a specific king and sometimes regrouping them as parts of a greater whole, as for example with the *Henry VI* plays, wherein *The First Part of the Contention betwixt the two famous Houses of Yorke and Lancaster* (a Q text dated 1594), became *The second Part of Henry the Sixt*, and *The True Tragedie of Richard Duke of Yorke and the Good King Henry the Sixt* (Q 1595) became *The third Part of Henry the Sixt*.

Comparing some of the quarto texts with those reprinted in the First Folio a reordering of the material may be observed, again as in the different translations of *Jeremiah*. Such is the case with *Henry V*, a play which has no 'Chorus' in its quarto version, and has thus acquired, or recovered, a linking device that joins together the disjointed battle scenes and simultaneously encourages the reader/spectator's imagination towards coherence and consistency of interpretation.[37] But this reordering and linking occurs on a grander scale across the ten collected 'Histories', for the editors reordered these plays in historical chronology, rearranging the random, non-historical order in which they were performed to produce a progressive sequence of events from *The life and death of King John* to *The Life of King Henry the Eight*, thus recreating a more 'natural', temporal order and a sense of historical continuity. Although *King John* and *Henry the Eight* are somewhat dislocated in time from the eight plays which they enclose, the two central 'tetralogies', as they have come to be termed, could now be read as a linked chain of events from the deposition of a rightful king – Richard II – to the overthrow, by Henry VII, of the devilish monarch – Richard III, a reading which endorsed a Tudor view of divine, providential order.

Like the *KJV*, this first step in the production of the Shakespeare canon thus eliminated by defamation the variant texts which might provide alternative readings; it grouped, rearranged and reordered the material not only to distribute the finest words of the author, but effectively to tighten possible interpretations. And at its core it created an epic dramatisation of English history, transforming ten discrete stories of the past into an all-embracing metanarrative whose resolution was secured by divine justice. The central body was thus tightly conjoined around a heart which appeared to have been divinely directed. To encourage readers to appreciate the value of their prestigious volume and the genius of its author, Heminge and Condell not only prefaced their publication with a dedication and a preface 'To the great Variety of Readers', they also included prefatory poems in memory, praise and honour of Mr William Shakespeare (Norton facsimile, pp. 9–15), and the Droeshout engraving of Shakespeare's likeness, to ensure that the reader approached the plays in due awe and admiration for the individualised figure of the 'Author'.[38] Yet in doing so, they unwittingly revealed themselves as the instruments and agents of the editorial process, the immediate authors of the great canonical metanarrative itself.

*

And the whole earth was of one language, and of one speach.

2 And it came to passe as they iourneyed from the East, that they found a plaine in the land of Shinar, and they dwelt there.

3 And they sayd one to another; Goe to, let vs make bricke, and burne them thorowly. And they had bricke for stone, and slime had they for morter.

4 And they said, Goe to, let vs build vs a city and a tower, whose top may reach vnto heauen; and let vs make vs a name, lest we be scattered abroad vpon the face of the whole earth.

5 And the Lord came downe to see the city and the tower, which the children of men builded.

6 And the Lord said; Behold, the people is one, and they haue all one

language: and this they begin to doe: and now nothing will be restrained from them, which they haue imagined to doe.

7 Goe to, let vs go downe, and there confound their language, that they may not understand one anothers speech.

8 So the Lord scattered them abroad from thence, vpon the face of all the earth: and they left off to build the Citie.

9 Therefore is the name of it called Babel, because the Lord did there confound the language of all the earth. (*Genesis*, 11.1-9)

And when the day of Pentecost was fully come, they were all with one accord in one place.

2 And suddenly there came a sound from heauen as of a rushing mighty wind, and it filled all the house where they were sitting.

3 And there appeared vnto them clouen tongues, like as of fire, and it sate vpon each of them.

4 And they were all filled with the holy Ghost, and began to speake with other tongues, as the spirit gaue them vtterance. (*The Actes of the Apostles*, 2.1-4)

These two great foundational narratives of Christianity map the cultural space occupied by the Bible and the *Complete Works of Shakespeare*.

In the Old Testament story of the Tower of Babel, the presence of a uniform language and an apparently limitless technological capability on the part of mankind presented YHWH ('Jehova'), the Old Testament God, with the serious threat of a unified human race conceiving in their 'imagined' aspirations towards superhuman power. Their unity of purpose, and their capacity to build skywards, together constitute the threat of another rebellion like that of Adam, who sought to seize the divine prerogative of infinite knowledge.[39] The Judaic God destroys both their Tower and their linguistic unity, demolishing the construction, scattering its builders across the face of the earth, and confounding their common language into an infinite diversity of tongues: Babel.

The story of Pentecost in the Acts of the Apostles represents a characteristically masterly Christian appropriation and assimilation of Old Testament materials. Pentecost reverses the Babel myth by restoring universal communication and the possibility of social unity, but this time on God's, rather than on mankind's, terms. By now God has, in the person of Christ, 'come down', not to destroy, but to reconstruct; not to overwhelm the world as in the Flood, but to establish the 'New Covenant' implicit in Christ's sacrifice and Resurrection; not to prevent the human ascension into heaven, but to facilitate it; not to scatter the people across the face of the earth, but to gather them together into the unity of the *ecclesia*. For that reason the Apostles are 'all with one accord in one place'; and with the gift of tongues, inspired by the Holy Spirit, they form the hub of a communications network that will enable common universal understanding to be restored. This time, however, it is not one language (the 'language of Canaan', the Hebrew language that had become identified with the cultural and religious exclusivity of Judaism), but the capability of speaking in all languages, that enables the restoration of lost pristine unity. And now what is uttered, in all those many languages, is not the proud ambition of an overweening human 'imagination', but the very Word of God.

The *KJV* and the *Complete Works of Shakespeare* are both cultural Towers of Babel. Though based in a variety and multiplicity of texts, in one case derived from several different languages, the editors sought to establish a common discourse, a uniformity of contents and a particular significant structure. In the case of the latter feature, there is again a striking parallel: since by including the Apocryphal (or as biblical scholars now term them 'deutero-canonical') books, which were so disliked by reformers as to be removed from bibles altogether, the *KJV* formed for itself a tripartite structure that parallels the generic trivium of *Mr William Shakespeares Comedies, Histories and Tragedies*, with the Old Testament functioning as History, the fanciful narratives of the Apocrypha as Comedy, and the Passion-narratives of the Gospels forming a final Tragic denouement.

With the *KJV* written in a 'language of Canaan', and the First Folio aiming to represent the perfect undifferentiated unity of Shakespeare's 'mind and hand', both texts were clearly seeking to re-establish, by their inclusive comprehensiveness and achieved uniformity, a lost perfection, and to conceal as far as possible the Pentecostal babbling of many tongues that went into their making.[40] It is, finally, perhaps inevitable that contemporary scholarship and criticism is subjecting both these great books, not for the first time, to processes of 'disintegration' that are calculated to release from their authoritarian structures the many and varied utterances out of which their respective canonical unities were initially composed.

Notes

1 In the First Quarto text of *Henry V* (1600) Flewellen asserts that there 'is no tittle-tattle, nor bible bable' in Pompey's camp (*The Cronicle History of Henry the fift*, edited by Graham Holderness and Bryan Loughrey (Hemel Hempstead, Harvester Wheatsheaf, 1993),

p. 64). The 1623 Folio text unhelpfully renders this phrase as 'pibble bable'; and the Arden edition distances it as far as possible from its origins by giving it as 'pibble-pabble' (see collation for 4.1.71–2 in *Henry V*, edited by T. W. Craik (London, Routledge, 1997), p. 263). What starts out, apparently, as a piece of wordplay on 'Bible' and 'Babel' eventually becomes a gibberish word for nonsensical prattle. The presence in the Quarto version of both 'Bible' and 'Babel' makes it a useful reference for our title.

2 The *KJV* was printed by Robert Barker, 'Printer to the Kings most Excellent Maiestie' in 1611. The title page reads: THE HOLY BIBLE, Conteyning the Old Testament, AND THE NEW: Newly Translated out of the Originall tongues: & with the former Translations diligently compared and reuised by his Maiesties speciall Comandment Appointed to be read in Curches'. William Aldis Wright, one of the late nineteenth-century editors of the Cambridge Shakespeare (W. A. Wright, W. G. Clark and J. Glover, published in nine vols., 1863–6, 2nd edn 1867, and 3rd edn rev. Wright 1891–3), and also co-editor with W. G. Clark of the single volume Globe edition of Shakespeare's works, published in 1864, was also the editor of an early twentieth-century reissue of *The Authorised Version of the English Bible 1611*, 5 vols (Cambridge, Cambridge University Press, 1909), an edition which retained the original spelling and marginal notes. A new edition of the *KJV* has recently been published: *The Bible: Authorised King James Version*, ed. by Robert Carroll and Stephen Prickett (Oxford, Oxford University Press, 1997), with modernised spelling and punctuation. Unless otherwise stated, all quotations from the *KJV* in this chapter are from the facsimile edition, ed. and introd. by A. W. Pollard, *The Holy Bible: A Facsimile in a reduced size of the Authorized Version published in the year 1611* (Oxford, Oxford University Press, 1911). Further references are included parenthetically in the text. The First Folio of Shakespeare's plays appeared as *Mr. William Shakespeares Comedies, Histories, & Tragedies. Published according to the True Originall Copies*, printed by Isaac Jaggard and Edward Blount in 1623. Unless otherwise stated, all references in this essay are to the facsimile reproduction *The First Folio of Shakespeare: Based on Folios in the Folger Shakespeare Library Collection*, prepared by Charlton Hinman (London and New York, W. W. Norton/Paul Hamlyn, 1968), and reissued with an additional introduction by Peter Blayney in 1996. Further references are included parenthetically in the text.

3 William Barlow, *The Summe and Substance of the Conference, which it pleased his Excellent Maiestie to haue with the Lords, Bishops and other of his Clergie, (at which the most of the Lordes of the Councell were present) in his Maiesties Priuy-Chamber, at Hampton Court, Ianuary 14, 1603* (printed in London by John Windet, 1604), as quoted in Pollard, *The Holy Bible*, 'Preface', p. 26; also included in J. R. Tanner (ed.), *Constitutional Documents of the Reign of James I* (Cambridge, Cambridge University Press, 1961), p. 63.

4 *Th'overthrow of Stage-Playes, by the way of a controversy betwixt D. Gager and D. Rainoldes* (Middleburgh, R. Schilders, 1599).

5 John Drakakis, 'Theatre, ideology and institution', in Graham Holderness (ed.), *The Shakespeare Myth* (Manchester, Manchester University Press, 1987), pp. 24–5.

6 'his Highnesse wished that some especiall paines should be taken in that behalfe', Barlow, as n. 3.

7 Frank Kermode, 'The canon', in R. Alter and F. Kermode (eds), *The Literary Guide to the Bible* (London, Collins, 1987), pp. 600–10, esp. pp. 601 and 604.

8 Rule 1 in 'The Rules to be observed in the Translation of the Bible', as reprinted in Pollard, *The Holy Bible*, p. 29. For the '*Bishops' Bible*', see 'English versions of the Bible', in Peter Ackroyd and Christopher F. Evans (eds), *The Cambridge History of the Bible* (Cambridge, Cambridge University Press, 1970), vol. 2, pp. 159–61.

9 See Gustavus S. Paine, *The Men Behind the KJV* (Grand Rapids, MI, Baker Book House, 1959), pp. 136–9.

10 See John C. Olin, *Desiderius Erasmus: Christian Humanism and the Reformation* (New York, Harper and Row, 1965), p. 105. See also Craig R. Thompson, 'Scripture for the ploughboy and others', *Studies in the Continental Background of English Renaissance Literature: Essays Presented to John L. Lievsay* (Durham, NC, Duke University Press, 1977), pp. 3–28.

11 See John Hollander and Frank Kermode, *The Literature of Renaissance England* (Oxford, Oxford University Press, 1973), p. 29.

12 See Geddes MacGregor, *The Bible in the Making* (London, John Murray, 1961), pp. 82–91. For Tyndale see David Daniell, *William Tyndale: A Biography* (New Haven, Yale University Press, 1994).

13 For the Geneva Bible see Ackroyd and Evans (eds), *The Cambridge History*, pp. 155–9.

14 'I. M. S.', 'On Worthy Master Shakespeare and his Poems', appeared in the 1632 Folio. See Stanley Wells and Gary Taylor (eds), *William Shakespeare: The Complete Works* (Oxford, Clarendon Press, 1986), p. xlv.

15 For a discussion of 'pre-performance' and 'post-performance' elements in dramatic texts see Wells and Taylor (eds), *Complete Works*, pp. xxxiii–xxxvii.

16 Barlow, *Summe and Substance*, as n. 3.

17 'Anglican writers agreed ... that the true meaning of Holy Scripture (as of any other text) was that intended by its author. That Scripture is a special case, written by divine inspiration, posed no serious theoretical problems for them. Scripture's meaning is that of its author, whether that author is God himself, or human penmen more or less consistently guided by him' (Marcus Walsh, *Shakespeare, Milton and Eighteenth-century Literary Editing: The Beginnings of Interpretative Scholarship* (Cambridge, Cambridge University Press, 1997), p. 36).

18 For Roland Barthes, in the 'Work', 'the *author* is a god' (*S/Z*, trans. Richard Miller (London, Cape, 1975), p. 5). Sean Burke argues that Barthes constituted the author as a 'tyrannical deity' in order to 'create a king worthy of the killing' (*The Death and Return of the Author* (Edinburgh, Edinburgh University Press, 1992), p. 26). See also Morse Peckham, 'Reflections on the foundations of modern textual editing', *Proof*, 1 (1971), pp. 136–7.

19 'TO. THE. ONLY. BEGETTER. OF. THESE. ENSUING. SONNETS. M^R. W. H. ALL. HAPPINESS. AND. THAT. ETERNITY. PROMISED. BY. OUR. EVER-LIVING. POET. WISHETH. THE. WELL-WISHING. ADVENTURER. IN. SETTING. FORTH.' See Wells and Taylor (eds), *Complete Works*, p. 848.

20 See Sidney Jellicoe, *The Septuagint and Modern Study* (Oxford, Clarendon Press, 1968); the older treatment by H. B. Swete, *An Introduction to the Old Testament in Greek* (Cambridge, Cambridge University Press, 1902), and the recent treatment by Morgeus Muller, *The First Bible of the Church: A Plea for the Septuagint* (Sheffield, Sheffield Academic Press, 1996). See also Ernst Wurthwein, *The Text of the Old Testament*, trans. E. F. Rhodes (Grand Rapids, MI, Eerdmans, 1979), esp. pp. 49–74.

21 See Wurthwein, *Old Testament*, pp. 3–41; and E. Tov, *Textual Criticism of the Hebrew Bible* (Minneapolis, Fortress Press; Assen, Van Gorcum, 1992), pp. 21–76.

22 See Emanuel Tov, *Hebrew Bible*, pp. 100–17.

23 See T. S. Pattie, *Manuscripts of the Bible* (London, British Library, 1979).

24 B. M. Metzger, *The Text of the New Testament: Its Transmission, Corruption and Restoration* (Oxford, Oxford University Press, 3rd edn, 1992), p. 131 and *passim*.

25 See David Ewert, *From Ancient Tablets to Modern Translations: A General Introduction to the Bible* (Grand Rapids, MI, Zondervan, 1983), pp. 65–83; and Metzger, *New Testament*, pp. 98–103.

26 Early modern Catholic and Protestant interpretations of scripture were of course entirely different from one another. While Protestants insisted on 'the determinate meaning, the

comprehensibility, and the reliability of transmission of Scripture', Roman Catholic scholars argued that the meaning of scripture was 'inherently equivocal and indeterminate' (see Walsh, *Shakespeare, Milton*, pp. 33–4). The Catholics drew attention, *inter alia*, to 'the great alterations which have happened ... to the Copies of the Bible since the first Originals have been lost' (Richard Simon, *A Critical History of the Old Testament* (London, 1682), sig. a3ᵛ–4ʳ, III.160).

27 Carroll and Prickett, *The Bible*, p. xxi.

28 For early modern Catholics effective translation of the scriptures was impossible, 'since no two la[n]guages jumpe equaly in their expressions, it is impossible that euerie word of the one should haue a full expression of euerie word of the other ... t'is impossible to put fully and beyond all quarrel the same sense in divers words' (William Rushworth, *The Dialogues of William Richworth or the Iudgemend of Common Sense in the Choise of Religion* (Paris, 1640), pp. 266–7).

29 Carroll and Prickett, *The Bible*, pp. xx and xxii.

30 Carroll and Prickett, *The Bible*, p. xxvii–xxviii.

31 The cost of the First Folio, depending on whether it was bound or unbound, was between 15s. and £1, around forty times more than the average single playtext in quarto format. For a more detailed analysis of costs see Peter Blayney, *The First Folio of Shakespeare* (Washington, Folger Library Publications, 1991).

32 See Katharine Eisaman Maus, in Stephen Greenblatt et al. (eds), *The Norton Shakespeare* (London, Norton, 1997), pp. 606 and 639.

33 See *The Norton Shakespeare*, pp. 3391–2.

34 The same A. W. Pollard, responsible for the facsimile edition of the *KJV* in 1911, was the first to classify these texts as 'bad quartos' in *Shakespeare's Folios and Quartos* (London, Methuen, 1909). For a reappraisal of the 'bad quartos', see Paul Werstine, 'Narratives about printed Shakespeare texts: "foul papers" and "bad quartos"', *Shakespeare Quarterly*, 41 (1990), pp. 65–86; Holderness and Loughrey, 'General introduction' to *The Cronicle History of Henry the fift*; and Laurie E. Maguire, *Shakespearean Suspect Texts: The 'Bad' Quartos and their Contexts* (Cambridge, Cambridge University Press, 1996). Wells and Taylor included both the Quarto and Folio versions of *King Lear* in their *Complete Works*; and the new Arden *Henry V*, ed. T. W. Craik (London, Routledge, 1997), also includes a photographic facsimile of the 1600 First ('Bad') Quarto text.

35 It should be noted that this basic account of theatrical manuscripts rests on very little material evidence, and that surviving contemporary examples of so-called 'foul papers' and 'promptbook' copies, being somewhat diverse, do not readily fall into such neat categories. See Werstine's 'Narratives about printed Shakespeare texts', and also his 'Plays in manuscript', in John D. Cox and David Scott Kastan (eds), *A New History of Early English Drama* (New York, Columbia University Press, 1997). See also Peter Blayney's 'The publication of playbooks', in the same volume.

36 Of the whole co-authored play, clearly a typical product of the collaborative authorship current in the early modern theatre, Wells and Taylor include in their *Complete Works* only the fragment identified as written in Shakespeare's hand. On collaboration see Jeffrey Masten, *Textual Intercourse: Collaboration, Authorship and Sexualities in Renaissance Drama* (Cambridge, Cambridge University Press, 1997).

37 For a discussion of the Quarto and Folio versions of *Henry V*, see Holderness and Loughrey, *The Cronicle History of Henry the fift*, 'Introduction'.

38 See Graham Holderness and Bryan Loughrey, 'Shakespearean features', in Jean E. Howard (ed.), *Appropriating Shakespeare: Post-Renaissance Reconstructions of the Works and the Myth* (Hemel Hempstead, Harvester Wheatsheaf, 1991), pp. 183–201.

39 The more obvious parallel with the rebellion and fall of Lucifer does not, despite very wide-
    spread assumptions to the contrary, appear at all in *Genesis*. It can be reconstructed from
    various references scattered throughout the Bible – in *Isaiah, Jude, Revelation* – and was
    elaborately narrated and expounded by the church fathers, notably St Augustine in *De
    Civitate Dei*. A very full and impressively dramatised account is to be found in Old English
    poetry, particularly in the poem known as *The Fall of the Angels* (Genesis A), long before
    Milton gave the story its now most familiar treatment in *Paradise Lost*. For a translation and
    commentary see Graham Holderness, *Anglo-Saxon Verse* (London, Northcote House,
    2000).

40 The story of Babel was of considerable interest to Jacques Derrida. It is, in Kevin Hart's
    words, 'a story that condenses much of what interests him under the rubric of "deconstruc-
    tion"' (Hart, 'The poetics of the negative', in Stephen Prickett (ed.), *Reading the Text:
    Biblical Criticism and Literary Theory* (Oxford, Blackwell, 1991), p. 312). First it gives 'a
    good idea of what deconstruction is: an unfinished edifice whose half-completed structures
    are visible, letting one guess at the scaffolding behind them' (Derrida et al, *The Ear of the
    Other: Otobiography, Transference, Translation*, ed. Christine V. McDonald, trans. Peggy
    Kamuf (New York, 1985), p. 102). Ironically for Derrida, in the Babel story the logocentric
    aspirations of humanity are crushed by a God who declares: 'you will not impose a single
    tongue; you will be condemned to the multiplicity of tongues' (*Ear of the Other*, p. 102).

Ghost writing: *Hamlet* and the Ur-Hamlet

Emma Smith

Hamlet is a ghost story. It, like its eponymous hero, is haunted by a spirit from the past. This spirit is also uncannily familiar: it bears the same name from the grave as the young prince who lives in its shadow. There are, of course, two Hamlets – one alive, the other dead – in *Hamlet*. But are there also two *Hamlets* in Hamlet? Just as Elsinore is haunted by the ghost of old Hamlet, so critics have argued for more than a century that Shakespeare's play is haunted by an old *Hamlet*, a play on the same subject, now lost, which predated the one we have now. *Hamlet*'s prehistory exists both within the play, in old Hamlet's (dis)embodiment of the past, and beyond and before it, in the persistent bibliographical evocation of a pre-*Hamlet*, a non-existent play known as the Ur-Hamlet. This phantom play has been variously deduced, discussed and even edited by textual scholars, and thus its imagined and imaginary textual history forms an analogue for *Hamlet*'s obsession with ghosts, memory, origins and the search for certainty around the traces of the past.

The suggestion that there was a *Hamlet* play before Shakespeare's *Hamlet* dates back to Edmond Malone's posthumously printed edition of Shakespeare's works of 1821. Like many later editors of Shakespeare, Malone dated *Hamlet* at around 1600, but recognised evidence which seemed to point to a *Hamlet* play more than a decade earlier in 1589. This evidence for a *Hamlet* in the late 1580s has been often rehearsed. Most famous among these early allusions is Thomas Nashe's satire, in his preface to Robert Greene's *Menaphon* (1589):

> It is a common practise now a dayes amongst a certain sort of shifting companions, that runne through euery art and thriue by none, to leaue the trade of *Nouerint*, whereto they were borne, and busie themselves with the indeuors of Art, that could scarcely Latinize their neck-verse if they should haue neede; yet English *Seneca* read by Candle-light yeelds many good sentences, as *Blood is a begger*, and so forth; and if you intreate

him faire in a frostie morning, hee will affoord you whole Hamlets, I should say handfuls of Tragicall speeches.[1]

Nashe goes on to refer to 'the kid in Aesop', usually read as an allusion to Thomas Kyd, author of *The Spanish Tragedy*, a play with which *Hamlet* can be seen to share certain preoccupations. As Kyd's father was a scrivener, and the neatness of his holograph manuscripts has been seen to suggest his own training as a '*Nouerint*', this identification of an early *Hamlet* play, already well-known by 1589 and possibly authored by Kyd, has been taken as decisive by many scholars. Other evidence may point to the same conclusion, although Nashe is the only writer to suggest an author, albeit obliquely, for this early *Hamlet*. In 1596 Thomas Lodge mentions a 'ghost which cried so miserably at the Theatre, like an oyster-wife, *Hamlet, revenge*', and this phrase, which appears nowhere in the play we have, seems to have become a byword. Perhaps this reference to an early *Hamlet* in performance relates to the play of the same name at which Philip Henslowe took 'viii s' at Newington Butts in June 1594. That there was a play called *Hamlet* or about Hamlet on the stage some time between 1589 and the mid-1590s seems clear. That this might have been by Shakespeare seems to have been largely discounted, due to ideas about *Hamlet*'s place in a developmental canon of Shakespeare's dramatic career, and to the absence of the mention of *Hamlet* from Francis Meres's catalogue of Shakespeare's plays. In *Palladis Tamia* (1598) Meres praises Shakespeare as 'the most excellent' in comedy and tragedy, and lists six plays in each genre, but not *Hamlet*. By 1598, then, there seems to have been a *Hamlet* without Shakespeare and a Shakespeare without *Hamlet*. At some unspecified date this anomaly is rectified. Gabriel Harvey's marginal note to a copy of Chaucer, acquired by him after 1598, states: 'The younger sort takes much delight in Shakespeares Venus, & Adonis: but his Lucrece, & his tragedie of Hamlet, Prince of Denmarke, haue it in them, to please the wiser sort.' Cumulatively, the evidence seems to suggest that there was a *Hamlet* play before that recorded in the Stationers' Register as 'a booke called the Revenge of Hamlett Prince Denmarke as yt was latelie Acted by the Lo: Chamberleyn his servante'[2] in 1602. There is, however, no evidence that this earlier play was ever printed, and no verifiable traces of its plot or language can be recovered.[3]

These absences, however, have not deterred textual bibliography from speculating about the play which preceded *Hamlet*. In the late nineteenth century, Anglo-German bibliographers, using the German prefix meaning 'original or primitive', dubbed this lost play of the late

1580s the 'Ur-Hamlet'. Like that other ghost of Shakespeare's play, old Hamlet, this textual phantom both is, and is not, Hamlet/*Hamlet*. Within a very few years of Gregor Sarrazin's 1895 identification of the lost drama with Thomas Kyd, however, a play which, at most, might be conjectured to have contained a ghost and the words 'Hamlet revenge' had gained a surprising corporeality. Numerous commentators sought to reconstruct its contours, primarily in order better to understand Shakespeare's own art in *Hamlet*. Three other plays – the German play *Der Bestrafte Brudermord* which exists in an early eighteenth-century manuscript but is generally believed to be of considerably earlier date, Thomas Kyd's *The Spanish Tragedy* and the 1603 quarto text of *Hamlet* – were crucial in determining the supposed content and theme of the lost Ur-Hamlet. Informed inference, the major ratiocinative process of the New Bibliography of the late nineteenth century, found in *Hamlet* and its textual problems the ur-text of its own method and rationale. In the mystery of *Hamlet* and Hamlet the discipline was able to extend its imaginative reach. In the absence of the play itself, textual bibliography wrote it, situated it among its putative sources and discussed its relationship to the extant *Hamlet*. What had seemed spectral and shadowy became a solid foundation on which could be stacked endless theories about *Hamlet* itself.

For around thirty years up until the end of the First World War, the Ur-Hamlet gained in solidity. Through deduction from existing texts, a surprising amount of detail about the missing play accrued. Arguing, for example, for Kyd's authorship of the Ur-Hamlet, his authoritative editor F. S. Boas wrote that 'the First Quarto of the Shakespearean *Hamlet*, whatever view be taken of the problems which it raises in other ways, reproduces, it may be reasonably inferred, at least the broad outlines of the earlier play on the subject. And in it we find the original saga developed into a complex dramatic structure curiously analogous to *The Spanish Tragedie*'.[4] Boas's recognition that the similarity between the inferred 'earlier play' and Kyd's revenge tragedy is 'curious' evades the logic of his own discussion: it is precisely because of a predisposition in favour of Kyd's authorship of the Ur-Hamlet that he imagines the play in a form so like that of *The Spanish Tragedy*. Boas's argument is typical of the self-fulfilling conclusions of bibliography's co-option of the Ur-Hamlet, in which the pre-play becomes a blank page in a textual history which the critic can inscribe as he pleases.

Many critics chose to use this bibliographic space to acquit Shakespeare of any fault in the writing of his most problematic play.

Often, traces of the Ur-Hamlet, always derogated as unworthy of him, were identified in *Hamlet*, and through this identification Shakespeare himself was exonerated of their solecisms. John Corbin's *The Elizabethan Hamlet* (1895) uncovered a 'crude tragedy of blood' behind Shakespeare's play.[5] The character of this lost play, the Ur-Hamlet, could be fixed by studying 'the two extant versions founded directly upon it, the German version [*Der Bestrafte Brudermord*] and the first quarto of Shakspere' (Corbin, 18). From this comparison, Corbin deduces that the lost play was 'a tragedy of blood', adding, 'nor does it take the ghost of the lost play to tell us this' (Corbin, 30–1). Corbin's play begins to take shape, in the markedly evasive syntax which reflects the processes of the text's invention: 'no conclusion is admissible that would make the Prince Hamlet of the lost play anything but a person who feigned madness to escape the jealousy of a usurping uncle' (Corbin, 31). The existence of this pre-play is comforting to Corbin's sense of Shakespeare's aesthetic distinction, as he is able to argue that 'all which is least according to Shakspere's taste proceeded from Kyd', thus 'for the first time exonerat[ing] Shakspere from the bizarre cruelty of many of Hamlet's deeds' (Corbin, 89). This process of exculpation is also behind Robert Russell Benedict's *The Mystery of Hamlet Prince of Denmark* (1910), in which the author notes conversationally that 'to many who have studied him, as well as to those who casually know him, the Prince is more or less a mystery'.[6] Like Corbin, Benedict attributes this mysteriousness largely to the underlying existence of the old Ur-Hamlet. He sees in the First Quarto *Hamlet* a play which is 'substantially the lost Hamlet after having received Shakespeare's preliminary touches', asserting that 'much of the poet's first work on Kyd's play was, without doubt, concerned with the elimination of its coarseness and crudeness, which prepared the way for the next version, the second Quarto, upon which he lavished all the richness of his poetic imagination' (Benedict, 42–3). This account of the genesis of *Hamlet* accounts for the inconsistencies in Hamlet's character, so that his textual history gives the Prince a kind of Jekyll and Hyde duality:

> Hamlet in his emotional aspect, his frequent abandonment to passion, his fierce longing for revenge, is the old Hamlet of the Kyd play; while, on the other hand, the Hamlet of refinement and sensibility who strives to draw aside the veil that hides the world of divine law and mystery is Shakespeare's creation and the highest manifestation of his genius. (Benedict, 44)

It is easy to see in Benedict's account clear assumptions about psychological and aesthetic, even metaphysical, consistency which enact a kind of double projection, absolving Hamlet the character of personality defaults by scapegoating an imagined dramatic and passionate predecessor, and thereby absolving *Hamlet* the play and Shakespeare as its author of any artistic failings. In transforming a 'crude drama of revenge' into a 'poetic tragedy of human frailty, aspiration, and failure', it is inevitable that 'some of the rude and half-barbaric elements of the ground-work are seen in the finished product' (Benedict, 116).

On similar ground some twenty years later is J. M. Robertson, one of many writers who tackled a perceived enigma around Shakespeare's play and particularly around its central characterisation. Hugh Grady has discussed how, for Robertson, a Scottish free-thinker and social radical, the textual-bibliographic project of disintegration 'was of a piece with the political and religious demystifications to which he had devoted his life'.[7] Disintegration, the questioning of the organic unity of the Shakespearean text and of its singular authorship, found in its non-existent Ur-Hamlet the proof positive not only of Shakespeare's genius, but also, implicitly, its own scholarly ingenuity. In a book entitled *The Problem of 'Hamlet'* (1919), Robertson also attributed the riddle of the play to the simultaneous existence of the current and a previous play. *Hamlet* is haunted, as 'the essential fact [is] that Shakespeare's *Hamlet* is an adaptation of an older play, which laid down the main action, embodying a counter-sense which the adaptation could not transmute'.[8] The ghostly past thus exerts a strange pull on the present material which even Shakespeare cannot counteract. Robertson's earlier *Hamlet*, like Corbin's, is by Kyd, and from this identification of authorship Robertson is able to infer much about the play. In his account, Kyd has done some of the work of complicating the source to prepare the ground for Shakespeare's inimitable genius to work on the story. Kyd's Hamlet feigns madness, and the 'play-within-the-play is another supererogation. Kyd loved to complicate his motives thus' (Robertson, 65). Despite the fact that only one original play, *The Spanish Tragedy*, can be attributed with certainty to Kyd, this author's style and interests are stated as if drawn from a substantial oeuvre: 'by thus confusing the original Hamlet-plot through his favourite Ghost-motive, Kyd, led to retain the mock-madness by his success with the semi-madness of Jeronymo, prepared the divagation which Shakespeare so wonderfully develops' (Robertson, 65-6). Robertson's construction of Kyd's recalcitrant Ur-Hamlet leads him to greater admiration for Shakespeare's achievement:

> What Shakespeare could not do, no man could have done. What he did remains a miracle of dramatic imagination. In place of one of the early and crude creations of Kyd, vigorous without verisimilitude, outside of refined sympathy, he has projected a personality which from the first line sets all our sympathies in a quick vibration, and so holds our minds and hearts that even the hero's cruelties cannot alienate them. (Robertson, 75)

All that is regrettable about Hamlet's character is reassuringly explicable to Corbin, Benedict and Robertson, as the atavistic survival of elements of an earlier, cruder and emphatically non-Shakespearean play. And as this play, and therefore the ready exoneration of Shakespeare which it conveniently offers, does not exist, it has to be invented. As H. H. Furness's variorum edition of the play (published in 1877 with new editions in 1905 and 1918) recognised in strikingly biblical cadences, a satisfactory account of the difficulties of *Hamlet* was crucial to the whole intellectual project of humankind:

> In the endeavour to solve the mystery of Hamlet, the human mind, not only in its clear radiance, but in the sad twilight of its eclipse, has been subjected to the most searching analysis. This ideal character, Hamlet, has been assumed to be very nature, and if we fail to reach a solution of the problem it presents, the error lies in us and in our analysis; not in SHAKESPEARE.[9]

Furness makes clear that Shakespeare's prodigious art is beyond question: explanations for the mystery must be sought elsewhere if the merely human intellect is to be vindicated.

Hugh Grady rightly associates disintegrationism with a pattern of private, non-institutional scholarship which flourished in the late nineteenth and early twentieth centuries. After the Great War, however, bibliographic times were changing. For J. Dover Wilson, writing his monograph on *The Copy for 'Hamlet' 1603 and The 'Hamlet' Transcript 1593* in 1918, the fact of the Ur-Hamlet, and of its inferiority to Shakespeare's *Hamlet*, can be taken for granted. Wilson asserts confidently that certain lines from the 1603 quarto 'represent botched "ur-Hamlet" stuff', and that Claudius's prayer and Hamlet's following speech were both present in the lost play.[10] Dover Wilson is in no doubt about the magnitude of the textual problems, including those of the Ur-Hamlet, which surround Shakespeare's play. As with Furness's lofty sentiments, there can be no doubt about the stakes of Dover

Wilson's bibliographic enterprise. Inviting criticism and comment on his bibliographic proposition, he aims 'to make the foundations so sure that the superstructure will stand the test of time. And, if so, we shall be in sight of a permanent solution to the greatest of all Shakespearian textual problems – the origin and history of the world's subtlest and most profound dramatic masterpiece' (Dover Wilson, 64). Dover Wilson's scientific editorial stance, however, with its insistence on the solid metaphors of construction, is inflected by the inescapable language of the uncanny when discussing the Ur-Hamlet: 'we are compelled … to posit the existence of a *tertium quid*, some intermediate text which will link the early "Hamlet" with its posthumous apparition in 1603' (Dover Wilson, 32).

Scientific language and procedure had frequently been co-opted to bibliography. In his *Shakespeare Manual* of 1876, F. G. Fleay had proposed, instead of the subjective aesthetics of literary criticism, the rigorous application of certain metrical tests to establish the authenticity of Shakespeare's texts. The 'great need for any critic who attempts to use these tests is to have had a thorough training in the Natural Sciences, especially in Minerology, classificatory Botany, and above all, in Chemical analysis' as 'the methods of all these sciences are applicable to this kind of criticism, which, indeed, can scarcely be understood without them'.[11] One example of the imagery, if not the methodology, of the sciences applied to the Ur-Hamlet is found in Henry David Gray's 'Reconstruction of a Lost Play', first delivered as the Presidential address to the Philological Association of the Pacific Coast in 1927. Gray establishes a disarming analogy for his labours: 'I remember nothing more unconvincing to me in my schoolboy days than the picture of an extinct animal as reconstructed from an unearthed bone'. Gray's palaeontological imagery, however, is used to create a kind of authority for his analogously reconstructed textual dinosaur, the Ur-Hamlet: 'though inevitably wrong in detail, a consistent deduction of the beast from the bone is admittedly both interesting and scientific.' Gray's rationale in this painstaking work is the conjecture that the puzzling inconsistencies of Shakespeare's play represent the fossilised remains of the earlier play. 'If by putting bit and bit together we can make Kyd's *Hamlet* live for us again … we shall come a long step nearer, I think, to solving the *Hamlet* problem.'[12] Gray works on the assumption that *Der Bestrafte Brudermord* is revelatory of an English *Hamlet* play, probably by Kyd, and from this starting point he is able to deduce something of the uses Shakespeare made of his source.

This leads to the unexceptionable conclusion that 'Shakespeare followed Kyd where he found interesting and dramatic material, and supplied new scenes of his own when, for one reason or another, he chose to depart from his source' (Gray, 264). Gray's Ur-Hamlet, reconstructed from 'the Belleforest story insofar as it was apparently followed, arrang[ed] in scenes to correspond to the scenes of *The Spanish Tragedy*' (Gray, 270), is set out in twenty-four scenes allowing for a considerable amount of detail. The play begins with a prologue 'substantially as in *Fratricide Punished* [the translation of *Der Bestrafte Brudermord*]', then has the ghost appear on the battlements to Horatio and Hamlet. In outline it is closely related to Shakespeare's play, including Fortinbras, the play within the play, Ophelia's madness and suicide, Hamlet's journey to England and the fatal duel between Hamlet and Laertes. What differentiates the plays is not their action but their motivation: psychology is Shakespeare's great gift to the story. The 'inconsistencies' of *Hamlet* can be attributed to the influence of Kyd's play, because 'Hamlet's assumed madness and the enclosed play belonged originally to a drama in which the hero was not Shakespeare's highly individualised Hamlet but Kyd's blood-thirsty though questioning protagonist' (Gray, 273). Gray's aim to sort out the question of the Ur-Hamlet is motivated by a desire to see proper authorial responsibility, as his concluding remarks make clear: 'to assign Kyd's motivation to Shakespeare is to rob Shakespeare of his claim to a genius of a higher order than Kyd's' (Gray, 274).

Much of the interest in the Ur-Hamlet can be seen as an preoccupation with questions of paternity and origin. Attaining some certainty about the play's origins is the project of Geoffrey Bullough's authoritative study *Narrative and Dramatic Sources of Shakespeare*. Bullough argues that 'it seems very probable that Shakespeare rewrote an earlier *Hamlet* (hereinafter called the *Ur-Hamlet*) written either by Kyd or an imitator of Kyd', and he identifies the Ur-Hamlet as a significant source for Shakespeare's play.[13] Deduction about this missing text is, therefore, inevitable, and Bullough is not short on inference, particularly about the shortcomings of the ur-play. *Hamlet*'s opening scene on the battlements 'reveals a degree of sophistication in Shakespeare's treatment entirely lacking in *The Spanish Tragedy* and probably only dimly foreshadowed in the *Ur-Hamlet*' (Bullough, 28). Here, as in many accounts of differences between *Hamlet* and its predecessor, increased sophistication is key to Shakespeare's perceived handling of his imagined source. The *Ur-Hamlet* is frequently conceived as a storehouse of dramatic events rather than literary finesse. 'We may imagine', Bullough asserts, 'that the *Ur-Hamlet* contained, in addition to the play-within-the-play, a fencing match in which sport concealed deadly earnest, Hamlet was wounded by a foul blow, the King was killed and the Queen died by drinking poison intended for her son' (Bullough, 48). Why we might want or need to imagine all these elements is not quite clear, except that their evident poetic and psychological deficiencies throw Shakespeare's own genius into sharper relief.

Kyd's role as the author of a nonexistent but thoroughly derogated play is a difficult one for his literary reputation to sustain, although Boas considers 'vindicating his claim to be the first playwright who put the story of *Hamlet* up on the stage' to be a task 'alluring' to Kyd's biographer.[14] Fredson Bowers developed the identification of Kyd and the Ur-Hamlet in his book *Elizabethan Revenge Tragedy 1587-1642*. The imagined Ur-Hamlet plays a crucial role in the development of the genre. Bowers confesses, 'I have written more about the *Ur-Hamlet* than Shakespeare's *Hamlet*',[15] and indeed, the lost play, together with *The Spanish Tragedy*, represents a chapter in the history of the revenge motif. 'In order to evaluate Kyd's *Ur-Hamlet* properly the major features of the plot and characterisation must be surmised' (Bowers, 86), Bowers reasons, and thus he postulates a plot derived from Belleforest's account of Amleth. With this material, Kyd 'was forced to make wide changes to adapt the action to the stage and to the tragic form' (Bowers, 88). Bowers argues that in order to be a tragedy, the lost play must have ended with the death of the avenger as well as that of the victim, in contrast to the survival of the revenging Amleth. So, Bowers reasons, Kyd begins his work with a 'simple story' very like that of the extant *Hamlet*, but with one major dramatic problem: 'for there to be any play at all, the revenger must delay'. In this respect, Belleforest, the source, is 'of little help. His Amleth delays, it is true, but only for the undramatic reason that he is awaiting the best opportunity'. Here, according to Bowers, Kyd's dramatic skills, as evidenced by *The Spanish Tragedy*, are brought into play. How can Hamlet be brought to know the truth of what has happened to his father? Bowers constructs his answer: 'Kyd, the ever-spectacular, broke wide with tradition and introduced into the action of the play itself a ghost who acquaints his son with the true facts of his death' (Bowers, 89). It is, of course, entirely appropriate that the interpolation which defines the Ur-Hamlet, this most ghostly of plays, should be the figure of a theatrical ghost. Just as the ghost of Hamlet's father appears as a link, sometimes one of dubious authority, with the

play's past, so the Ur-Hamlet as ghost is evoked as an explanation of
Hamlet's origins. Marjorie Garber describes 'a ghost [as] the con-
cretization of a missing presence, the sign of what is there by not being
there';[16] in the textual history of the Ur-Hamlet the quality of 'not
being there' takes on a shape which, like the Ghost within *Hamlet* itself,
is at once definite ('in the same figure like the King that's dead', 1.1.39)
and ghostly ('the very coinage of your brain', 3.4.128).

Bowers continues to flesh out his imaginary ur-play. Kyd's Hamlet
also meets the king at prayer and has a chance to kill him, as 'Kyd dar-
ingly presents this opportunity but under such circumstances that
Hamlet cannot accept it' (Bowers, 91). Bowers even posits sources for
Kyd's invention, citing Machiavelli and some Italian prose stories as the
story of this imagined play reverts to the present tense. 'Kyd therefore
plans to create his catastrophe', Bowers writes, as he silently transfers
authority for this textual creation from his own imagination to that of
his surrogate author. 'The lengths to which Kyd went to maintain the
audience's sympathy for his protagonist make Hamlet one of the least
guilty of all Elizabethan stage revengers' (Bowers, 93); but in spite of
this certainty, it is apparently 'very likely Kyd would have killed off
Hamlet' (Bowers, 94). This detailed account of the Ur-Hamlet com-
pletely evades its own fiction. Reading Bowers's influential study of the
revenge tragedy genre, it is a continual effort of will to remember that
this same play has been spirited up from the smallest clues furnished by
Nashe and Lodge's equivocal allusions. Ironically, nowhere in his
account of the play does Bowers quote the only line which may reasonably be assumed to have been part of the lost play – the ghost's injunc-
tion 'Hamlet revenge'. In fact, Bowers's imagined play is curiously like
the play we already have. Kyd's *Hamlet* seems very like Shakespeare's
Hamlet. The ghostly text which, for Bowers, preempts the extant one
seems rather its duplicate than its primitive ancestor.

It is in a volume from the Bankside-Restoration Shakespeare, published for its subscribers by the Shakespeare Society of New York in the
early years of the century, that the Ur-Hamlet receives its most concrete imprimatur. In 1908 Appleton Morgan introduced a parallel text
of the 1604 quarto of *Hamlet* and an imagined text of the Ur-Hamlet,
complete with a suitably smudged mocked-up title page bearing the
date 1597. Morgan's introduction is evasive on the origins of this originary text, although he refers to *Der Bestrafte Brudermord*, arguing that
'here at last we find a vestige of the very ur-Hamlet we are searching
for; and that, if we retranslate this Brudermord back into English we

will arrive at a very fair conception indeed of what that required ur-Hamlet was like'.[17] This explanation emphasises that finding the fugitive ur-text is an imperative and its discovery is 'required'. And the result of this compulsion is the Bankside-Restoration text, produced as a companion volume to another dual *Hamlet*, a parallel text of the First Quarto and Folio editions. *Hamlet* becomes a multiple play, and in the interests of completeness the full suite of *Hamlet*s must include the elusive Ur-Hamlet. Morgan tries to preempt criticism: his conjectural text is, he admits, 'not in sixteenth-century diction at all' (although he has silently antiqued his text by mimicking a sixteenth-century use of u/v and i/j). He answers this objection modestly, arguing that he would not wish to eclipse the story by the manner of its telling: 'to have counterfeited sixteenth century phrasing, had I been equal to it – would by its flavour of tour de force have defeated the impression I seek to emphasize – namely, that only the action of the play would have been presented on London boards' (Morgan, xxxvi).

Morgan's Ur-Hamlet is a strangely incoherent document, whose silences and gaps are emphasised by the blank pages which punctuate its representation alongside parts of *Hamlet*. It runs to around 900 lines, less than half the length of Shakespeare's play. Its lettering is gothic, as opposed to the roman type of the Shakespearean quarto, perhaps alluding to its Germanic origins in *Der Bestrafte Brudermord*. As in Bowers's lengthy account of the Ur-Hamlet, Morgan inexplicably leaves out the only line which might vouch for its existence: 'Hamlet revenge'. At the points where its action is closest to *Hamlet*'s, the Ur-Hamlet has the air of a reductive paraphrase. Alongside Claudius's facing speech:

> Though yet of Hamlet our dear brother's death
> The memory be green, and that it us befitted
> To bear our hearts in grief and our whole kingdom
> To be contracted in one brow of woe,
> Yet so far hath discretion fought with nature
> That we with wisest sorrow think on him
> Together with remembrance of ourselves.
> Therefore our sometime sister, now our queen,
> Th'imperial jointress of this warlike state,
> Have we as 'twere with a defeated joy,
> With one auspicious and one drooping eye,
> With mirth in funeral and with dirge in marriage,
> In equal scale weighing delight and dole,
> Taken to wife

(1.2.1-14)

the Ur-Hamlet has the more prosaic:

> although our brother's death is still deep in all our memories, and
> although custom requires us to go into deep mourning and hold no state
> pageants or ceremonials we have thought best to nevertheless change
> our sombre funeral suits for suits of crimson, purple and scarlet because
> my late brother's widow has become my most dear consort and wife.
> (Morgan, 16)

The Ur-Hamlet duplicates certain scenes and speeches from
Shakespeare's play, beginning with the encounter with the ghost on the
battlements and including the episode of the players, Hamlet's chance
to kill the king at prayer, the stabbing of Polonius – called Corambis
after the 1603 *Hamlet* quarto – in the queen's bedroom, the fencing
match and the poisoned foil. Hamlet dies urging Horatio to take the
Danish crown to Norway and to 'Fortembras'. Horatio has the final
sententia, but it is, like the rest of the play, awkwardly phrased: 'A King
who seizes the crown by treachery / Shall in the end have nothing for
himself but scorn and mockery' (Morgan, 226).

Morgan, like other contemporary critics of the play, judges the Ur-
Hamlet to be inferior and therefore non-Shakespearean. Or at least he
hopes this is the case, as he concludes his introduction:

> it seems the tares must always grow with the wheat. Prince Hamlet
> addresses to poor Ophelia a remark so excessively coarse and vile that,
> even in the Warwickshire dialect in which it is smothered, it is unprint-
> able for the popular reader! Let us hope that this passage is a survival
> from the lost ur-Hamlet! (Morgan, xxvii)

The purported existence of the Ur-Hamlet functions here as a guarantor
of the aesthetic purity of the Shakespearean text: on it, and its unknown
author, can be placed the blame for anything which cannot be admitted
Shakespearean. Shakespeare emerges from the exercise of reconstruction as paradoxically both a greater and a lesser playwright, able to transform the leaden stuff of his source into the pure gold of his dramatic art,
but simultaneously unable to erase all traces of his base material.

That the search for the Ur-Hamlet may reveal something about the
play itself is suggested by Terence Hawkes. In his essay 'Telmah' –
which is, of course, 'Hamlet' backwards – Hawkes notes 'the extent to
which looking backwards, re-vision, or re-interpretation, the running of
events over again out of their time and sequence, ranks, in effect, as a fundamental aspect of *Hamlet*'.[18] He notes that 'subsequence, posteriority,
these are the substantive modes of the opening'; and indeed, these are the
key terms in the bibliographic discussion of the Ur-Hamlet. The textual

history of Shakespeare's play is thus highly pertinent to its own recursive mode, in which the past is interrogated and reformed as Hamlet meditates on his relationship with an earlier Hamlet, his father. The case of the Ur-Hamlet is also, however, an illuminating case study in the methods of traditional bibliography. In its stress on 'the material properties of the book',[19] the New Bibliography sought to return to the idealised and immaterial originals of Shakespeare's plays, stripping away the interventions of printed publication to arrive at a manuscript. In its retrogressive search for the Ur-Hamlet, the hypothetical nature and the seductive, primogenitary allure of all such inferred textual origins and originals are laid bare. The various accounts of the Ur-Hamlet by eminent textual scholars seem to be entirely learned, entirely rational and entirely plausible, and yet their foundations are extraordinarily insubstantial. Its presumed crudeness highlights Shakespeare's artistry; its bloodthirstiness explains some vestiges of sanguinariness. The Ur-Hamlet is at once inferior to the greatness of *Hamlet*, and a prerequisite of that greatness. As this textual foil does not exist, it has been invented. As a scapegoat it can take on itself those qualities from which bibliographers want to dissociate Shakespeare: it functions as an ongoing, even a necessary supplement to the canonic centrality of *Hamlet* itself. Like Henry Gray's extinct animal reconstructed from a single bone, the Ur-Hamlet is a creature of fantasy dressed in the pseudo-science of late Victorian bibliographic invention and of Bardolatry. It is a ratiocinative aberration, as if the Ur-Hamlet's near contemporary Sherlock Holmes had spun an entirely fallacious deduction on a couple of faint clues. A ghost of *Hamlet* like the spirit of Hamlet's father, the Ur-Hamlet, 'th'extravagant and erring spirit' (1.1.135) enjoys an uncanny hold over the textual history of Shakespeare's play. Hamlet's words conferring a textual authority to the Ghost's version of the past could stand for the bibliographic efforts to invent the play's own ghostly Ur-Hamlet: 'and thy commandment all alone shall live / Within the book and matter of my brain' (1.5.101–2). Hamlet, and *Hamlet*, it seems, both need their ghosts.

Notes

1 Ronald B. McKerrow (ed.), *The Works of Thomas Nashe* (Oxford, Basil Blackwell, 1958), p. 315.

2 Stanley Wells et al, *William Shakespeare: A Textual Companion* (Oxford, Clarendon, 1986), p. 396.

3 For the argument that Q1 of *Hamlet*, printed by Valentine Simmes in 1603 as THE / *Tragicall Historie of* / HAMLET / *Prince of Denmarke*, represents the Ur-Hamlet, see Eric

Sams, 'Taboo or not taboo? The text, dating and authorship of *Hamlet*, 1589–1623', *Hamlet Studies*, 10 (1988), pp. 12–46. In her chapter 'Bad taste and bad *Hamlet*' in *Unediting the Renaissance: Shakespeare, Milton, and Marlowe* (London, Routledge, 1996), Leah S. Marcus has discussed the ways in which textual bibliography has derogated Q1 as corrupt, 'bad' and fraudulent, at once a 'beckoning ghost' (p. 138) and 'an embarrassment, a potential blot on the reputation of Shakespeare' (p. 134). This provocative analysis of Q1 gives it a weighted bibliographic function similar to that I am proposing here for the fictive Ur-Hamlet, although the absence from Q1 of the line 'Hamlet revenge', cited by Lodge in 1596 in one of the major sources for the existence of an early *Hamlet* play, seems to me to undermine the case for eliding Q1 and the Ur-Hamlet. It is the imaginary status of the Ur-Hamlet that is of interest here.

4 Frederick S. Boas (ed.), *The Works of Thomas Kyd* (Oxford, Clarendon, 1901), p. xlvii.

5 John Corbin, *The Elizabethan Hamlet: A Study of the Sources, and of Shakespeare's Environment, to show that the Mad Scenes had a Comic Aspect now Ignored* (London, Elkin Mathews, and New York, Charles Scribner's Sons, 1895), p. 3. Further references are included parenthetically in the text.

6 Robert Russell Benedict, *The Mystery of Hamlet Prince of Denmark* (Philadelphia, Lippincott, 1910), p. 5. Further references are included parenthetically in the text.

7 Hugh Grady, *The Modernist Shakespeare: Critical Texts in a Material World* (Oxford, Clarendon, 1991), p. 51.

8 J. M. Robertson, *The Problem of 'Hamlet'* (London, Allen & Unwin, 1919), p. 11. Further references are included parenthetically in the text.

9 H. H. Furness, *A New Variorum Edition of Shakespeare: Hamlet*, vol. 1 (Philadelphia, Lippincott, 1918), p. vii.

10 J. Dover Wilson, *The Copy for 'Hamlet' 1603 and The 'Hamlet' Transcript 1593* (London, Alexander Moring, 1918), p. 25. Further references are included parenthetically in the text.

11 F. G. Fleay, *Shakespeare Manual* (1876, repr. AMS Press, New York, 1970), p. 108.

12 Henry David Gray, 'Reconstruction of a lost play', *Philological Quarterly*, 7 (1928), p. 254. Further references are included parenthetically in the text.

13 Geoffrey Bullough, *Narrative and Dramatic Sources of Shakespeare*, vol. 7 (London, Routledge & Kegan Paul, 1975), p. 16. Further references are included parenthetically in the text.

14 Boas (ed.), *Works*, p. xlv.

15 Fredson Thayer Bowers, *Elizabethan Revenge Tragedy 1587–1642* (Gloucester, MA, Peter Smith, 1959), Preface, n. p. Further references are included parenthetically in the text.

16 Marjorie Garber, *Shakespeare's Ghost Writers: Literature as Uncanny Causality* (London, Methuen, 1987), p. 129.

17 Appleton Morgan (intr.), *Hamlet and the Ur-Hamlet* (New York, The Shakespeare Society of New York, 1908), p. xix. Further references are included parenthetically in the text.

18 Terence Hawkes, *That Shakespeherian Rag: Essays on a Critical Process* (London, Methuen, 1986), p. 96.

19 Margreta de Grazia, 'The essential Shakespeare and the material book', *Textual Practice*, 2 (1988), p. 70.

Texts and textualities: a Shakespearean history

Andrew Murphy

What kind of a thing is this concept or episteme called 'text', and how can its properties and its histories be known?[1]

the text is more than just the shadow or trace of a thought already shaped; in a literate culture, the textual structures that have evolved over the centuries *determine* thought almost as powerfully as the primal structure that shapes all expression, language.[2]

communications technologies are ... acidic to prior modes of traditional cultures.[3]

In his 1924 British Academy Shakespeare lecture, E. K. Chambers sought to defend the unitary Shakespeare text against what he perceived as two critical approaches which served to undermine it. In the first instance, he opposed the stress of 'disintegrators' (such as F. G. Fleay and J. M. Robertson) on collaboration as the normative mode of Renaissance theatrical composition and, in the second, he resisted John Dover Wilson's notion of 'continuous copy', which conceived of theatrical texts as mobile, shifting entities, their surface traversed by diverse hands. The issues at stake were, for Chambers, stark and clear, as we can see from his concluding comment on Wilson's theory. Noting the mutational character of the envisaged 'continuous' text, Chambers observes that it constitutes 'a perpetual form; an evanescent υλη! Who is the author of such a play? We cannot tell. The soul gets a "dusty answer", when hot on that particular certainty.'[4] The real problem with such approaches for Chambers is thus that they serve to render the question of authorship uncertain. Agency multiplies; authority becomes dispersed; the unitary text dissolves in the interstices between complex sets of social relationships.[5]

No one would now claim that either the disintegrators or Wilson were wholly right and that Chambers was wholly wrong. Nevertheless, we can find certain interesting resonances between the broad general outlines of the positions Chambers opposed and some of the theoretical issues raised by more recent generations of textual critics. Thus Gary Taylor, for instance, offers Thomas Middleton as the paradigmatic instance of the Renaissance writer who 'provides us with an inescapably collaborative model of textual production', suggesting that it is, in part, the imposing integrity of the Shakespeare First Folio volume itself that has promoted and sustained the notion of Shakespeare as a unique, isolated, singular author:

> the massive authority of the Shakespeare Folio has tended to impose an autonomous model – despite overwhelming evidence to the contrary, both within the Shakespeare canon itself, and in literary history generally. Attempts to identify collaborators in the Shakespeare canon have been characterized as 'disintegration' – [a] spatial metaphor, which takes the sheer physical oneness of the many bound copies of the 1623 volume as an accurate reification of an ideal authorial wholeness. Middleton's canon, by contrast, is dispersed among many volumes, making the editorial study of authorship – and hence, of collaboration – not a dubious indulgence but a clear necessity.[6]

Taylor has emphasised this point in a practical way by including some texts traditionally regarded as being proprietorially 'Shakespearean' – *Macbeth*, *Timon of Athens* and *Measure for Measure* – in his Oxford edition of the complete works of Thomas Middleton. Jeffrey Masten has broadened this argument, suggesting that

> in a way that has not been fully recognized or conceptualized by scholars trained to organize material within post-Enlightenment paradigms of individuality, authorship, and textual property, collaboration was a prevalent mode of textual production in the sixteenth and seventeenth centuries, only eventually displaced by the mode of singular authorship with which we are more familiar. This is especially true ... of texts associated with early modern theatres.

For Masten, 'collaboration was the Renaissance English theatre's dominant mode of textual production'.[7]

We might also, of course, look at Renaissance collaboration from a broader perspective. Renaissance playwrights certainly worked together to assemble texts – the *Booke of Sir Thomas More* can be taken as an exemplary instance of this process in action. But we can see certain Renaissance texts as being 'collaborative' in a more general sense also. The Renaissance playtext often functions as a kind of composite of materials configured and reconstituted into a new entity.[8] One thinks, for instance, in the case of the Shakespeare canon, of the passages from Plutarch refashioned into iambic pentameter; of chronicles mined for material for the histories; of classical stories reworked into new plays; of the recycling of materials and themes already treated by contemporary fellow writers and dramatists, whether English or European. The Renaissance playtext is thus not a bounded, unique, singular entity, but rather is permeable, often having other texts woven through its fabric.

I will return, in due course, to the issue of the 'permeability' of the text and its significance within general Renaissance conceptions of textuality. For the moment, however, I wish to turn my attention to the second point of resistance offered in Chambers's lecture. Wilson's notion of 'continuous copy' may well, as Chambers argues, be unsupported by direct evidence. But the broader point which his theory implies – that the Renaissance dramatic text is always located within a general cultural matrix – is surely valid. As Paul Werstine has argued (and as Peter Stallybrass argues in this volume in relation to the question of the reassignment of speeches), the texts of the Shakespeare canon 'were open to penetration and alteration not only by Shakespeare himself and by his fellow actors but also by multiple theatrical and extra-theatrical scriveners, by theatrical annotators, adapters and revisers (who might cut or add), by censors, and by compositors'.[9] Indeed, we might say that many of the interventions which Werstine signals here constitute the *conditions of existence* of the Renaissance playtext, since the text's very ontological status depends upon them. In offering this argument I am, of course, drawing heavily on Jerome McGann's 'social theory of texts'. In the seminal statement of his position – the *Critique of Modern Textual Criticism* – McGann argues that the initiation of literary authority

> takes place in a necessary and integral historical environment of great complexity. Most immediately ... it takes place within the conventions and limits which exist for the purpose of generating and supporting literary production. In all periods those institutions adapt to the special needs of individuals, including the needs of authors (some of whom are more comfortable with institutions than others). But whatever special arrangements are made, the essential fact remains: *literary works are not produced without arrangements of some sort.*[10]

It may well, indeed, be the case, as McGann argues here, that structures of production and dissemination are necessary to the very existence of *all* literary works, but we can say that such structures are indisputably essential to works of dramatic fiction, since, without the institution of the theatre and the greater social and administrative networks within which it is located and permitted to function, the play as a work of drama simply has no existence. In this sense, the play is necessarily a social entity – a fact recognised more than three decades ago by M. C. Bradbrook, when she observed of the 'interlude' (the form which, as she puts it, served to 'sire' Elizabethan drama) that it was 'not made to be read but to be performed' and concluded that

> Elizabethan drama was likewise an embodied art, and existed for performance. To treat it as book-art is to do it great violence. By a 'play' it is probable that no Elizabethan would have meant the script or 'book', but always an *event*, the play-in-being, the enacted mime in which players and audience shared. This deep and natural immersion in performance, this assumption of a common activity, was the most precious inheritance from the theatre of the Middle Ages.[11]

Bradbrook's emphasis on the play as a performative occasion, as an event, serves usefully to highlight not just the social and broadly collaborative nature of the Renaissance playtext, but also its distinctive textual status. The drama in this period was primarily an oral form, in the sense that its primary mode of presentation and reception was the declaimed performance. But it was also, as Bradbrook indicates, 'oral' in another sense, in that its roots lay in the pre-print and, to some extent, non-literate traditions of medieval drama and artforms. Thus, as Leah Marcus has observed, 'English theatrical culture was [in the Renaissance] a milieu in which oral and written forms jostled up against each other and competed for the allegiance of audiences'[12] and George T. Wright has noted that

> Shakespeare's plays ... appear at a moment in Western culture when drama still has strong ties to oral traditions but has begun to establish its claim to reception as an art of letters. Shakespeare's apparently faint interest in publishing his plays suggests that his art worked mainly from the stage and that the language we find in the plays ... had its primary reality for actors and audience as sounded words.[13]

As Wright indicates here, the Renaissance play can be shown to share certain qualities in common with artforms produced within oral societies. Thus, for instance, writing of Yugoslav oral poetry, John Miles Foley has observed that

The history of such oral traditional poetry is not a search for stemmata or prescriptions for *termini ad quem*, but rather of the dynamic and essentially timeless shape-shifting of a living, evolving multiform of a tale or cycle of tales. Just as no one performance is 'original' or archetypal but only an avatar of an ongoing process, so the structures within the performance are also momentary realizations of multiforms.

Foley goes on to note that 'we are always dealing with occurrences of multiforms and never directly with the multiform itself.'[14] The quality that Foley isolates here as characteristic of the oral artform is precisely the quality that Chambers fears as being indicated by Wilson's 'continuous' theatrical text. In neither case can a stable entity be isolated and assigned to a unique proprietor. The text shifts and mutates over time, as it is passed on among the *guslari* of Foley's contemporary Serbia, or mediated through the complex set of Renaissance theatrical agents identified by Werstine ('actors ... scriveners ... annotators, adapters and revisers ... censors', etc.).

Of course, the drama of the period was not 'oral' in the strictest sense of being circulated within a society that lacked a written culture. The Renaissance play is always, in the first instance at least, a written entity before it becomes an oral performance. But, as Walter Ong has argued, writing in this period is itself still deeply inflected by the culture of orality. Thus Ong observes of scribal culture that 'manuscripts, with their glosses or marginal comments (which often got worked into the text in subsequent copies) were in dialogue with the world outside their own borders. They remained closer to the give-and-take of oral expression'. He further argues that

> Manuscript culture [took] intertextuality for granted. Still tied to the commonplace tradition of the old oral world, it deliberately created texts out of other texts, borrowing, adapting, sharing the common, originally oral, formulas and themes, even though it worked them up into fresh literary forms impossible without writing.[15]

The connections between manuscript culture's conception of textuality and the conception of textuality indicated within the culture of Renaissance drama should, by now, be clear. As we have already noted, the Renaissance playtext is open and appropriative. Like Ong's manuscript, it creates texts out of other texts, borrowing, adapting and sharing common formulae and themes. And just as the scribe frequently enters into dialogue with the text being copied and thus establishes a kind of 'collaborative' relationship with the text, so too is the

Renaissance playtext in a variety of different ways the work of diverse hands.

In its written form, then, the Renaissance play is permeable to and symbiotic with neighbouring texts and contexts. As a performance event, it is mobile, fluid and subject to change. As Leah Marcus notes of Shakespeare's plays:

> rather than flowing effortlessly and magically from Shakespeare's mind onto the unalterable fixity of paper, the plays were from the beginning provisional, amenable to alterations by the playwright or others, coming to exist over time in a number of versions, all related, but none of them an original in the pristine sense promised by Heminge and Condell [in the preliminaries to the First Folio].[16]

Renaissance dramatic textuality – in the broadest sense – is thus predicated on an understanding of the text as unbounded, multiplicitous, malleable, adaptive and mercurial. These are all qualities which mark the text as a product of what we can characterise (drawing on Raymond Williams's classic formulation) as a culture in which oral and scribal values are, if no longer dominant, then certainly strongly residual. But this is also, of course, a culture in which alternative textual values are clearly emergent. As Martin Elsky has noted, 'the Renaissance must be seen as occupying a unique "marginal position" ... between oral and manuscript culture on the one side and typographic culture on the other'.[17] Printing had, of course, been in existence in Europe for more than a hundred years by the time the professional drama began to emerge in England but, as Elizabeth Eisenstein has observed, it took about a century for the contours of print culture to become solidly established.[18] In the earliest years of the theatre, print was very much a secondary channel of distribution. As Jeffrey Masten has noted, printed texts

> work[ed] in this culture as the silent surrogates for the ostensible thing itself, theatrical performance. The emphasis in these publications is not on a 'reading' text (that is, a work authorized by its putative status as dramatic literature) but rather on a text that functions as a record of – *reconstitution* of – a particular theatrical performance a reader/consumer may have heard of or attended.[19]

It has been argued that in some instances the printed text was no more than a way for a theatre company to raise extra capital in times of financial stringency.[20] For all that, the new culture of print did effect radical changes in the way in which textuality itself was conceived in the

Renaissance – changes whose impact was felt as much in the field of drama as elsewhere.[21]

Marshall McLuhan was one of the first to recognise that '[t]he invention of typography … provid[ed] the first repeatable commodity, the first assembly-line, and the first mass-production'.[22] Walter Ong has built on this insight, observing that print 'embedded the word itself deeply in the manufacturing process and made it into a kind of commodity', thus creating 'a new sense of the private ownership of words' (118). As a result, he observes, 'the old communal oral world … split into privately claimed freeholdings' (131). The mobile, multiplicitous, unbounded Renaissance text does not fit easily within this new dispensation which tends, as Ong puts it, 'to feel a work as "closed", set off from other works, a unit in itself' (133). The conflict prompted by the dramatic text's positioning at this juncture of a residual oral culture and an emergent print culture can clearly be seen in the publication record of texts from the Shakespeare canon from the final decade of the sixteenth century through the opening decades of the seventeenth century. Many of the texts which later generations have taken for granted as singular coherent entities appear in this period in multiple versions, some of them drastically divergent from each other. We have learned over the centuries to sort and hierarchise these versions, to discount some of them as 'bad' texts, to promote others as the genuine article as Shakespeare finally intended it.[23] In this sense, we have engaged in a similar process of privileging to that which Jack Goody sees occurring in societies where traditional oral artforms come to be encoded in written and print forms:

> One version recorded on a particular occasion (and about whose status … one can say very little) tends to become the model by which others are judged. In the Bagre case [in the LoDagaa society of west Africa], the production of variants has not ceased but these are often now seen against the background of my written version. Not only seen, but judged, for the written version acquires a truth value that no single oral version possesses.[24]

Rather than judging the early variant texts in this way and sorting them into categories of good and bad, true and false, authentic and derivative, we might well be better served – given the historical conditions of the constitution of Renaissance textuality that we have just been exploring – to see these individual printed versions as providing particular arrested moments of textual formation, in which the fluid text, traversed by a range of diverse inputs, has become fixed by the regime of print. Such publications are thus, to draw on a metaphor which Graham Caie deploys elsewhere in this collection, like snap-shots of the moving text, holding it still in one of its shifting forms.

Print, we can thus say, arrests the mobile text, securing it in a static moment.[25] In the liminal phase where the regimes of print and orality/chirography assert competing claims, the fixity that print offers is often multiple. But as Ong has observed, 'print is comfortable only with finality' (132), and so, as print culture begins to achieve a position of ascendancy, such multiplicity is rejected in favour of a search for the singular, the definitive. As far as the Shakespeare text is concerned, this process begins as early as 1623, when we find the First Folio text staking a claim to authority by declaring that the singular texts it provides are 'absolute in their numbers, as [Shakespeare] con-ceived the[m]', thus centralising the author as the unique source of a unique – and definitively stabilised – meaning.[26]

There is, of course, a certain irony in the fact that the signatories to the First Folio preface should have been John Heminge and Henry Condell – Shakespeare's acting colleagues from the King's Men – close collabo-rators, we might say, in the shifting performative life of the text. As the Shakespeare editorial tradition got underway in the opening decades of the eighteenth century, however, Alexander Pope savaged the First Folio, attacking it specifically because it was a text assembled by actors and thus was, he believed, grossly tainted by actorly concerns.[27] Pope charges the actors with adding to and deleting from the text in order to serve their own theatrical convenience. He observes, for instance, that

> a number of beautiful passages which are extant in the first single edi-tions, are omitted in this: as it seems, without any other reason, than their willingness to shorten some scenes: These men (as it was said of *Procrustes*) either lopping, or stretching an Author, to make him just fit for their Stage.[28]

As Gary Taylor has noted, throughout his edition, Pope 'repressed the theatricality of the plays in favor of their readerliness'[29] and this anti-theatrical bias was reaffirmed in the work of Pope's successors, with Johnson, for instance, in his *Proposals* of 1756, famously complaining that, once written, the texts of the plays had been

> immediately copied for the actors, and multiplied by transcript after transcript, vitiated by the blunders of the penman, or changed by the affectation of the player; perhaps enlarged to introduce a jest, or mutilated to shorten the representation; and printed at last without the

concurrence of the author, without the consent of the proprietor, from compilation made by chance or by stealth out of the separate parts written for the theatre.[30]

The hostile anti-theatricalism of the eighteenth-century editors can be seen as indicative of an increasing tendency to marginalise the multiplicitous oral and social lineages of the text, refashioning it as an isolable and wholly 'literary' object, assimilable to and intelligible within the emerging codes of an increasingly print-centred culture. Alvin Kernan has stressed the extent to which this shift in the way textuality was conceived was part of a broader reconceptualisation of the entire literary system which occurred over the course of the eighteenth century, whereby '[a]n older system of polite or courtly letters – primarily oral, aristocratic, amateur, authoritarian, court-centered – was swept away ... and gradually replaced by a new print-based, market centered, democratic literary system'.[31]

As Mark Rose has indicated, this rise of a print-based textual culture and literary system contributed to and was facilitated by the concomitant emergence and evolution of a new understanding of copyright during the course of the eighteenth century. It is notable, in the present context, that the first piece of English copyright legislation should have been passed in 1709 – the year in which the first eighteenth-century edition of Shakespeare (Nicholas Rowe's) was published by Tonson. Rowe's edition seeks to systematise the text, reducing its pluralistic codes to uniformity by, for example, standardising character names and locations and imposing consistency in act and scene divisions. As Rose has argued, the entire copyright debate and the legislation which issued from it served similarly to effect a general cohering of the text, stabilising it as the unique product of a unique author and cutting it free from the interlaced matrix of social and productive relations within which it had emerged:

The proponents of perpetual copyright focused on the author's labor. Those who argued against it focused on the results of the labor, the work. Thus the two sides established their positions by approaching the issue from opposite directions. Yet, however approached, the question centered on the same pair of concepts, the 'author' and the 'work,' a person and a thing. The complex social process of literary production consisting of relations between writers and patrons, writers and booksellers, booksellers and readers was rendered peripheral.[32] Abstracting the author of the work from the social fabric in this way contributed to a tendency already implicit in printing technology to reify the literary composition, to treat the text as a thing.[33]

[interested] in establishing a text; few of their notes concern anything but textual questions. Thus they may be credited with opening up a space for purely textual study'.[39] As Werstine further notes, the space thus opened was occupied, in the opening decades of the twentieth century, by the New Bibliographers, whose intense focusing on the strictly textual served further to reinforce the disjunction between the isolated text and its oral and social contexts.

In contrast to a great number of their predecessors from Pope to Sidney Lee,[40] the New Bibliographers defended the First Folio as, in the main, a substantially reliable text, rejecting, as John Dover Wilson puts it, the 'gloomy [doctrine] of the old criticism' that 'Heminge and Condell were either knaves in league with Jaggard to hoodwink a gullible public, or else fools who did not know how to pen a preface'.[41] But the defence of Heminge and Condell mounted by the New Bibliographers did not indicate a new affirmation of the actorly or social text. In fact, the new emphasis on the fundamental soundness of F1 signalled, if anything, the onset of a more comprehensive, multifaceted attack on the oral and social dimension of the Shakespeare canon. As Hugh Grady has demonstrated, the New Bibliographic investment in F1 was all of a piece with Chambers's project in his Shakespeare lecture.[42] Like Chambers, the New Bibliographers sought to oppose the disintegrationists by reconfirming Shakespeare as the solitary author of a coherent body of unique proprietary texts assembled in the Folio in good faith by Shakespeare's colleagues.[43]

The rejection of disintegration was not, however, the only reason for the New Bibliographers' investment in F1, as we can see by examining some of the central textual analyses advanced by A. W. Pollard and W. W. Greg. Pollard's ground-breaking 1909 defence of F1 was predicated on his (in)famous division of the early quarto editions into the 'good' and the 'bad'. The 'good' quartos he described as constituting a 'family [with] no single black sheep in it ... every member of it [being] of good average morals and utility'. Of the 'bad' quartos, he noted that 'any desirable amount of scorn and contempt' might be applied to them.[44] Pollard thus both carries forward and systematises here the traditional editorial quest for the singular, authorially sanctioned text. Within the terms of his analysis, any texts from a broader social context which cannot specifically be tied directly to the figure of the author must be rejected not just as 'inauthentic' (as Malone might have put it), but, indeed, as in some sense morally repugnant – to be repressed into a kind of textual unconscious.[45]

For W. W. Greg, Pollard's *Shakespeare Folios and Quartos* once again 'marked the opening of a new era in Shakespearian studies' and Greg himself certainly explored further the possibilities indicated by his colleague's work.[46] In the year following Pollard's book, Greg published his *Shakespeare's Merry Wives of Windsor 1602*, in which he offered the first suggestion of a possible account of how the texts characterised by Pollard as 'bad quartos' might have come into being. Greg proposed that the basis of the First Quarto *Merry Wives* was a reconstruction of the play from memory by the actor who had played the part of the Host, working in collaboration with the printer, John Busby. Greg's original suggestion here was, of course, subsequently worked up into a general theory of 'memorial reconstruction'.[47] As Laurie Maguire has stressed, subsequent reductive deployments of this term have often served to mask the complexity of Greg's original formulation. Maguire breaks down Greg's analysis of the imagined process of assemblage and transmission of Q1 *Merry Wives* into a total of thirteen distinct stages. It is worth quoting her account at some length, to indicate both the complexity of the projected process and the extent to which it indicates the variety of different influences which are imagined as shaping the text at every stage:

1) Shakespeare writes *The Merry Wives of Windsor* 'substantially as we know it', but with greater prominence accorded the plot in which the Host is cozened of his horses. 2) Minor cuts are made for performance. 3) It becomes necessary to remove the horse-stealing plot, and the task of altering the play is entrusted to another playwright in the Chamberlain's Men; Act 5 is totally recast and two alternative endings supplied (for public and Court performance) ... 4) The actors are lazy and do not learn the new dialogue properly. 5) Furthermore, resentful of the extra work, the actors deliberately introduce allusions to excised material. 6) The Chamberlain's Men are in disgrace because of topical scandal attached to the original version of the play ... and they exile themselves from London. 7) The 'hired man' who played the Host remains in the Capital. 8) An 'unscrupulous stationer' suborns the hired man-Host to recreate the play. 9) In the first place the Host had learned his part imperfectly and by ear. 10) The Host possibly dictates the play to someone in the stationers' office. 11) The Company further alters the original play ... 12) Later, Shakespeare revises the phrasing of the earlier scenes ... 13) After Shakespeare's death, in preparation for the First Folio ... this playhouse copy was 'prepared for the press with such care as the circumstances seemed to demand'. (*Shakespearean Suspect Texts*, 75–6)

What is significant here, from the perspective of the present analysis, is that what Greg maps out is a narrative in which a complex network of factors serves to produce a range of different textual versions over the course of the early lifetime of *Merry Wives* – seven of the thirteen stages identified by Maguire can be seen as producing some sort of change to the play.[48] One of these variant versions makes its way into print in 1602 – a version conceived as being heavily reliant for its genesis and dissemination both on a complex of social factors and on a set of oral procedures (reconstruction and reconfiguration based on memories of a particular enacted performance).

Greg's 'memorial reconstruction' is thus, in a way, not unlike the 'generative reconstruction' that Jack Goody has identified as occurring within the cultural transmission process in oral societies (179–80). Writing of the Bagre tradition of the LoDagaa, he observes that since there is 'no single keeper of the oral tradition, the Bagre expands, develops and contracts with each ceiling, in a "generative", "creative" way that characterizes much oral activity of a "literary" kind' (189). The difference between Greg and Goody, however, is that the whole point of anatomising this narrative of 'generative reconstruction', from Greg's perspective, is not to demonstrate the composite factors which necessarily serve to make and remake variant textualities in the Renaissance, but rather to mark such textual reconstructions as aberrant (rather as the Bagre variations which differ from Goody's own transcription have come to be seen as aberrant). Social engagement and oral lineages are, in themselves, determining markers of illegitimacy for Greg. In his view, the multiplicitous, shifting social text is an 'errant' text, wandering into complexes of variation and multiplicity, compounding error with error. Like Spenser's wandering monster, *Error*, this process produces a malignant multiplication of textuality ('Her vomit full of bookes and papers was, / With loathly frogs and toades, which eyes did lack'[49]). Like the Red Crosse Knight, the editor faces the difficult duty of cutting through this multiplicity, to pledge fidelity to a textual Una, a singular Truth.

Thus we can say of two of the pillars of the emergent New Bibliographic orthodoxy – the categorisation of the quartos into good and bad, and the theory of memorial reconstruction – that both aimed at setting the singular text on firm footing by first isolating and then discounting and invalidating the greater oral and social history of the text. In a way, this tendency within New Bibliography is none too surprising, given the movement's intense dedication to the world of print.

As Greg puts it in *The Editorial Problem in Shakespeare*, the 'fresh approach to textual problems' which New Bibliography offered was distinguished by the fact that it laid 'stress upon the material processes of book-production, concerning itself primarily with the fortunes of the actual pieces of paper on which the texts were written or printed, and the vagaries of scribes and compositors'.[50]

The deep ironies of the 'materialism' espoused by the New Bibliographic movement have been much commented on over the past several years, as it has been noted that, for all their interest in the mechanics and particularities of the printed text, the New Bibliographers ultimately subordinated that material physical entity to a notional authorial ideal which they imagined as lying behind what they famously and repeatedly referred to as the 'veil of print'.[51] The ultimate end that New Bibliography held in view was the idealised realm where the author's work could float free not only from its multi-faceted social context, but even from its very vehicle of transmission – the printed text. In a sense, we can view this vision as the culmination of a long tradition, whereby the culture of print, fully ascendant in the Western textual tradition, denies even its own social and material context as a productive force. The autonomous author is brought to transcend not just his or her own social moment, but even the very means of production whereby the text enters into circulation within the regime of print. *Ars est celare artem*: the end, at the last, disavows the means.

In our own time, of course, we have experienced a further shift in textual culture – a shift characterised by, as George Landow puts it, a rejection of 'some of the fundamental assumptions of the information technology that [has] increasingly dominated – and some would say largely created – Western thought since Gutenberg'.[52] In Landow's view, the advent of computer-based textuality 'leads to an entirely new conception of text' (15) – a conception 'which demands new forms of reading and writing [and] has the promise radically to reconceive our conceptions of text, author, intellectual property, and a host of other issues ranging from the nature of the self to education'.[53]

As Landow himself argues, drawing on Ong and McLuhan, and as Graham Caie registers elsewhere in this volume, this new electronic regime has many features in common with the textual dispensation of the pre-print (or emergent print) era.[54] We have, for instance, noted in this chapter that the Renaissance text is often woven from a range of prior textual materials, and Landow argues that the electronic text likewise 'blurs the distinction between what is "inside" and what is "outside" a text'. Thus, in electronic textuality

> As an individual lexia loses its physical and intellectual separation from others when linked electronically to them, it finds itself dispersed into them. The necessary contextuality and intertextuality produced by situating individual reading units within a network of easily navigable pathways weaves texts, including those by different authors and those in nonverbal media, tightly together. (*Hypertext*, pp. 63, 53)

Likewise, Jay David Bolter notes that the tendency towards fixity which characterises the printed text tends not to be shared by the electronic text, which, he argues,

> is the first text in which elements of meaning, of structure, and of visual display are fundamentally unstable. Unlike the printing press or the medieval codex, the computer does not require that any aspect of writing be determined in advance for the whole life of a text. This restlessness is inherent in a technology that records information by collecting for fractions of a second evanescent electrons at tiny junctions of silicon and metal. All information, all data, in the computer world is a kind of controlled movement, and so the natural inclination of computer writing is to change, to grow, and finally to disappear.[55]

Peter Donaldson spells out some of the implications of electronic and multimedia reproduction for the Shakespeare text, when he argues (drawing on his experience as director of the Shakespeare Interactive Archive) that

> Multimedia hypertext reconfigures the relationship between an authoritative cultural *source* (a Shakespeare play) and its belated, aesthetically and culturally divergent contemporary *versions*, changing the ways we think about such matters as 'the original text' and its reproduction in 'authoritative' versions and productions. Much that has been written about hypertext assumes that the computer will be an ally of the contemporary literary theories that unseat the 'author', spread meaning out into a web of traces and associations, and change the relation between cultural center and margin.[56]

As Gary Taylor cautions us in his contribution to this volume, however, the future may not be quite as rosy as theoretically informed enthusiasts of electronic textuality would wish to believe. Taylor notes the very real difficulties associated with computer textuality – including problems of obsolescence, selectivity, access and cost. Beyond this, we might note that, as we have seen in the case of the printing press, all technologies bring with them regimes of constraint as well as of liberation. Don Idhe's comment on the emergent scientific technologies of the Renaissance (principally the telescope) might well be of relevance here: 'what is revealed within the aura of fascination tends to override what is often less clear, the dimension of what is *concealed* or reduced by the instrument-enhanced vision.'[57] We are still, at this time, caught in the 'aura of fascination' of the electronic text and the possibilities which it indicates for a world beyond the constraints of print. What remains to be established, however, is the exact parameters of what this new regime of textuality by its nature conceals or reduces. This is a territory that future historians of textuality must address themselves to delineating.[58]

Notes

1 D. C. Greetham, 'Textual forensics', *PMLA*, 111:1 (Jan. 1996), p. 47.

2 George P. Landow and Paul Delany, 'Hypertext, hypermedia and literary studies: the state of the art', in Delany and Landow (eds), *Hypermedia and Literary Studies* (Cambridge, MA, MIT Press, 1991), p. 3.

3 Don Idhe, *Postphenomenology: Essays in the Postmodern Context* (Evanston, IL, Northwestern University Press, 1993), p. 45.

4 E. K. Chambers, 'The disintegration of Shakespeare', *Proceedings of the British Academy 1924–1925* (London, British Academy/Oxford University Press, 1925), p. 104.

5 On Chambers's response to the Disintegrators, see Leah S. Marcus, *Puzzling Shakespeare: Local Reading and Its Discontents* (Berkeley, University of California Press, 1988), ch. 1.

6 Gary Taylor, 'The Renaissance and the end of editing', in George Bornstein and Ralph G. Williams (eds), *Palimpsest: Editorial Theory in the Humanities* (Ann Arbor, University of Michigan Press, 1993), p. 135.

7 Jeffrey Masten, *Textual Intercourse: Collaboration, Authorship, and Sexualities in Renaissance Drama* (Cambridge, Cambridge University Press, 1997), p. 4.

8 One might, of course, say 'bricolage' rather than 'composite', especially bearing in mind Gayatri Spivak's clarification of Levi-Strauss's conception of the *bricoleur* as someone who 'makes do with things *that were meant perhaps for other ends*' (translator's preface to Jacques Derrida, *Of Grammatology* (Baltimore, Johns Hopkins University Press, 1976), p. xix; emphasis added).

9 'Narratives about printed Shakespeare texts: "foul papers" and "bad" quartos', *Shakespeare Quarterly*, 41 (1990), p. 86.

10 Jerome J. McGann, *A Critique of Modern Textual Criticism* (Chicago, University of Chicago Press, 1983; reissued Charlottesville, University of Virginia Press, 1992), p. 48 (emphasis added). For a useful critique of McGann's work, and of other 'social theory' approaches, see G. Thomas Tanselle, 'Textual criticism and literary sociology', *Studies in Bibliography*, 44 (1991), pp. 83–143.

11 M. C. Bradbrook, *The Rise of the Common Player: A Study of Actor and Society in Shakespeare's England* (Cambridge, MA, Harvard University Press, 1964), p. 38.

12 Leah S. Marcus, *Unediting the Renaissance: Shakespeare, Marlowe, Milton* (London, Routledge, 1996), p. 155. I am deeply indebted to the work of Leah Marcus throughout this section of the chapter.

13 George T. Wright, 'An almost oral art: Shakespeare's language on stage and page', *Shakespeare Quarterly*, 43 (1992), p. 161.

14 John Miles Foley, 'Editing Yugoslav epics: theory and practice', *TEXT*, 1 (1981), pp. 79, 81.

15 Walter J. Ong, *Orality and Literacy: The Technologizing of the Word* (London, Methuen, 1982; reissued Routledge, 1989), pp. 132, 133. Further references are included parenthetically in the text.

16 Marcus, *Puzzling Shakespeare*, p. 44.

17 Martin Elsky, *Authorizing Words: Speech, Writing, and Print in the English Renaissance* (Ithaca, Cornell, 1989), p. 114.

18 Eisenstein observes in *The Printing Press as an Agent of Change: Communications and Cultural Transformations in Early-Modern Europe* (Cambridge, Cambridge University Press, 1979) that 'one must wait until a full century after Gutenberg before the outlines of new world pictures begin to emerge into view' (vol. 1, p. 34).

19 Masten, *Textual Intercourse*, p. 115.

20 Gary Taylor notes in his 'General introduction' to Stanley Wells and Gary Taylor, *William Shakespeare: A Textual Companion* (Oxford, Clarendon, 1987) that 'an exceptional number of texts owned by the Chamberlain's Men seem to have been sold [for publication] around the time of their move to the Globe Theatre in 1599–1600' (p. 33). But see also Peter W. M. Blayney, 'The publication of playbooks', in John D. Cox and David Scott Kastan (eds), *A New History of Early English Drama* (New York, Columbia University Press, 1997), pp. 385–7.

21 It is, of course, important to resist seeing printing as an entirely determinative factor in textual change. As a corrective to this view, see Ruth Finnegan, *Literacy and Orality: Studies in the Technology of Communication* (Oxford, Basil Blackwell, 1988), esp. p. 41.

22 Marshall McLuhan, *The Gutenberg Galaxy: The Making of Typographic Man* (London, Routledge & Kegan Paul, 1962), p. 124.

23 See Werstine, 'Narratives' and, most recently and comprehensively, Laurie E. Maguire, *Shakespearean Suspect Texts: The 'Bad' Quartos and their Contexts* (Cambridge, Cambridge University Press, 1996). The issue is further discussed on pp. 202–3 below.

24 Jack Goody, *The Interface Between the Written and the Oral* (Cambridge, Cambridge University Press, 1987), pp. 298–9. Further references are included parenthetically in the text.

25 Even a printed edition is not, of course, *wholly* static, since, as a result of the manner in which corrected and uncorrected sheets were bound together, virtually no two copies of a Renaissance edition are identical in every detail. Thus Peter Blayney has observed in *The First Folio of Shakespeare* (Washington, DC, Folger Shakespeare Library, 1991) that 'no two copies [of the First Folio] have yet been found to contain exactly the same mixture of early and late pages' (p. 15). On the theoretical implications of such variations, see Marion Trousdale, 'A second look at critical bibliography and the acting of plays', *Shakespeare Quarterly*, 41 (1990), p. 94.

26 'To the Great Variety of Readers', A3r.

27 By 'editorial tradition' here, I mean the tradition of having named, foregrounded editors for the text. All of the seventeenth-century folios had 'editors' also, but their presence in the text and their work of emendation went unannounced. For a useful summary of the changes made by these anonymous editors, see Paul Werstine, 'William Shakespeare', in D. C. Greetham (ed.), *Scholarly Editing: A Guide to Research* (New York, MLA, 1995), pp. 255–6.

28 'The Preface of the Editor' in *The Works of Shakespear* (London, 1725), p. xvii. Here, as elsewhere, I have regularised long 's'.

29 Gary Taylor, *Reinventing Shakespeare: A Cultural History from the Restoration to the Present* (New York, Weidenfeld & Nicolson, 1989; reissued Oxford, Oxford University Press, 1991), p. 82.

30 *Proposals for printing, by subscription, the dramatic works of William Shakespeare, corrected and illustrated by Samuel Johnson* (London, 1756), repr. in facsimile as *Johnson's Proposals for his Edition of Shakespeare* (Oxford, Oxford University Press, 1923), p. 3 (Oxford text). Johnson was largely repeating here the narrative of theatrical dispersal and corrupt reconstruction that Theobald had proposed in his edition of 1733 – see, in particular p. xxxviii of Theobald's 'Preface' to his edition. A similar anti-theatrical strain can be detected in, for example, the preface to Hanmer's 1743–4 edition (pp. III–IV) and also Warburton's 1747 preface (pp. vii–viii).

31 Alvin Kernan, *Printing Technology, Letters and Samuel Johnson* (Princeton, Princeton University Press, 1987), p. 4.

32 In the case of the dramatic text we might, of course, also add the set of relations among the various other agents specified by Werstine: actors, scriveners, adapters, revisers, censors.

33 Mark Rose, 'The author as proprietor: *Donaldson v. Becket* and the genealogy of modern authorship', *Representations*, 23 (1988), pp. 62 3. See also, more generally, John Feather, 'The publishers and the pirates: British copyright law in theory and practice, 1710–1755', *Publishing History*, 22 (1987), pp. 5–32.

34 Kernan, *Printing Technology*, p. 100.

35 There are, of course, exceptions to this general trend. In *Authorizing Words*, Elsky sees Michel de Montaigne and Robert Burton as figures who exploit a certain potential for 'unfixity' within the regime of print, as they take advantage of new editions to offer changes – and sometimes contradictions – to what they have previously written. On Burton, see also Jonathan Sawday, 'Shapeless elegance: Robert Burton's anatomy of knowledge', in Neil Rhodes (ed.), *English Renaissance Prose: History, Language, and Politics* (Tempe, AZ, Medieval and Renaissance Texts and Studies, 1997), pp. 173–202.

36 See Margreta de Grazia, *Shakespeare Verbatim: The Reproduction of Authenticity and the 1790 Apparatus* (Oxford, Clarendon, 1991).

37 The quotation appears in part 2 of the first volume of Malone's edition, on the verso page facing the title page of *The Tempest*.

38 Allardyce Nicoll, 'The editors of Shakespeare from first folio to Malone', in *Studies in the First Folio* (London, Humphrey Milford/Oxford University Press, 1924), p. 178.

39 Werstine, 'William Shakespeare', p. 264.

40 A. W. Pollard's *Shakespeare's Folios and Quartos: A Study in the Bibliography of Shakespeare's Plays, 1594–1685* (London, Methuen, 1909) was prompted in part by the pessimistic assessment of the First Folio offered by Lee in his introduction to the 1902 Clarendon Press facsimile of F1.

41 Wilson, 'The task of Heminge and Condell', in *Studies in the First Folio*, p. 77.

42 See Grady, 'Disintegration and its reverberations', in Jean I. Marsden (ed.), *The Appropriation of Shakespeare: Post-Renaissance Reconstructions of the Works and the Myth* (Hemel Hempstead, Harvester, 1991), p. 120. See also Grady, *The Modernist Shakespeare: Critical Texts in a Material World* (Oxford, Clarendon, 1991), especially, pp. 57–63.

43 Ironically, it was within this same period that the first suggestions were made that the handwriting of one of the contributors to the *Booke of Sir Thomas More* fragment might be Shakespeare's. See Edward Maunde Thompson (ed.), *Shakespeare's Handwriting* (Oxford, Clarendon, 1916) and also A. W. Pollard (ed.), *Shakespeare's Hand in the Play of 'Sir Thomas More'* (Cambridge, Cambridge University Press, 1923). Pollard arranged for the pages in question to be exhibited at the British Museum.

44 Pollard, *Shakespeare's Folios*, p. 80.

45 The stress on a kind of familial morality is perhaps not so surprising here – Pollard was, after all, the (anonymous) author of *Life, Love and Light: Practical Morality for Men and Women* (London, Macmillan, 1911).

46 W. W. Greg, 'The *Hamlet* texts and recent work in Shakespearian bibliography', *Modern Language Review*, 14 (1919), p. 383.

47 Margreta de Grazia notes – in 'The essential Shakespeare and the material book', *Textual Practice*, 2 (1988), p. 76 – that 'the explanation was extended by Pollard and Wilson to the rest of the "Bad Quarto" family in 1917, so that by 1939 Greg could claim that reporting was involved in the production of all the "Bad Quartos".'

48 The question of the validity of Greg's complex narrative does not concern me here (Maguire takes up this issue at pp. 76–8 of her analysis). Rather, I am concerned (a) with the various agents of intervention posited by Greg and with his determination to subordinate their roles to that of the centralised, isolated author and (b) with his desire to account for the text at hand in a way that detaches it from an imagined ideal authentic text, of which the 1602 quarto is merely a singularly poor reproduction.

49 Thomas P. Roche and C. Patrick O'Donnell (eds), *The Faerie Queene* (New Haven, Yale University Press, 1981; first pub. London, Penguin, 1978), 1.1.20.6–7. Derrida summarises the Socratic view that writing itself is 'condemned … to wandering and blindness, to mourning' (*Of Grammatology*, p. 39).

50 W. W. Greg, *The Editorial Problem in Shakespeare: A Survey of the Foundations of the Text* (Oxford, Clarendon, 1942; 3rd edn, 1962), p. 3.

51 See, for instance, de Grazia, 'Essential Shakespeare' and de Grazia and Peter Stallybrass, 'The materiality of the Shakespearean text', *Shakespeare Quarterly*, 44 (1993), pp. 255–83.

52 George P. Landow, *Hypertext: The Convergence of Contemporary Critical Theory and Technology* (Baltimore, Johns Hopkins University Press, 1992), pp. 17–18. Further references are included parenthetically in the text.

53 George P. Landow, 'Twenty minutes into the future, or how are we moving beyond the book?', in Geoffrey Nunberg (ed.), *The Future of the Book* (Berkeley, University of California Press, 1996), p. 225.

54 For a detailed consideration of the connections between modern and Renaissance interpenetrations of technology and textuality, see Neil Rhodes and Jonathan Sawday (eds), *The Renaissance Computer* (London, Routledge, 2000).

55 Jay David Bolter, 'Topographic writing: hypertext and the electronic writing space', in Delaney and Landow (eds), *Hypermedia*, p. 116.

56 Peter S. Donaldson, 'The Shakespeare Interactive Archive: new directions in electronic scholarship on text and performance', in Edward Barrett and Marie Redmond (eds), *Contextual Media* (Cambridge, MA,: MIT Press, 1995), p. 125.

57 Idhe, *Postphenomenology*, p. 44.

58 My thanks to Neil Rhodes for his feedback on an earlier draft of this chapter.

Afterword: Confessions of a reformed uneditor

Leah S. Marcus

As Laurie Maguire's haunting chapter here suggests, editing is a matter of life and death. It aims at revitalising its author, but, through its strong desire for memorialisation, risks entombing the author anew. All editing worthy of the name is at the same time unediting insofar as it challenges the authority of pre-existing forms in which a given text had been made available to readers; but the two activities are especially symbiotic at present, when both the ontological status of what we used to call the 'literary text' and the previously standardised editorial templates by which it was promulgated have become subject to widespread scholarly interrogation. The divide between editors and literary critics about which I complained in *Unediting the Renaissance: Shakespeare, Marlowe, Milton* (1996) has increasingly been effaced as more and more of us find ourselves doing both. Indeed, my writing of that book was undertaken on a self-imposed furlough from the larger project of an edition – *Elizabeth I: Collected Works* forthcoming from the University of Chicago Press, and co-edited with Janel Mueller and Mary Beth Rose. I was the 'theorist' in charge of creating an appropriate format for the edition, and though I did not realise it then, I am now certain that my time out from the edition – which set it back at least three years – was essential for the conceptualisation of a format that would make Elizabeth's collected writings available to a broad spectrum of readers and at the same time responsive to recent developments in the ways we conceptualise texts.

The present volume has much to offer editors/uneditors. Ramona Wray's chapter on the early modern female voice calls attention to the much enlarged field of texts considered worthy of editing, as women who were writing four centuries ago are rediscovered and made available for modern readers. As she suggests, it is not only the subject matter but also the implicitly gendered protocols for determining attribution and meaning that have to change when we edit early modern

women authors. I would venture to say that an edition of the writings of
Queen Elizabeth I would not have been undertaken by literary scholars
as recently as twenty years ago: what she wrote was often not 'literature' in the strict sense of the term, and it is often impossible to determine the precise degree of her agency, particularly in letters and
devotional writings that are co-produced in a commonly held 'corporate' style with officials of her government and of the church.

As discussed here by John Pitcher, Samuel Daniel was remarkably
solicitous for the period in terms of his 'ownership' and ordering of his
writings – even to the point of enlisting his friends and patrons as a
living record of the transformations undergone by his lyrics as he polished them and prepared them for publication. When it came to her
own lyrics, Elizabeth took a very different approach that was self-
effacing even by the standards of the day. Although she composed
verses in several languages, she seldom allowed them to escape the intimate court circles within which they were composed. A common feature of her verses as anthologised in manuscript miscellanies of the
period is that the words attributing the authorship to the queen – and
sometimes an accompanying description of their occasion or, indeed,
the entire poem itself – will be carefully crossed out in a way that leaves
these interesting matters legible beneath the erasure. This characteristic feature is not, as previous editors have assumed, a sign that the
copyist has changed his mind about the queen's authorship, but rather
a self-protective device by which the copyist accedes to her well-known
dislike for having her verses enter into manuscript circulation. How
does one solve issues of attribution in working with a culture that was
chary and sometimes downright evasive about authorship? Many of
Elizabeth's writings survive in her own hand, which usually implies her
authorship or at least her agency as translator. For those writings that
do not, our solution, like that proposed by the preparers of a new edition of the verses of Sir Walter Ralegh, is to define authorship culturally rather than through minute (and fallible) stylistic analysis: we
define as Elizabeth's those writings that circulated as hers – even if *sous
rature* – during her lifetime, so long as the attribution appears plausible
on other grounds.

Like John Pitcher and many other very recent editors, we refuse to
produce conflated versions of Elizabeth's writings, even though conflated editions have previously been the rule, especially (and surprisingly) in the work of historians producing modernised versions of her
speeches. Instead, we opt for a format that preserves the particularised

form of a given manuscript version. In cases in which there are pronounced differences between early texts that appear to possess equal authority, we frequently print more than one version, so that readers can examine the differences for themselves. This is particularly necessary for Elizabeth's speeches, which were seldom if ever written out in advance but delivered from notes or impromptu. For many of Elizabeth's speeches, the only versions we have are (O dreaded phrase!) memorial reconstructions transcribed by auditors shortly after her delivery of the speech, either for the purpose of preserving it as part of the historical record or with the aim of circulating it to a wider audience. Many editors might well condemn our printing of multiple versions as violating a key responsibility of editing, which they would define as the offering of a single authoritative version of an author's work so as not to confuse readers and complicate citation. We have greater trust in our readers' capacity – and even appetite – for an array of textual possibilities. To centre an edition on textual differences and instability is to respond to a new set of paradigms by which texts have recently been redefined. In many ways, of course, the best format for such a display is the online edition, and I still hope, despite the fact that my enthusiasm is not shared by my co-editors, that at least some elements of our edition may eventually be posted on the World Wide Web. But as Gary Taylor's eloquent lament here admonishes, we need to become electronically expert ourselves if we hope to produce workable hypertextual editions: to leave the niceties of encoding to outside experts is to court disaster, since such technicians are increasingly lured off to lucrative positions, many of them in the corporate world. But whatever the speed at which editing goes online, there is arguably still a place for the traditional book format. Indeed, the printed book is perhaps the most rhetorically effective locus for editorial innovation just now, since to offer such innovation online is in large part to preach to the converted.

How much editorial information is too much? Even if editors choose to offer two or more variant versions of a given text, however, we still have the problem of how to deal with other, more minor variants among manuscript and printed copies. As the differing opinions expressed in this volume amply indicate, there is considerable disagreement at present about the degree to which what Lewis Mumford characterised as the 'barbed wire' of traditional editorial annotation should be preserved in our new editions. I subscribe to W. Speed Hill's view that the traditional editorial apparatus as used in modern editions is less an aid to readers than an imprimatur conferring legitimacy upon the work of the editor.[1] The logic goes like this: if the editor demonstrates that he or she has consulted, with detailed attention, all the varying editions or manuscripts used in the compilation of the list of variants, then he or she has earned the right to be trusted to determine the final text. In our edition of Elizabeth, we have adopted a different logic. A comprehensive list of variants, especially for the speeches, many of which exist in paraphrased versions that may have as few as one third of their words in common, is simply not practical. In the case of texts that we do not present in multiple versions, we do frequently offer variants, but these are printed clearly among the explanatory notes, and in a manner, we hope, that will not alienate readers who dislike barbed wire but will rather cause them to become intrigued by the differences among texts. We are quite candid in such cases about the fact that we do not present all variants, but only the ones we consider most significant. Such a procedure is, of course, idiosyncratic and high-handed in that it is based on individual judgement, but arguably somewhat less so than the traditional methods by which editors have introduced variant readings into their final texts in the name of correcting the 'errors' of the author.

To regularise is often to efface. Our generation has a strong appetite for the very quirkiness and multilayeredness that made early manuscript and printed copies appear disfigured and devalued for many previous editors and collectors. As this volume's chapters by Stephen Orgel and Peter Stallybrass amply illustrate, there is much to be gained by consulting – and reproducing – textual materials in a form that preserves rather than effaces important signs of their production and reception. In the nineteenth and early twentieth centuries, early modern books were often advertised for sale as *bien lavé* and thereby cleansed of the interventions of early readers and sometimes (as in the Milton example cited by Orgel) even of the correcting intervention of the authors. It is melancholy to think how many marginal interactions of the type documented in Orgel's research have been lost because collectors demanded clean copy, although recent bibliographical projects to catalogue surviving marginal annotations to some extent make up for the loss. Luckily, with printed materials we are less deprived: recent 'unediting' has recovered many instances of early modern gender instability that are retrievable by recourse to the First Folio of Shakespeare and other early modern manuscript and printed texts. Similarly, Stallybrass discusses patterns of naming in the folio that may, with equal plausibility and interest, be taken to signal authorial intent or scribal or printing-house practice, but which can scarcely be held to be inconsequential. How does one go about incorporating marginalia or other textual anomalies into a modern edition? Medieval scholars, as discussed in the chapter by Graham Caie, are ahead of early modernists here, since they have long been interested in the dialogic relations between a text and its (often indispensable) commentary. In our edition of Elizabeth's writing, we incorporate what we judge to be significant early marginalia, headings and endorsements as part of an attempt to convey at least some of the historical milieu of the copytext. We are also very reluctant to emend what appear to us odd locutions and even errors, preferring to signal them through notes rather than silently to amend them. And no doubt our work, as it displays the differing intentions of three editors, copyeditors and other elements of the cumbersome process by which archival research somehow manages to make it into the form of a book, will display many startling inconsistencies and limitations like those in earlier editions chronicled in the present volume. How much ripening time does it take before a regrettable editorial inconsistency can be reinterpreted as a noteworthy indicator of the historical situatedness of the editor and edition?

There is one vexed matter that we have had to face that is not taken up in much detail in the present volume: that is the problem of modernisation of textual elements like spelling and punctuation. Ideally, an edition designed for a broad audience would have both original-spelling versions for the use of scholars and modern-spelling versions for the ease of everyone else. But in practice editors are usually forced to choose between one and the other, and the choice of original spelling – particularly for sixteenth-century materials whose original spellings are often erratic in the extreme – often condemns an edition to a very narrow audience when the materials are potentially of wide interest. Our edition of the writings of Elizabeth I, despite the many ways in which it attempts to remain close to the historical milieu of its materials, presents modern-spelling versions of all of its texts and (in a compromise based largely on monetary and marketing considerations) offers original-spelling versions additionally in a separate volume only for materials in Elizabeth's hand and for foreign-language materials that we have offered in translation in the modern-spelling part of the edition.

How can we justify the massive interpretive intervention represented by our modernisation of spelling and punctuation in our manuscript (and occasionally printed) copytexts? The answer is that, increasingly, feminist scholars and others have been calling for texts that do not continue the marginalisation of early modern authors by other means. If we wish for these materials to enter into the canon and compete for a broad spectrum of reader attention along with other more familiar materials from the period that have long since been subjected to the indignity of modernisation, then we need to modernise as well. But there are degrees of modernisation: we have strived to retain much of the cultural aura of the materials we reproduce despite our difficult decision to shape the ways in which they are interpreted through the imposition of modern spelling and punctuation. And at least we have managed to preserve the original spellings of the author's holograph texts. The spelling and punctuation of early modern manuscript copies are arguably more dispensable in that they so freely altered their originals, although such copies are often of enormous historical importance on other grounds. Every editor has to strike a delicate balance between a fond dream of faithfulness to the past and a hope for utility in the present. As the chapters here by Andrew Murphy and by Graham Holderness, Stanley Porter and Carol Banks amply testify, all editing is ephemeral. Indeed, the very edition which looks most dated to us now may well be that which once strove the most adamantly for permanence.

Michael Steppat's discussion here of *Unediting the Renaissance* proceeds on the assumption that my critique of modern editions was aimed primarily at editors, and that I considered it possible to achieve a 'value-free' editing in which the scholar in charge could magically excise him or herself from her or his own cultural situation. Nothing could be further from the truth. My target was not so much editors as scholar-critics and other informed readers, and my question to them was: how do you justify your passive tolerance of editions inscribed with outmoded aesthetic, social and gender assumptions at the same time that you work to uproot such assumptions in and through your own critical work? We can none of us escape our present, but with a little hard textual work, we can at least escape some of our past. It is toward that endeavour that the present volume was collected, and toward that endeavour that, increasingly, uneditors are becoming editors.

Note

1 See W. Speed Hill' s essay 'The theory and practice of transcription', in Speed Hill (ed.), *New Ways of Looking at Old Texts: Papers of the Renaissance English Text Society, 1985–1991* (Binghamton, NY, MRTS in conjunction with the Renaissance English Text Society, 1993), pp. 25–32.

Index

Letter-by-letter filing order has been used (articles at the beginning of an entry are disregarded for this purpose). Shakespeare's works and works by other authors given more substantial discussion are shown as entries in their own right. Other titles are shown under authors' names.

Note: 'n' after a page reference indicates a note number on that page. Page numbers in italics refer to illustrations.